# Web Project Management for Academic Libraries

JODY CONDIT FAGAN
AND
JENNIFER A. KEACH

Chandos Publishing

*Oxford • Cambridge • New Delhi*

Chandos Publishing
TBAC Business Centre
Avenue 4
Station Lane
Witney
Oxford OX28 4BN
UK
Tel: +44 (0) 1993 848726
Email: info@chandospublishing.com
www.chandospublishing.com

Chandos Publishing is an imprint of Woodhead Publishing Limited

Woodhead Publishing Limited
Abington Hall
Granta Park
Great Abington
Cambridge CB21 6AH
UK
www.woodheadpublishing.com

First published in 2009

ISBN:
978 1 84334 503 9

British Library Cataloguing-in-Publication Data.
A catalogue record for this book is available from the British Library.

Typeset by Domex e-Data Pvt. Ltd.
Printed in the UK and USA.

# Contents

# List of figures and tables

## Figures

## Tables

# About the authors

**Jody Condit Fagan**, MLS, MA, currently serves as Content Interfaces Coordinator and Associate Professor at James Madison University Libraries & Educational Technologies. In this role she leads initiatives to improve user access to collections across library systems such as the library catalog, database and journal portals, and link resolvers, and also coordinates usability testing efforts. She previously worked on web projects as a librarian at Southern Illinois University, Carbondale, where she also obtained a Masters degree in history. At both JMU and SIUC, her positions have also included reference, instruction, and collection development responsibilities. She is a proud graduate of the College of Information Studies at the University of Maryland, College Park.

Jody is currently the editor of the *Journal of Web Librarianship* and Chair of the American Library Association Poster Sessions Committee. Her research interests surround user behavior in library web interfaces. She has recently published articles in *Information Technology and Libraries, Computers in Libraries*, and *The Charleston Advisor*, and has presented regularly at conferences such as the American Library Association, the American Society for Information Science and Technology, Computers in Libraries, and Electronic Resources & Libraries. Additional information about her extensive publications and presentations can be found on her website, *http://jcf-hp.blogspot.com/*.

Jody is a proud aunt of three and enjoys visiting her family in Florida, Washington, DC, and Southern Illinois. In her spare time, she enjoys reading, watching the St. Louis Cardinals, and obsessing about her cats. She currently lives in Broadway, Virginia, with her husband, Bryan Fagan, a freelance writer and copyeditor.

**Jennifer Keach**, MLS, is currently Director of Digital Services and Associate Professor at James Madison University Libraries & Educational Technologies. In this role, she manages a 12-person department focused on the library website, staff computing, and public computing. She also provides library instruction and collection development for the Media Arts & Design program, and traditional reference service for all subjects.

Her passions include brainstorming with colleagues to solve their problems, coordinating the creation of technology solutions, and organizing information in useful ways. Her research interests include organizational communication and leadership. She has presented at the EDUCAUSE Annual Conference and Computers in Libraries. Jennifer earned her MLS from the University of Alabama in 1994.

Jennifer's career path includes service both with the public and behind the scenes, in libraries large and small. In her previous positions at James Madison University, Bridgewater College, and Hampden-Sydney College, she coordinated web development and management, research databases, online reference, collection development, serials, instruction, and an integrated library system. During most of her 15 years in libraries, she has also provided reference service. This diversity of experience encourages her to see web projects from diverse perspectives.

Jennifer is originally from the suburbs of Baltimore, Maryland, and has made her home in rural Virginia with her husband, Dave Scott, a high school English teacher. In her spare time, she enjoys international travel, friendly poker, classic films, her dog Otis, and the great outdoors.

# Acknowledgements

We'd like to thank our colleagues and users at James Madison University (JMU) for their encouragement and participation in our project management education. We'd especially like to thank the current and past members of JMU Libraries' Digital Services department. We'd also like to thank Sandy Maxfield, Associate Dean, and Ralph Alberico, Dean of Libraries and Educational Technologies, for their support.

Additional colleagues who have played a significant role in our project management education and support include Cheri Duncan and Bill Hartman, with whom we have worked on many web projects; Brian Cockburn, who introduced Jennifer to Ashley Friedlein's book, *Web Project Management*; and Lida Larsen, Susan Logue, and Keith VanCleave, who served as Jody's first library web mentors.

The following people directly contributed to this book by reading chapters and serving as consultants: Greg Brown, Lydia Dixon, Greg Spitzer, and Stefanie Warlick. We'd also like to thank Elizabeth Kline for her indefatigable editorial assistance.

Finally, thanks go to our husbands, Bryan Fagan and Dave Scott, for their encouragement, advice, and patience while we wrote this book (and during all other times, too).

# Introduction

## Who should read this book?

*Web Project Management for Academic Libraries* focuses on the realities of academic libraries and provides practical project management tools and techniques. Most academic librarians do not have the time or the need to become certified project managers. Some formal project management techniques make more sense for the academic library than others. This book offers a menu of options for busy web project managers to choose from that can be adapted to any setting.

This book offers advice for all kinds of library staff serving in the web project management role. You could be a reference librarian who has taken the lead in pioneering a new virtual reference service. You could be a cataloger who has been asked to lead a task force to investigate next-generation catalog interfaces. You could be your library's regular webmaster leading an entire website overhaul. This book is also suitable for those who have not yet managed a project, but hope to do so. Perhaps you are a library school student and want a job in the web world. Finally, this book is useful to library administrators who are looking for more effective ways for their libraries to manage web projects.

The authors of this book are both academic librarians who have served on the reference desk, taught library instruction classes, and performed collection development responsibilities all while engaging seriously in web projects. Between the two of us, we have also worked in acquisitions, electronic resources, interlibrary loan, serials, and systems. Like most librarians, we entered into project management with no training or formal preparation for this role. We picked up techniques one-by-one, adapting formal project management practices to our library environment.

By reading advice on everything from team building to writing technical specifications in this book, you may think that you don't have time to practice project management in your library. Even for us, putting all these techniques into practice for every single project remains an elusive goal. Like us, you are likely torn between many roles at work. Instead of thinking you must try everything, experiment with just one new idea from this book with your next project. Whether you need help getting started on a project, want to finally complete a project on time, or want to improve the process as a whole, this book will help you.

## Overview of this book's contents

The first section of this book focuses on the context of web project management in academic libraries. Chapters 2 and 3 discuss the role of web project manager and consider how the academic library environment shapes project management practices. Chapter 4 talks about how web projects get started and how the project manager can shape a vaguely formed idea into a project.

The second section of the book is all about 'team.' Chapter 5 talks about the various roles needed for a web project team in an academic library. Even small libraries will need to think about how each role will be filled, even if many roles are fulfilled by one or two people. Chapter 6 discusses the personalities found in academic libraries that will influence the dynamics of your team. Chapter 7 talks about how you can communicate effectively with your team, again with consideration for the different needs of different personalities.

Chapters 8 and 9 continue the theme of communication for the web project manager. Chapter 8 covers the importance of effective organizational communication in academic libraries. Chapter 9 provides an overview of methods to gather user input and incorporate it into the process.

The next three chapters cover project specifications in three areas: design, technical, and content. These chapters present simple yet powerful project management tools that anyone can use without special software or training. Only after you understand exactly what you are creating can you begin to create your end product.

Finally, chapters 13 and 14 talk about 'doing the work.' You will learn about project management tools that help you plan for when the work will happen and who will do it. You will learn about monitoring the work in progress and bringing it to a final conclusion.

If you'd like to read even more about web project management in academic libraries, please visit the authors' website, *http://sites.google .com/site/pm4web/*, where you will find supplemental content and updates about related projects and presentations.

# Why are web projects in academic libraries different?

Many functions of academic libraries operate on a routine basis: we have daily hours; we check items in and out; we acquire, license, and catalog electronic resources. On top of these regular activities, today's academic libraries are engaging in more *projects*. To stay current with rapidly changing times, we are piloting and implementing new service models, starting new intracampus partnerships, and creating institutional repositories. Planning and assessment are of high interest: which of our new ideas match up to the strategic plan? How do we fit the project-oriented work into our already busy schedules? Which new endeavors give our organizations the most return on investment?

*Web projects*, in particular, are increasingly more impressive in scope and more costly in staff skills. In the early days of the web, many librarians learned HTML and enthusiastically converted print bibliographies to web pages. It didn't really matter if one online pathfinder didn't match others, and it was relatively easy to keep everything up to date. Today, we supplement robust database-driven applications with web services that pull data from multiple locations to formulate on-the-fly miracles. The technical skills needed are no longer as simple as HTML and are increasingly difficult to add 'on the side' of an existing full-time job. Some libraries have hired web professionals to handle CSS, database design, and web programming, or even created entirely web-oriented departments.

Even in libraries with web departments, however, many types of people may find themselves directing the execution of a web-related initiative through its lifecycle. A reference librarian with a good idea collaborates with the web department. An associate dean spearheads a new initiative with a well-formed implementation team. An innovative systems staff member writes some code for one department, and that work is swiftly adopted by the entire organization. Increasingly, anyone within the library may manage a web project.

Web projects are also increasingly more central to the academic library mission. Every aspect of the library—from services to collections to instruction—is delivered at least in part through the website. In addition, our students, faculty, and library colleagues are increasingly online, integrating Web 2.0 tools into their work and social lives. Our users and our colleagues rightfully expect our academic library websites to keep up with this increased use of the web. Especially with Web 2.0 tools, we can add new online services more quickly than ever before. These technologies, though, still need clear goals and planning to be successful and sustainable.

Web projects in academic libraries do not usually consume vast financial resources, but they always cost libraries dearly in staff capital. In addition to the obvious expense of technical staff salaries, the entire organization also expends emotional and mental energy keeping up with changes. Whether you and your colleagues find it exciting or frightening, constant technological change is frequently stressful. If an institution is focused on institutional repositories one year, it might not have enough organizational energy to also work on social network services that year. A smart institution, then, plans carefully for changes—prioritizing, communicating, scheduling, evaluating, and celebrating—to minimize those stresses on the organization.

Because web projects create stressful forces within an organization, the role of project manager is critical. A project manager looks out for the needs of a *project* as opposed to a specific department's or individual's goals. Project management contains techniques useful in and of themselves, but project management can also help us be good colleagues. Project management helps to clarify expectations, prevent misunderstandings, and get work done efficiently and effectively. It can help staff reap the rewards of hard work and avoid burnout. It can help good librarians to be great librarians. In sum, web projects in academic libraries are a *big deal*. They are no longer something that can be handled easily on an ad hoc basis with no planning. If you are already high performers in the web world, we hope this book will help you refine your skills and offer you some new ideas. If you struggle to fit in even the simplest web projects, we hope this book provides basic tools to help you navigate successfully through the complexity of modern academic library web projects.

# The web project manager in academic libraries

## Introduction

If you are already working in an academic library on web projects, you very likely have other major responsibilities as well. If you're in library school looking at job ads with web responsibilities, these jobs likely also include other aspects of library work, such as reference, instruction, collection development, cataloging, or even all of the above. In a study of library job advertisements, library school curricula, and professional library organization workshops, Jane Kinkus found that project management qualifications and responsibilities in academic libraries have been increasing and are 'here to stay' (2007, 361). Web-related jobs in libraries continue to evolve, with project management roles increasingly available in 'electronic' and 'digital' areas, not just in administrative positions (Croneis and Henderson 2002, 236).

The purpose of this chapter is to define the role of the web project manager in an academic library, make the case for academic libraries' need for full-time web project managers, and discuss the knowledge, education, and traits necessary for a web project manager.

## The definition of a web project manager

With the advent of the web, the first library websites were often created by librarians who learned HTML 'on the side.' Webmaster duties were often not included in official job descriptions (Taylor 2000). A full-time librarian could realistically maintain a small suite of HTML pages for the entire website. Many librarians who are now engaged in web project management gained this responsibility as an assignment or as a volunteer. As web technologies became more complex and library websites became increasingly large, staff now have difficulty performing their original jobs plus web design and development responsibilities, let alone managing the web work of others.

In a survey conducted by the authors (Keach and Fagan 2008), of 121 people who responded to the question 'In the last two years, about how many different people in your organization have led web projects?,' the majority (64%) said that a few different people have led web projects as opposed to one person (14%) or many people (22%). In fact, if you've been reading job ads, you've probably not seen academic library positions literally titled 'web project manager.' More commonly, you've seen titles such as 'web librarian,' 'web services librarian,' 'digital services librarian,' and 'webmaster.' In the authors' survey, 50 of the 121 respondents said they managed 'all' or 'most' of their libraries' web projects. A selection of their varied job titles is shown in figure 2.1.

Jobs with similar names vary greatly in duties and qualifications. For example, one web services librarian might work in reference and serve primarily as a liaison to technical personnel in a systems department who actually do the HTML and CSS work. Another web services librarian might spend most of the day writing HTML and CSS code themselves under the direction of a library-wide web committee. These two jobs

**Figure 2.1** Job titles of those responsible for all or most web projects

| | |
|---|---|
| Web Services Librarian (5) | Information Technology Coordinator |
| Web Development Librarian (3) | Knowledge Management Librarian |
| Digital Services Librarian (3) | Lead Application Developer |
| Web/Reference Librarian (2) | Manager of Digital Library Services and |
| Web Coordinator (2) | Information Systems |
| Systems Librarian (2) | Reference Librarian |
| Webmaster (2) | Web Applications Manager |
| Assistant Reference Librarian | Web Content Reference Librarian |
| Automated Services Librarian | Web Developer and Graphics |
| Digital Initiatives Librarian | Web Development Coordinator |
| Electronic Resources Librarian | Web Librarian |
| Electronic Services Librarian | Web Program Manager |
| Head of Information and Access | Web Services Team Leader |
| Services | Web Specialist II |
| Head of Libraries Web Services | Web Support Librarian |
| Head, Collection Management & | |
| Technical Services | |

require different skills and you would likely enjoy one more than the other, depending on your personality.

Of the 50 respondents who said they managed 'all' or 'most' of their library's web projects, 39 respondents additionally listed three to five responsibilities of their positions. We attempted to create broad groupings of responsibilities; table 2.1 shows the results. Notice that only five respondents listed a job responsibility in the category of 'project management,' while an additional four listed some responsibility related to leading teams. Even when grouping these together, only nine of those 39 respondents (23%) listed project management as a job responsibility.

We also asked respondents how much of their time they spent managing web projects. Figure 2.2 summarizes the responses from the

**Table 2.1** Grouped responsibilities of those who manage all or most web projects

| Responsibility | Number of respondents | Responsibility | Number of respondents |
|---|---|---|---|
| Non-web related (instruction, reference) | 14 | Support web publishing | 6 |
| Supervise/manage people | 10 | Communication/ primary contact | 6 |
| Content systems, including CMS | 10 | Project management | 5 |
| Responsible for library public web | 10 | User needs evaluation/usability | 4 |
| Web management | 10 | Training | 4 |
| Electronic resources, including access | 9 | Develop web applications | 4 |
| Server administration/ maintenance | 8 | Learn/maintain knowledge | 4 |
| Vision/oversight | 7 | Lead teams | 4 |
| Web development (direct) | 7 | Information architecture | 2 |
| Web maintenance (direct) | 7 | Responsible for staff intranet | 2 |
| Interface design | 7 | Web standards/ accessibility | 1 |
| | | Public computing | 1 |

**Figure 2.2** Amount of time spent managing web projects (n=87)

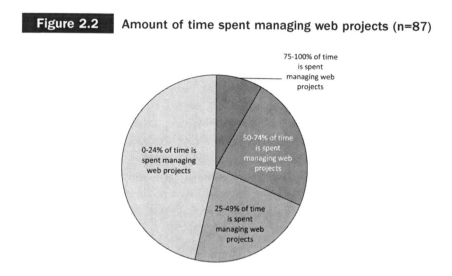

87 respondents to this question. Almost half of the respondents spent less than 25% of their time managing web projects, while only seven respondents spent more than 75% of their time managing web projects.

This chapter, therefore, attempts to disregard actual position descriptions and instead focuses on the *role* of web project management: coordinating a web project from start to finish. For those looking for a tidy, one-sentence definition:

> A web project manager in an academic library is the person who directs the execution of a web-related initiative through its lifecycle, including defining the project, collaborating with stakeholders and team members, facilitating meetings, managing the timeline and deadlines, and overseeing all aspects of communication among the technical team and within the organization.

While a web project manager could be a technical expert in HTML, CSS, or other web-related skills, using these skills is separate from the project management role. For the purposes of this book, web project management is *not*:

- programming web applications
- coordinating usability tests
- writing and editing web content for the library website
- fielding day-to-day website troubleshooting issues

- administrating web and database servers
- answering the library website's 'Contact Us' e-mail.

In an academic library, the person who commonly manages web projects might also perform one or more of the bullet points above as part of a job, but this book focuses solely on project management responsibilities.

# The many job descriptions of web professionals

Although 'web project manager' is not yet a usual job title in academic libraries, 'webmaster,' 'web services librarian,' and 'web development librarian' are more common. In today's academic libraries, this person often tries to manage web projects as well as develop websites, assist web authors, and perform maintenance.

Although job descriptions for web librarians will continue to differ from one another, some common trends are beginning to emerge. First, web librarians in academic libraries continue to have hybrid jobs. In a 1998 survey of ARL Libraries about webmasters, Mary K. Taylor found that almost 60% of ARL webmasters spent fifteen hours or less per week on their web duties (2000, 118). In a 2007 study of webmasters in medium-sized libraries, Jason Kneip reported that most library webmasters perform other duties in addition to web development, and spend less than twenty hours a week fulfilling their web-related responsibilities (2007, 11). Furthermore, in the medium-sized libraries he surveyed, one-quarter of respondents had a job title that contained the word 'director,' 'associate director,' 'head,' or 'manager,' suggesting they have other management or supervisory responsibilities. Figure 2.3 lists some example hybrid job titles from the authors' survey (Keach and Fagan 2008).

**Figure 2.3**   **Hybrid job titles of those managing all or most web projects**

Access Services/Web Design Librarian
Assistant Librarian/Head of Web Services
Electronic Reference Services and Web Development Coordinator
Information Resources Manager/Web Services Coordinator
Instructor of Library Services/Instructional Technology Librarian
Reference/Instruction and Web Development Librarian
Reference/Instruction Librarian
Systems and Web Development Librarian

If you're serving as a webmaster in an academic library, therefore, you can expect to have a blended position incorporating traditional library functions, technical skills, and project management duties. It will be critical for you to learn and practice good project management techniques in order to bring some sanity to existing web workflows as well as your own.

The location of a webmaster within the organization is also different depending on the organization. Technology-related positions have changed locations within the organization with the advent and development of the web. In 1990, surveys found 'electronic' and 'digital' positions only in public service departments. By 1998, these types of positions were also in technical services, systems, and digital projects (Croneis and Henderson 2002, 235). In Taylor's 2000 study of ARL webmasters, she found that 31% were affiliated with the library's systems department, while the next highest percentage were from a public services department (118). In his 2007 survey, Kneip had similar findings, with 30% in 'systems/automation/technical services,' 22% in 'reference/instruction,' and 14% in 'technology/digital services' (9).

In the authors' survey (Keach and Fagan 2008), 50 respondents who said they managed 'all' or 'most' of the web projects at their library answered the question, 'In what department/unit of your library do you work?' There were similar results to the previously cited surveys, with some new, specialized departments. The most common departments listed were public services and information technology/systems, followed by some variant of 'digital services' (see table 2.2). Other departments listed were 'web services,' 'information services,' and 'library information systems.' Web project managers continue to identify with diverse units throughout the organization.

If you are considering a new position, think about what type of department might best fit your own goals. Do you want your daily work to include working directly with users in a public services unit or would you prefer a focus on technology in a systems department? Consider, too, that departmental focuses will vary by institution. Make sure to get a feel for the work environment in the specific department or unit you're considering.

Both Taylor and Kneip argued that library webmasters should be given more time to work on web-related responsibilities. In her recommendations, Taylor recommended that 'libraries should have one person responsible full time for website development issues, and they should financially support continuing education and travel to conferences where new trends are discussed' (2000, 122). In his discussion of medium-sized

| Table 2.2 | Departments where web project managers work |

| Department | Number of respondents |
|---|:---:|
| Public Services/Reference | 10 |
| Digital Library Initiatives/Services/Programs | 6 |
| Information Technology Services/Systems | 5 |
| Information Services | 4 |
| Web Services | 4 |
| Administration | 3 |
| Library Information Systems | 3 |
| Technical Services | 3 |
| Access Services | 2 |
| Informatic Center | 2 |
| Instructional Technology/Instructional Support | 2 |
| No departments in library | 2 |
| Library Automation and Technology | 1 |

libraries, Kneip writes that more time to experiment, attend professional development workshops, and less top-down control would help medium-sized library webmasters (2007, 15–16).

From this discussion, you can see that academic libraries are still grappling with the complexity of web work and the challenge of fitting it within existing organizational structures. The role of 'webmaster' within libraries, which has been studied for at least ten years, varies greatly; the role of managing web projects is only beginning to be defined.

# Project management in libraries

Recent research points to increased interest in the topic of project management for all types of projects within libraries (Winston and Hoffman 2005; Bunch et al. 2006; Kinkus 2007). In a 2007 study, Kinkus found that by 2003, academic library job advertisements increasingly used the terms 'project management' or 'project manager' rather than merely implying project management through other terminology (361). She proposed that libraries' 'increased interdependence across multiple library units' will ensure an ongoing need for project teams and, therefore, project managers. She also points to current workshop

## Moving your web project manager role from ad hoc to official

 Have you volunteered to help with the library website only to find that web project management has taken over your former job? Perhaps you were enjoying life as a cataloger or a reference librarian, but you happened to have the most web skills (or the least fear of web technologies), and were pressed into service. If this scenario sounds familiar, you may be an 'ad hoc' web project manager operating on a per-project basis. If you're reading this book, it probably means you enjoy your web work. So how do you convince your library administration that they need to formalize some of your duties or change your job description to make more room to lead web projects well?

One critical element to your case will be careful documentation. As you go through your day, keep track of how much time you spend on different web activities and categorize the time in terms of the various roles you play. Document your projects along with evaluative information like changes in web statistics, user comments, and survey results. In time, you will amass hard evidence in support of your argument that web project management is worth the investment of staff time.

Your library may not be willing to create a position dedicated to web project management; however, don't overlook the opportunity for other kinds of support. Student workers, graduate assistants, release time from other duties, or even a laptop might help you get through your ad hoc work. Our best advice is to schedule web projects alongside your other work carefully. Request release time from other duties for the duration of large projects. It is all too easy to let web projects take over your life and burn you out, so only undertake any new project with a clear understanding of how it affects your other commitments. In some libraries, there may never be enough staff support to allow for a dedicated web project librarian. Or, you may be content with a hybrid position. You can be an effective ad hoc web project manager as long as you recognize that project management doesn't just happen. It takes time and you must balance it with your other work.

offerings of organizations such as the American Library Association, the Special Libraries Association, and the Association of College and Research Libraries as a sign of the importance of project management skills in libraries. In the UK, the Chartered Institute of Library and Information Professionals also offers training in project management for library staff (*http://www.cilip.org.uk/training*). Yet in the three years' of job advertisements Kinkus examined (1993, 2003, and 2004), the number of jobs specifying project management-related responsibilities was a small percentage (2007, 361). Project management within libraries is still an emerging role.

## Academic libraries need web project managers

Although subject bibliographers, catalogers, archivists, reference librarians, and other staff will all contribute to the website, these full-time jobs leave little room for project management responsibilities. Web teams and committees are wonderful, but are usually composed of stakeholders who already have full-time jobs. Technical experts, while clearly critical to web projects, may or may not have the right interpersonal or group communication skills to execute a well-managed project across an organization. Furthermore, in organizations where library units and functions compete for resources, academic libraries need a champion for their web presence. Dan Brandon describes this much-needed role of the project manager succinctly: 'integrator, communicator, and problem solver' (2006, 12).

As web project manager in an academic library, you fill this need. You do the legwork in getting stakeholders and technical teams to work together across the organization, and have the time and authority to do so. While various individuals will speak up for specific areas of the library, you defend the needs of the project itself. You ensure good communication, effective tracking and evaluation methods, and coordination among the team members. You employ consistent project planning methods and lead one or more teams in the effort of producing websites, web applications, and other web-related initiatives. You break down a web project into manageable phases, set timelines, and evaluate and improve project management practices. As web project manager, you conduct regular evaluations of how the project management processes are working, improve team efficiency, and increase the effectiveness of organizational communication about web projects.

If you are serving as the hub for all the organization's web-related projects, some other responsibilities may come with the job. Here are just a few of the additional opportunities for which you may be expected to assume responsibility:

- fostering organizational knowledge related to the library web
- setting standards and encourage adherence
- coordinating content providers and technical teams
- forming partnerships and alliances on campus related to the web presence
- evaluating the website on an ongoing basis
- marketing the library web presence.

Large academic libraries may need multiple full-time positions to address the list above, with the project manager playing a coordinating role. In many libraries, however, many of the tasks in the list above fall to one person. Web teams, discussed in more detail in chapter 5, 'The academic library web team,' can help distribute many of the activities above and more.

# Qualifications and education for web project managers

So, if you want to be a web project manager in an academic library, what qualifications do you need? Depending on the size and type of academic library, position advertisements will list a variety of educational requirements, personality traits, and technical skills. If you're searching for a job, play to your strengths and apply for jobs that are seeking someone with your skill set! If you're writing a job description, consider which of the qualifications below are most important for your institution and for the role you envision the position taking.

## Education for the web professional

Just as you won't find job descriptions for 'web project managers' in academic libraries, you'll also find no single educational path to become a web project manager—or even a webmaster, which is a recognized role—in an academic library. Recent surveys of academic libraries show that most currently employed webmasters rely on job experience, self-instruction, and continuing education to fulfill at least part of the requirements of their position. While three-quarters of the respondents to Taylor's and Kneip's surveys held an MLS or equivalent degree, not many had certificates or degrees in computer science or web-related fields (Taylor 2000, 117; Kneip 2007, 8). According to both Taylor and Kneip's studies, webmasters gained knowledge of web technology in both medium and large academic libraries mostly from self-instruction, including books and websites (Taylor 2000, 116–17; Kneip 2007, 12). Kneip's respondents reported feeling a high level of expertise with HTML and CSS, but not as much expertise with design, graphics, web programming, and database management (2007, 11). Although a library-related degree is common for webmasters, other academic degrees, coursework, and certifications can also be relevant. After you are in a position, you will still engage in numerous workshops to continue your education.

## *Professional qualifications*

In the USA, a master's degree in library science (MLS) is often required for professional library jobs, including those with web project management responsibilities. Although what you learn in library school may not directly prepare you to manage web projects, an MLS degree is helpful for understanding the larger organization and other roles such as reference, instruction, and collection development. While webmasters and other highly skilled technical staff may or may not have an MLS, librarians with MLS degrees are more likely to be the successful candidates in jobs with project management responsibilities due to their need to interact as peers with librarian colleagues, report to faculty groups, and to be familiar with library-specific systems such as the OPAC and research databases.

In the UK, a postgraduate qualification in librarianship or information science is also often a requirement, with a membership in the Chartered Institute of Library and Information Professionals (*http://www.cilip .org.uk/qualificationschartership/*) considered the 'gold standard'. CILIP has a reciprocal agreement with the American Library Association and the Australian Library and Information Association allowing graduates holding American, Canadian, or Australian bachelor's and master's degrees in library and information studies to apply for positions in the UK (*http://www.cilip.org.uk/qualificationschartership/Qualifications fromoverseas*).

If you're a newly minted professional with solid web skills but without much work experience, you should get some additional education or experience of managing projects under your belt. If you like the idea of being a big fish in a small pond, plenty of small or medium-sized academic libraries need a webmaster or web librarian. These web positions are frequently combined with another library function, but this might be just the thing for an early professional job. Web librarians who have done at least some cataloging, reference, instruction, or other library work will have more credibility with their colleagues in those roles. If, on the other hand, you don't feel ready to put yourself out there in the spotlight as 'the' web librarian, you could look for entry-level positions in academic libraries with large web departments, where you would learn from others in your department or through teams. You would be able to work directly on web projects right away as well as learn from the proven experience of your new colleagues. You might also expand your search to web jobs in other departments at a university, including those working on the university website itself.

Most importantly, don't assume that a big university library or even a big university has no need for your fledgling web project management skills. Many institutions have been slow to allocate staff and reorganize departments to support web functions. They may have some individuals such as programmers or graphics experts, but may not yet have someone who can coordinate those people. Your MLS degree and interest in managing projects may be all it takes to get you a leadership position supported by a highly skilled team.

## Other academic degrees

Several degrees at undergraduate and graduate levels can prepare you for web project management (see figure 2.4). The Project Management Institute (PMI) offers accreditation to colleges and universities for project management programs. These programs are often offered through a business department and prepare the student for any type of project management. See *http://www.pmi.org/CareerDevelopment/Pages/Degree-Directory.aspx* for a current list. Computer science and information science programs are increasingly offering degrees in information architecture and human-computer interaction. While these programs may not provide you with the project management foundations, they will provide you with many of the skills needed for working with websites.

**Figure 2.4** Academic degrees relevant to the web project manager

| Degree | Institution | URL |
|---|---|---|
| BS in Informatics | University of Washington | http://www.ischool.washington.edu/informatics/ |
| BS in Business with Project Management specialization | Capella University | http://www.capella.edu/schools_programs/undergraduate_studies/business/project_management.aspx |
| MS in Information Architecture and Knowledge Management | Kent State University | http://iakm.kent.edu/studentservices/prospective.html |
| MS in Interaction Design and Information Architecture | University of Baltimore | http://iat.ubalt.edu/idia/ |
| PhD with specialization in Human-Computer Interaction | University of Maryland College Park | http://www.cs.umd.edu/hcil/academics/graduate-studies.shtml |

Various undergraduate degrees offer additional preparation for a web project manager in an academic library. Although a general computer science curriculum will certainly boost your understanding of technology, a degree in a liberal arts subject with a significant research requirement, such as history or sociology, will help you understand students' use of library resources. Applied degrees such as marketing or communications can also provide excellent preparation for project management by teaching you about communication with internal and external stakeholders. If you expect to focus on writing or editing web content, you might take classes or get a degree in technical communication. Some media studies and graphic design curriculums include concentrations in interaction and web design. If you're on the job hunt after earning your degree, be sure to highlight how your degree or coursework might have application to your role as a web project manager. Unlike some other careers, web project management does not yet require one undergraduate degree to the exclusion of all others.

## Academic coursework and project management certifications

If you already work in an academic library, chances are that your institution allows you to take classes for free or for a reduced fee.

Coursework in business, computer science, or media studies will increase your skills, knowledge, and understanding in those areas. Look for classes dedicated to project management in your institution's business and computer science departments.

If you are interested in pursuing project management beyond the library, you might also consider certification as a project manager. Certification also has the potential to help web project managers within academic libraries clarify their roles. Several certification programs are listed in figure 2.5.

**Figure 2.5**    Selected project management certifications

| Organization | Certifications | Website |
|---|---|---|
| Project Management Institute (PMI) | Program Management Professional Project Management Professional Certified Associate in Project Management | *http://www.pmi.org/ CareerDevelopment/ Pages/Obtaining-Credential.aspx* |
| The International Association of Project and Program Management (IAPPM) | Certified Project Manager Certified Project Professional Certified Project Director Certified International Project Auditor | *http://www.iappm .org/cpm.htm* |
| International Project Management Association (IPMA) | Certified Projects Director Certified Senior Project Manager Certified Project Manager Certified Project Manager Associate | *http://www.ipma.ch/* |

## Education for information architecture

Information architecture is a closely related field to web project management. Information architects structure, organize, and label information within information systems. The ASIS&T Information Science Education Committee is currently gathering information about existing courses and programs in this field and has a website where they've listed their work so far: *http://www.asis.org/educationprograms.html.*

## Workshops

Workshops will help you continue your education without a huge time commitment, although the fees for such workshops can be high and travel costs are usually involved. Learning Tree (*http://learningtree.com/*), for example, teaches week-long courses in numerous cutting-edge technologies in the USA. Less expensive options include workshop opportunities at conferences (see callout). If you are a librarian traveling to one or more of these conferences anyway, the pre-conference fee and a night or two extra at the hotel may be the only extra costs.

---

## Conference and workshop opportunities for project management and web technologies

 ### Project management

The Association of Research Libraries (ARL) offers a sponsored institute on project management in libraries, 'Library Project Management Institute: Getting Things Done or Getting the Outcomes You Want' (*http://www.arl.org/ leadership/institutes/*).

The Chartered Institute of Library and Information Professionals (CILIP; *http://www.cilip.org.uk/training/*) offers workshops such as 'Managing Projects in the Library and Information Context.'

The International Project Management Association (IPMA; *http://www.ipma.ch/edutcationtraining/*) has a project management program targeting countries that do not have a national project management association, and offers economic support to universities or government agencies that want to organize a training program. While the host covers local expenses, IPMA generally covers the cost for preparing the training material as well as travelling expenses and fees for the trainers.

### Web-related technologies

The US federal government offers several workshops and short courses through 'Web Manager University,' all in the Washington, DC area (*http://www.usa.gov/webcontent/resources/training/university .shtml*). These workshops are focused on web issues such as usability, clear writing, and accessibility.

---

In the UK, UKOLN offers an annual 'Institutional Web Management Workshop' which 'provides an opportunity for those involved in the provision of institutional Web services to hear about institutional case studies, national initiatives and emerging technologies' (*http://www.ukoln.ac.uk/web-focus/events/workshops/*)

### Ongoing library and information professional conferences

These conferences often include project management topics:

- the Library and Information Technology Association (LITA), *http://www.ala.org/ala/mgrps/divs/lita/litaevents/litaeventsprograms.cfm*
- Computers in Libraries, *http://www.infotoday.com/conferences.asp*
- the American Library Association, *http://www.ala.org/ala/conferencesevents/index.cfm*
- the Association for College and Research Libraries, *http://www.ala.org/ala/mgrps/divs/acrl/events/index.cfm*
- the Chartered Institute for Library and Information Professionals, *http://www.cilip.org.uk/training/confcalendar/*.

# Personality traits for the web project manager

Certainly no single personality profile exists for a web project manager. Nevertheless, there are several important characteristics that will make the job easier. You need excellent interpersonal communication skills, planning and organization skills, a high tolerance for change, and the ability to work in a high pressure environment. You also need to re-think your job in terms of enabling others to do their work, rather than maintaining a sole focus on your own work.

In 1987 Barry Z. Posner conducted what would become a landmark study, 'What it takes to be a good project manager,' in which he surveyed 287 men and women in the USA. Based on their responses, he compiled a list of six 'skill areas' for project managers, which are shown in figure 2.6; 84% of his respondents highlighted good communication skills as essential

**Figure 2.6**  Skill areas for project management

| Skill area | Components |
|---|---|
| Communication | Listening, persuading |
| Organization | Planning, goal-setting, analyzing |
| Team-building | Empathy, motivation, esprit de corps |
| Leadership | Sets example, energetic, vision (big picture), delegates, positive |
| Coping | Flexibility, creativity, patience, persistence |
| Technology | Experience, project knowledge |

*Source*: Posner 1987, 53

for a project manager. Posner also found that problem solving was seen as an important skill, and 'problem finding' was even more critical—that is, becoming aware of issues before they became problems (52).

## Interpersonal communication

You should enjoy working with people and feel comfortable talking one-on-one and in groups. If you're shy, you'll need to develop strategies to overcome your fears. Project managers need to be able to motivate others, to explain complicated projects and technologies to both technical experts and laypeople, and often, to translate between groups with disparate vocabularies. A library staff member may only have vague ideas; the programmer needs specific instructions. It's your job to figure out how to clarify the customer's needs and make them specific enough for the programmer. In academic libraries, this ability to serve as a bridge between public services staff and technical experts is critical.

Although you need to be comfortable expressing ideas verbally, you will also need to be a good listener. Academic libraries are full of intellectuals, some of whom need to 'think out loud' or develop their ideas by examining copious research. Patience in listening will pay off. You will gain an understanding of goals, concerns, interests, and buy-in by listening. This area is so important that we've included a section on the topic of active listening in this chapter's list of recommended readings.

## Planning and organization

If you're already a natural list-maker and use a day planner religiously, you're on the right track. If you think you might need improvement in this area, you'll want to check out the 'personal organization' section in the recommended readings at the end of this chapter or take a workshop on this topic. In any organization, your colleagues will have varying levels of interest and skill with personal organization and time management. Be careful to remain open to other work styles even as you may be tightening up your own personal organization skills.

## High tolerance for technological vicissitudes

To be a web project manager in an academic library you need to embrace the challenges of technology. Websites and applications will always have limitations, bugs, and error messages. Programmers may spend a week trying to code something that seemed like it was going to be easy, only to find out that security restrictions on campus make the desired result impossible. Not only will you need to overcome your own frustrations with technology, you'll have to encourage others to do so as well. Many of your colleagues in academic libraries will be interested in the latest technologies, but they will be even more interested in their subject and service areas. You'll need to help and encourage them as you introduce technological change.

## High pressure, high profile environment

Managing web projects takes leadership, and being in a place of leadership will mean you have a high profile. A web project manager in an academic library needs to feel comfortable—or at least prepared—to operate in a position where every decision will face scrutiny. Reactions to your decisions are likely to be immediate, public, and often surprising. Most projects will be met with both praise and criticism. Thanks to the variety of communication methods in academic libraries, and a general feeling of academic freedom, you may end up receiving critiques in front of a large group of people, while receiving the nicest compliments in the privacy of your e-mail inbox.

Web project managers also operate under time pressure from several sources. You will be setting deadlines which others may be less than willing to follow, and operating under deadlines which are difficult to meet given your other job responsibilities. Since you're likely working with a team, they too will contribute to how 'on track' a project is, and it will be your role to negotiate with them about changes to the schedule.

## Enabling others to do their job

Thomas Shelford and Gregory Remillard emphasize the importance of the web project manager's role as a positive 'enabler' (2003, 4–5). By spending time actively listening to a colleague, you may be enabling her to better visualize ideas. You may be spending time getting feedback from stakeholders, analyzing their input, and revising specifications to enable the programmers on your team to proceed with more specific details and avoid time-consuming meetings. In these examples, you are moving the goals of the project forward by helping participants meet their own goals more efficiently.

This enabling role means you don't end up with a tangible product at the end of every day, nor will finished projects be your successes alone. You'll need to be able to find satisfaction from helping others to do *their* jobs in order to truly enjoy project management. Project managers may discover new challenges in documenting accomplishments for performance evaluations and promotions. Just as with managing personnel, the project manager's success is often wrapped up in the success of others.

Many academic libraries use teams, committees, and permanent work units to accomplish significant amounts of work. Routine work and other projects compete for work time and energy. You will be relying on others to get projects done, and will need some 'soft' skills to succeed. Ashley Friedlein lists several 'soft skills' necessary for a project manager (2001, 14–15). Check with your human resources department to see if they offer training classes in some of these skills. Various academic departments on campus may also teach courses that cover these topics, including business, communication studies, and public administration.

Friedlein's 'soft' skills that characterize a good web project manager are:

- being a good communicator and educator
- being a team player; leading by example; willing to work hands-on
- being able to empathize
- having enthusiasm for the web
- having a good sense of humor; ability to stay calm under pressure
- being able to fight your own battles; having grit and determination
- being good at handling relationships; recognizing emotional credits and debits for use with client and team to steer project forward
- being able to take responsibility and learn from one's own mistakes
- paying attention to detail

- being pragmatic—having a strong grip on reality
- being solution-oriented.

## Technical skills for the web project manager

So, what are the technical requirements for a library web project manager? While practical experience with web technologies is definitely a plus, your understanding of how web technologies work and how they can be applied to solve problems is also critical. You can understand

---

### Motivating people emotionally

 In public institutions, stellar achievement is infrequently rewarded with direct financial rewards. Since you can't hand out end-of-year bonuses or raises, you'll need sensitivity to what motivates people emotionally. So, how do you build up your 'emotional credit?' Here are some ideas:

- Remember what's personally important to the people on your team, and bring it into conversations. Is John excited about his new hybrid vehicle? Ask about its recent gas mileage achievements.
- Volunteer for others' teams and give them the kind of contribution you would like to receive from your team members.
- When your colleagues send out a request for feedback on their project, make sure you always respond.
- When others contribute to your project, be generous, specific, and immediate with your praise. Consider explaining your appreciation for them in a letter with a copy to their supervisor.
- Modify the praise you offer to others based on what you know about the person. A shy person may not welcome public praise, but may instead value a small thank-you lunch.
- If you are working with tenure-track faculty members who are making major contributions, write formal thank-you notes on letterhead so they can include them in their dossiers. Again, you'll want to send a copy to their supervisor as well.
- Bringing homemade food to meetings can not only send a positive emotional message, but also raise people's energy level.

---

what JavaScript can do and what its advantages and disadvantages are without being an expert in writing code.

How much you use technical skills directly in your daily work will depend largely on the size of your library and its web staff. In a larger library, your knowledge of HTML and CSS may come into play only as you are coordinating a team of staff who actually code the pages. In a smaller library, you may end up creating stylesheets and coding HTML yourself. No matter the size of your library, though, you should have at least a working knowledge of the following technologies and knowledge areas:

- HTML and XHTML
- CSS
- JavaScript
- graphic design as it relates to the web
- database design
- web programming in sufficient detail to have an intelligent conversation with an expert.

If you are lacking in one of the above areas, you are not alone. Kneip's study of library webmasters in medium-sized libraries found that 72% felt 'very experienced' with HTML but only 45% had experience using CSS (2007, 14). Less than 20% said they felt very familiar with web programming and database management. For the web project manager, the most critical skill is the ability to conceptualize technologies and understand how they can be applied to real-world problems. Although you'll want to be knowledgeable about each of these areas, you do not need to be an expert in them all to be a good project manager.

## So, do you want to be a web project manager?

Just because you like working with web technologies does not mean that project management needs to be in your future. You can have ample opportunities for web-related work on web teams or in another role. There are several challenges that go along with the web project management role that you should consider:

- Operating under deadlines is stressful even when everyone agrees the deadline is critical. Depending on your organizational culture, you may be the only one who thinks those deadlines are actually important. Meeting deadlines is one of the satisfactions that come with successful project management—but in an academic library, deadlines might be out of your control.

- No matter how great your project management process and communication is, there will always be someone in your organization, or even many people, who overlook your repeated messages—and blame you.

- Since academic librarians usually feel ownership of some part of their library website, you may need to make decisions that are unpopular with colleagues.

- In academic libraries, web projects frequently depend on others to contribute to the project. You may have carefully structured the timeline to provide time for staff input or for them to upload content. In an academic library, your contributors will usually have other responsibilities that may take priority. Delayed responses from your colleagues then means a delay for your project.

- If you are a tenure-track librarian, you may be under additional pressure to publish and to meet senior librarians' expectations. This peer-evaluation pressure may increase the stress of the process.

- By being the project manager, you may not spend as much time 'hands on' with web development, graphics, or usability testing as you would like. You may be coordinating those who do, and find less time than you thought to actually practice your own web skills. If you want to both manage and work directly on projects, you'll probably want to work in a smaller organization.

- If you were a librarian before you were a web project manager, you may miss being more involved in prior roles such as serving on the reference desk, teaching classes, or cataloging. Your previous colleagues who continue to fulfill more traditional librarian roles may no longer feel you are 'one of them.'

The many rewards of being a web project manager can balance out the challenges. Ashley Friedlein lists several of the rewards for being a web project manager. First on his list is creative thinking: 'Creative does not necessarily mean wacky ideas and original designs; it means creative business thinking, coming up with novel and better ways of doing business using the Web' (2001, 15). In libraries, our business is serving our patrons, and coming up with new and better ways of doing our business to facilitate their work is rewarding. Integrating traditional print collections and legacy systems with our other online resources using web interfaces is just one of the creative challenges in academic libraries. To support your creativity, you also have the chance to learn new skills. With the fast pace of change in web technologies, staying current with new trends is an intrinsic part of the job. Not only do you get to be one of the first to try out new things, you get paid to do it!

The chance to communicate with the world beyond your institution is also something that many find attractive about the role of web project management. Although you may think of local users as your audience, server log files will show site traffic from all over the world. Particularly if your library has special collections or unique online content, you facilitate the work of scholars everywhere. Finally, one of the most valuable rewards for working with the web in an academic library is joining the virtual community of others in similar roles. Web project managers in academic libraries are among the most progressive, change-oriented people you'll meet. They are generally willing to share their experiences, formally and informally. Since colleagues at other institutions are not competitors, they are likely to share code, processes, suggestions, and advice with nothing expected in return. Furthermore, you'll have avenues into other groups, such as human-computer interaction researchers, usability testers, and information architects. These professionals also enjoy helping others achieve their goals through creating and improving web interfaces. By joining the ranks of web project managers, you will gain friends, colleagues, and mentors at other institutions worldwide.

# Conclusion

While libraries were able to publish early websites on an ad hoc basis, today's academic library requires web project management expertise. Whether the project management role is one person's sole area of responsibility or just a small part of someone's job, these responsibilities should be part of someone's formal job description. Furthermore, due to their position as a 'hub' in the organization, web project managers may engage in activities other than project management that are critical for the organization. To fulfill these roles, web project managers will need a solid library education, knowledge of current web technologies, and a resilient personality. The challenges and the rewards of the position are both great. If you are destined to be a great project manager, you will have the satisfaction of bringing individuals together to achieve something greater than the sum of their separate goals.

## Life skills for the web project manager

 Being a web project manager in an academic library is tough! Based on our personal experiences, here are some practical tips that might make your day—and your life—much smoother!

### Time management

- Spend the first few minutes of each day making a 'day list' of the things you'd like to accomplish this day—and be realistic!

- Choose the 'top three' items on your day list. Promise yourself that even if you get nothing else but these items done, you will be satisfied.

- Schedule specific 'planning times' in whatever calendar you use. For example, if you have a project team meeting coming up, reserve 30 or 60 minutes prior to the meeting for planning purposes. Never run in breathless to a meeting again!

- Schedule fifteen minutes after each meeting to take care of any immediate action items that came up during the meeting.

- You are guaranteed to spend some of your evening and weekend hours 'on the job' during crunch times. Make sure to keep track of these hours and, if your institution allows, take compensation time during a lower-intensity period. In academic libraries, the summer session is usually a good time for this.

### Personal organization

- Consider creating a private wiki to keep track of your personal ideas, to-do lists, meeting notes, and brainstorm sessions. Think of it as your virtual brain.

- Working in an academic library usually means attending conferences and possibly writing conference reports. Save yourself lots of time by blogging at the conference, then using your blog as your conference report! No more paper notes!

## Staying positive

- You will need to send necessary but unwelcome e-mails. Whether you are announcing the delay of a project completion or announcing a 'compromise decision' that is only popular with some, be succinct and upbeat in your communications.

- Pay attention to thanking others. At least once a week, set aside a time to think of someone you appreciate, and send them an e-mail telling them how much you appreciate them as a colleague, and why.

- Don't be shy about nominating your team, a recent project, or colleagues for an award through your library, your university, or professional organizations. Even if your nomination doesn't win, your colleague(s) or team members will know that *you* think they deserve the award. Wouldn't you feel proud if someone told you they'd nominated you for an award?

# Recommended readings

## Personal organization

Adair, John (2003) *Concise Time Management and Personal Development*. London: Thorogood.

Allen, David (2001) *Getting Things Done: The Art of Stress-free Productivity*. New York: Penguin.

Nauman, Ann K. (1991) *Making Every Minute Count: Time Management for Librarians*. Berkeley Heights, JC: Library Learning Resources.

Pickering, Peg (2001) *How to Make the Most of Your Workday*. Franklin Lakes, NJ: Career Press.

Pollar, Odette (1999) *Organizing Your Work Space*. Los Altos, CA: Crisp Publications.

## Active listening

Harris, Richard M. (2006) *The Listening Leader: Powerful New Strategies for Becoming an Influential Communicator*. Westport, CT: Praeger.

Hoppe, Michael H. (2006) *Active Listening*. Greensboro, NC: Center for Creative Leadership.

# References

Brandon, Dan (2006) *Project Management for Modern Information Systems*. Hershey, PA: IRM Press.

Bunch, Nancy J., Anne Marie Casey, Frances A. Devlin, and Lana Ivanitskaya (2006) Project management and institutional collaboration in libraries. *Technical Services Quarterly* 24 (1): 17–36.

Croneis, Karen S., and Pat Henderson (2002) Electronic and digital librarian positions: A content analysis of announcements from 1990 through 2000. *Journal of Academic Librarianship* 28 (4): 232–236.

Friedlein, Ashley (2001) *Web Project Management: Delivering Successful Commercial Web Sites*. New York: Morgan Kaufmann.

Keach, Jennifer, and Jody Condit Fagan (2008) *Survey of Web Project Managers in Academic Libraries*. Web survey conducted June 9 – July 1, 2008.

Kinkus, Jane (2007) Project management skills: A literature review and content analysis of librarian position announcements. *College & Research Libraries* 68 (4): 352–363.

Kneip, Jason (2007) Library webmasters in medium-sized academic libraries. *Journal of Web Librarianship* 1 (3): 3–23.

Posner, Barry Z. (1987) What it takes to be a good project manager. *Project Management Journal* 18 (1): 51–54.

Shelford, Thomas J., and Gregory A. Remillard (2003) *Real Web Project Management: Case Studies and Best Practices from the Trenches*. Boston: Addison-Wesley.

Taylor, Mary K. (2000) Library webmasters: Satisfactions, dissatisfactions, and expectations. *Information Technology & Libraries* 19 (3): 116.

Winston, Mark D., and Tara Hoffman (2005) Project management and libraries. *Journal of Library Administration* 42 (1): 51–61.

# 3

# Environmental realities

## Introduction

The organizational environment, including your library's administration, organizational culture, and communication practices, affects your ability to manage a project in an academic library. You'll also face issues that come from being situated within a larger organization and working with students, faculty, and staff. These issues will vary greatly between institutions and even seasoned project managers will take time to learn about the larger organization.

## Organizational placement and size

The administrative placement of your library within your college or university can have big implications for the web projects in your academic library. The library may be part of an academic affairs division, headed up by a provost. Or, it could be situated in a student support services division. In each case, the larger organization will see both the library and the people who work in it differently. Librarians at libraries within academic affairs may be regarded as faculty partners, which raises both obligations and opportunities. Libraries grouped with student support services may be freed from some obligations to participate as an academic unit, but may not have the same connection with faculty colleagues. Also consider what this means for your library's dean or director. Does she sit on an academic council with academic deans? What kinds of meetings does she attend across campus? Who is her boss? Learning about your dean's or director's context will help you be a savvier manager.

The size of your institution will also have a profound effect. Libraries at small institutions may be entirely dependent on their campus IT department for advanced technical skills and servers. Librarians in smaller institutions typically take on many different roles than at larger institutions, providing less time for each responsibility. Smaller institutions frequently do not have as many financial resources available for experimentation, but must still provide a suite of web services similar to those at large institutions. On the positive side of the equation, when resources are limited, identifying priorities and feasible solutions can be easier. You simply don't have as many options available to you. Also, your web project at a small institution may be the only project currently under way. You will have the attention of your colleagues. A project at a smaller institution also means there are fewer stakeholders to coordinate and potentially fewer disagreements.

## Campus web environment

Your campus may handle web projects for the entire organization through one or many different offices. A central computing office may handle academic and administrative computing—hardware, software, and web. A marketing office may provide publishing support and templates.

On your campus, the library may handle all library-related web work. Your library may, in fact, manage some aspects of web publishing for the entire campus. Each campus is different. Regardless of your obligations to work with others throughout campus, as a savvy project manager, you should get to know your colleagues who provide web support for the campus. Not only do you need to learn about policies, you also want to build their trust as colleagues. You may also find yourself relying on their resources such as a usability testing lab, web programmers, content management systems, or knowledge about campus systems. To simplify the discussion, in this chapter we will refer to the 'campus web office.' On your campus, the 'campus web office' could be one person or many people distributed throughout information technology, marketing, and academic offices.

## Working with guidelines and requirements

Find out if your institution has guidelines or requirements related to your project. Some campus web offices control all design considerations for the library website. Others have web templates and style guides that every part of the institution must follow (Lombard and Hite 2007).

Others simply ask their units to use a standard logo in the same place on each page.

A 2005 article by Sarah Houghton spelled out several ways a library's website can be limited by the larger organization's web; we have added some more to create the list below:

- Technical limitations that apply to the larger organization's site also apply to the library's site. This may even mean the library's site cannot meet accessibility standards or be cross-browser compatible if the larger organization's site elements or content management systems are not up to standard.

- Visual elements of the larger organization may limit the library's screen real estate. A large header which brands all pages as part of the school's website, for instance, may squeeze out branding that you would like to include for your library.

- Global navigation required for the larger organization may distract from your own local navigation.

- Users may have difficulty distinguishing between library and non-library links. For example, if the header and footer feature contact information, links may send reference questions to a university's main e-mail address.

- The library may have limited access to the web servers where its website resides. This restriction may limit your ability to include applications and access database content.

One of the most challenging of environments in which to work is that where your library has little influence over the library website other than the words on the page. An institution which is marketing-heavy might require the library to load up its home page with graphics that show off rare books and other treasures, while you would like more real estate for undergraduate research tools and subject guides. The templates chosen by the web office on campus might work fine for academic offices which primarily provide information about major requirements and contact information, but not work for the library's instructional and research focus.

In any of the above areas, the goals of your web project and the environment at your institution may conflict. As web project manager, you should decide how important each potential battle might be and what support you might be able to muster. If you think it's worth fighting against a campus-wide mandate, you'll need to involve your library administration early on to measure their support. Consider a case where your project conflicts with the requirement to use a university template. Your administration may not support your case at all, in which case you should start modifying your expectations for your project. Your administration might instead support a liberal interpretation of the university requirements, hoping that the university won't care (or notice). Your administration might also be willing to have a direct conversation with the requisite office(s) to make a case for the desired exception, or support your desire to do so. Regardless of your administration's stance, you'll want to know where you stand before you begin to develop such a project.

When the relationship between your library and the campus web office is not what you'd like, as web project manager, what can you do?

## Challenge assumptions

If your team members have been at the university for years, you may have to question assumptions: 'There's just absolutely nothing we can do with the way *they* have it set up,' your team members may say. '*They* never have any time for our needs.' This is when your strength as a communicator must come into play. Listen to your team and then explain your goals and explore options with your colleagues in the campus web office. You may find fewer obstacles than your team led you to believe.

## Get to know the policy makers and enforcers

Find out who is responsible for creating the organization's templates, setting the organization's web guidelines, and establishing project priorities. Get to know them and their team members. Perhaps they are frustrated with some of the current limitations as well, and would welcome an ally in an ongoing dialogue with a high-level administrator. Perhaps they are unaware of tools they could use to verify accessibility compliance, or would welcome help with a usability test of the university navigation. Perhaps they don't actually know about your needs.

## Get to know your campus peers

There are likely numerous webmasters across the organization. If they don't already meet regularly, consider creating a regular lunch meeting to discuss issues of common interest. They may be the only one in their department facing technical or policy issues and may welcome the opportunity to network with others in related positions. This group may find common interests and recommend changes to higher levels.

## Research your university's peers

A strong argument for exceptions to campus web policies and for technology support is to demonstrate the library websites of your university peers. You will undoubtedly get questions from colleagues about why *our* website is not more like some other college website. Different resources, student populations, and missions will affect what different institutions can provide. Find out from your library administration if your library or university has identified a peer group. This peer group may not prove the best for *your* purposes, but it is a good place to start.

## Enlist help

After trying to make as much headway as you can on your own, enlist the help of your library administration. Be sure to present a clear list of things you think need to be changed, and submit hard research to back up your argument. An issue like accessibility compliance, for instance, is something they will certainly be able to support, since it relates to legal concerns as well as user needs. They may also be interested in ways that your requested changes can save staff time. Show how your peer libraries are able to accomplish what you recommend.

# Competing for technical support

Your situation may be almost the complete opposite: you may have few guidelines and little technology or design support. Larger libraries have the luxury of attracting and developing programmers and graphic designers dedicated to library projects. If you work in a smaller library, though, you may rely entirely on an IT office or marketing office.

Again, try to get to know the people across campus whose job is to assist with web projects. Ask what they need to know from you if you are requesting their assistance on a project and follow through on providing that information. Regularly inform that person about projects you are considering, even if you aren't asking for help. You may be surprised how many times the person will be interested in your work and needs. Ask them for advice about workshops, listservs, and other resources that you or a colleague might use to increase technical or design understanding. Doing so will help you understand what projects are feasible on your campus and which ones just aren't practical.

Your computing support colleagues from outside the library may simply be too busy supporting the university website and academic computing to be able to participate on more than an occasional project. If this is the case, consider selecting projects that fit with your in-house skill set. If you do not have a programmer available to you, do not plan on creating an application. Instead, look for turnkey commercial products from vendors that provide technical support to you as part of the purchase price. If you do not have a server available to you, look for hosted solutions where the vendor handles backups and maintenance. If you do not have a server, programmer, or money, consider how you might leverage one of the many free online resources available to individual web users such as blogs or wiki software.

Your campus marketing office may also be too busy with university-wide publications and initiatives to dedicate significant design time to your project. For both programming and design needs, consider looking for individuals on campus who would like to build their portfolio or provide service to the library. Faculty and students in computing, art, technical writing, and media departments might be interested in contributing their time. If funds allow, you can also hire outside professionals to provide these services. You should also develop in-house skills, though, to support future revisions and updates to the project—or be prepared to outsource skills again.

---

### Involving your administration with communication across campus

 Involving your library administrators can have a profound effect on your project. Part of their job is to network across campus, so they frequently have extensive campus knowledge, resources, and relationships. They can:

- identify partners across campus for web projects
- interpret university requirements and policies for web pages
- be aware of other projects related to your project.

Regardless of whether your library administrators are directly involved with your web project, make sure they see a project description so they can help you to stay in the campus loop.

# The academic environment: faculty and students

No discussion of the academic library environment would be complete without considering the two largest groups in that environment: faculty and students. Chapter 9 will discuss getting input from these user groups. Other than their role as your primary user groups, how do these users affect web project management in an academic library?

## *Faculty*

For web projects that directly impact university faculty, you and your web team should keep the following things in mind:

- Faculty are not necessarily library experts even though they may have advanced needs. The last time a particular faculty member used the library for research may be when he completed his PhD. Faculty have a wide spectrum of technological abilities. Some will have high knowledge and complex demands; others will be frustrated with even simple interfaces. Therefore, most projects intended for faculty will need to plan for both novice and advanced users.

- Faculty are experts in their subject area and may think of the library only in terms of that subject. For example, history faculty may see the library as an archive for books and special collections, while biology faculty may think first of online journals. If your project will support multiple disciplines, consider these different perspectives.

- Although some faculty thrive on change, there will be many faculty for whom change causes stress. Expect some resistance to change from faculty.

- Faculty operate according to the academic timeline. The academic timeline affects students, too, so we will address it in more detail below.

## *Students*

What is it about students that changes the environment within which you are managing web projects?

- Most students are not library experts and have a wide range of technological abilities. Just as with faculty, most projects will need to plan for both novice and advanced users.

- Students' needs and behaviors are changing rapidly and will continue to do so. Consider a given project's 'usefulness horizon.' That is, how much time do you want to invest in a specific fix, given the potential length of a given solution's utility?

- Since students graduate every four years, this group is much more tolerant of change.

- Like faculty, students operate according to the academic timeline.

OCLC's *College Students' Perceptions of Libraries and Information Resources* (De Rosa et al. 2005) provides a wealth of information about today's college students and is highly recommended reading for any librarian.

## Academic timeline

The academic calendar can have a great impact on your project management environment. When are people on campus? When are they busy? When will they care the most about your project? Students go through typical phases each year. Moving in, attending orientation events, and settling into their new class schedule dominates the first week, but then there are relative lulls between when major assignments are due. Unless faculty are new, their semester will be busiest when their students turn in assignments and during final exams. They may also spend their summer months working on research. Librarians are also affected by the academic timeline, with heavier instruction loads early in each semester. You may need to schedule your web project to accommodate the academic timeline. User studies, for example, need to occur when there are plenty of students and faculty on campus, but not immediately before final exams! You should also time the launch of major projects affecting services and research for the times when your students and faculty aren't at their busiest.

# Your library's environment

When we asked web project managers at academic libraries 'what are the top three to five factors or variables *most* likely to create challenges in managing a web project at your academic library?', many of the responses related to their particular library environment. The most common challenges to successful web project management listed by respondents (n=65) were a failure to set clear priorities by upper administration (or changing priorities) and inadequate staffing. The next highest group of challenges came from the need to build consensus, including difficulties getting people to provide input and getting people to agree. Close on the heels of the issue of consensus was the challenge of others' personalities and opinions. Comments related to colleagues included 'resistant to change' or 'difficult people to work with;' fourteen of the 65 mentioned their technical situation, such as difficult software, a challenging server environment, or an inherited 'technical nightmare;' thirteen of the 65 respondents had staff who lacked the necessary expertise. Table 3.1 shows the full list of responses.

Academic libraries vary greatly in their organizational culture and communication style. Your library may have supportive upper management, an efficient organizational communication structure, clear decision-making, and adequate staff resources. Or, your library may have problems with these issues and others. With each of these challenges, though, come corresponding opportunities. Consensus-building is challenging because library staff are eager to contribute and passionate about what they do. A lack of understanding about web project management may correspond to a high level of understanding in other important areas. As project manager, your job includes working within

**Table 3.1**     Challenges to successful project management in the academic library

| Challenge | Respondents (n=65) |
|---|---|
| Shifting/unclear priorities | 25 |
| Inadequate staff/budget/resources | 25 |
| Consensus/strong opinions/the effort required to get input | 18 |
| Personalities/camaraderie/buy-in | 17 |
| Specific technical situation | 14 |
| Technical staff lack expertise | 13 |
| Lack of time | 13 |
| Larger organizational environment | 11 |
| Project management missing/not understood | 10 |
| Poor organizational communication | 8 |
| Need user testing | 7 |
| Scope creep | 6 |
| Challenges inherent to the field of librarianship | 5 |
| Poor management | 4 |
| Poor team composition | 1 |

your particular environment. You'll find advice in this chapter as well as in chapter 8, 'Planning for organizational communication,' on working with common organizational challenges.

## Responsibility and authority

One issue common to many library staff members who also serve as web project managers is the separation of responsibility and authority. Most project managers have responsibility, but not authority, for the people and resources which contribute the bulk of the work to a project. Many members of a project team have volunteered as a temporary assignment. The members may be peers of the project manager or even one step higher in the organizational chart. A team member's supervisor may not fully support the member's work on the project. As for financial resources, your library administration will approve library budget expenditures; project managers do not usually have budgets of their own. The project manager, then, is in the awkward position of controlling neither the people nor the money on which their project depends.

This situation is not a result of poor decision-making or poor management. J. Davidson Frame (2003, 30) lists several considerations for why this situation is an efficient way for organizations to operate:

- Projects are temporary, whereas the organization endures. Thus, assigning staff and resources to a specific project management team full-time may not make the most sense.

- Projects are unique, and address momentary needs. Each has its own resource requirements.

- Projects are composed of many pieces linked together in complex ways. This is especially true in academic libraries, where people with specialized skills, such as catalogers, reference librarians, and archivists, work on individual pieces.

Indeed, as Frame notes, 'the person who can be usefully employed full-time on a project is the exception rather than the rule' (2003, 31). In most academic libraries, even with web work such as project management, programming, and design written into position descriptions, each person's role on a single web project will likely not encompass an entire working day. For the web project manager, it doesn't always make sense to supervise the people who will be rotating on and off a web project team.

A project manager can evoke authority formally through organizational structures as well as informally through political, social, technical, and leadership skills. Here are just some of the resources you may have which enhance your authority outside of formal structures:

- knowledge about your organization's current web projects
- the support of your project sponsor (see chapter 4)
- strong communication skills (see chapter 8)
- diligent research including user studies (see chapter 9)
- good project documentation (see chapters 10–12)
- a proven track record
- the support of your library administration.

Project managers need to ensure they know where their authority begins and ends and what recourse they have when they have a need outside of their sphere of influence. They must learn to exert power in ways that do not depend on a supervisory relationship. And they need to learn how to separate the responsibility for getting the project done from the responsibility of evaluating personnel assigned to the project.

---

### What is important to library administrators?

 All library deans and directors are concerned with specific measures of organizational success. As web project manager, you should find out what measures and methods are used by your library administration. If you can frame your needs in terms of those measures, it will be that much easier for them to decide to send resources or help your way.

For Association of Research Libraries members, the 'ARL ranking' is one measure that is important to deans, provosts, and other high-level administrators. Other libraries may report statistics to the Association of College and Research Libraries (ACRL) and prepare annual reports based on these numbers. Library administrators may also be required to submit strategic plan objectives in response to a university strategic planning effort. Or, they may need to guide the organization with a strategic plan handed down from above. If you tie your web project management work and the objectives of specific projects to these larger institutional measures, you make a strong case for your work.

# Conclusion

The academic library is filled with intellectuals working together to increase human knowledge, educate students, and support research. You will benefit from understanding the issues outside of your immediate surroundings and practicing political savvy. The campus, academic, and library environments affect your web project's success. This chapter highlighted some of the common issues that can arise. No institution is alike, but the strategies presented here will help you overcome challenges in your environment and make the most of opportunities.

# References

DeRosa, Cathy, Joanne Cantrell, Janet Hawk, and Alane Wilson (2005) *College Students' Perceptions of Libraries and Information Resources*. Dublin, OH: OCLC, *http://www.oclc.org/reports/pdfs/studentperceptions.pdf*.

Frame, J. Davidson (2003) *Managing Projects in Organizations*. San Francisco, CA: Jossey-Bass.

Houghton, Sarah (2005) I've been framed! Designing a library web site within a government frame. *Computers in Libraries* 25 (6): 6–8.

Lombard, Emmett, and Lesley A. Hite (2007) Academic library web sites: Balancing university guidelines with user needs. *Journal of Web Librarianship* 1(2): 57–69.

# 4

# Defining your project

## Introduction

The process of identifying and starting a web project varies from library to library and project to project. You may receive a request from a person or committee who has both the interest and authority to add a new area to your website. You may hear a smattering of comments and suggestions from your colleagues, none of whom have the authority to approve changes. You may receive a directive from your supervisor or the administration. You may notice the need yourself and initiate the project.

As you begin to suspect that you have a project on your hands, you need to decide if it really is a project or just a task that can be accomplished in short order. If you have the liberty to do so in your organization, you also need to decide if other projects take priority. You may even discover that you shouldn't do a particular project—now or ever. Finally, once you've committed to doing the project, you need to ensure that everyone involved understands what exactly you are trying to create.

In this chapter, you will learn about the beginnings of projects and how the lucky ones move from a sketch on a napkin to more detailed project specifications and eventual success.

## Learning about projects

Central support departments in large organizations, including university campuses, frequently use project request forms to enable customers dispersed throughout campus to request assistance. If you are in a similar organization or if you receive new project requests frequently, you may choose to do the same. For most libraries, though, requiring a lengthy form for every new request is probably excessive. In fact, the impersonal approach of a project request form may meet with resistance.

Different organizations may assign different individuals or groups to investigate and solicit new projects, for example:

- you, as project manager
- other individuals playing the role of project manager
- the department head of the unit with web responsibilities
- a web committee or team
- an IT business analyst.

You read about both full-time and ad hoc project managers in chapter 2, 'The web project manager in academic libraries.' Chapter 5, 'The academic library web team,' is dedicated to web teams of all sorts. The IT business analyst option merits some explanation in this chapter, however, because it is a relatively new role.

An IT business analyst works directly with project stakeholders to gather and communicate information about potential and current projects to the rest of the project team and the project manager. The International Institute of Business Analysis (IIBA) describes the relationship between project manager and business analyst on their website in the following way: 'The role of the BA differs from the role of the Project Manager in that the BA is responsible for defining and managing the scope of a business solution, while the PM is responsible for the work necessary to implement that solution.' In many environments, including libraries, the project manager typically performs the business analyst duties. This book recognizes this combination by collapsing the two roles. Organizations are beginning to recognize business analysis as a separate discipline; the IIBA was formed in 2003. If you would like to learn more about the field of business analysis, visit the website of the IIBA at *http://www.theiiba.org/*.

Regardless of how you collect it, you need basic information about a project so that you can evaluate the feasibility of the project, understand the resources required, and decide if and when to start the project. If your responsibilities include learning about and evaluating new projects, gather information through one or more conversations with your colleagues when they come to you with an idea. Take notes while you talk, using an internal copy of a project request form. Type it up later into a finished document, within a blog or discussion board, or whatever method works for you. After you've documented everything, share it with the requestor to ask if you got it right. The next sections detail the briefest information you might gather.

## *The project sponsor*

Every project should have a project sponsor—one or more people who have the authority to sign off on the project plan as well as the end result. In the simplest of projects, one or two people are the clear sponsors. Projects that support a staff function or will only affect a small number of end users are good examples of this situation. Occasionally, you yourself may be the project sponsor. You may work in a small library where it's your job to initiate all things relating to the web. Or, the nature of the project may not fall in any particular area *other* than 'web,' such as conducting a complete review of the website's accessibility. You might want to chat with your supervisor or some other library leaders to confirm that you are, in fact, the project sponsor.

In an academic library, where the responsibility for content on the website is often distributed widely, you will frequently find that identifying your project sponsor is challenging. Your project sponsor may or may not be the person who has requested the project. For instance, one or more members of the reference department may suggest a redesign of the form that students use to request items be put on hold. As the project manager, you may need to speak to members from reference, circulation, and systems in order to identify the person who has the authority to sign off on changes to the form. You may also need to involve upper-level administration to settle disagreements or review library-wide policy implications. In such a case, the colleagues that have requested the change are end users or other stakeholders rather than the sponsors. An upper-level administrator may actually be the sponsor.

The most politically challenging web project within an academic library is the redesign of a popular or prominent portion of your public website such as the front page or the catalog. These high-profile projects need project sponsors most of all. The request for a high-impact project may come from anyone: the library director, yourself, or colleagues from any part of the organization. It may also come directly from users or through the observation of users having problems with the site. As a member of the organization, you will be aware (or will quickly become aware) of a large number of competing views that may be impossible to reconcile. In these instances, ask the library director or other top level administrator to serve in the role of project sponsor. You will be soliciting input from throughout the organization, but you are seeking a project sponsor to provide final approval for contentious decisions.

## Key stakeholders

Key stakeholders are the individuals or groups you will want to communicate with throughout the project—for input as well as buy-in. Stakeholders include users as well as colleagues.

## Other interested people (if any)

Include any individuals who are tangentially involved including colleagues working on similar projects, secondary users, and key administrators.

## Skills requested

Your project sponsor or key stakeholders may be prepared to perform some of the work even if they are not on the project team. Examples include writing content, creating graphics, soliciting input from users, marketing, and training. Identify what this project requires your project team to provide by listing the following information.

## Brief description

Write a concise description of the project to be used in describing it to others.

## Objectives

List what the project sponsor wants to achieve. If your project sponsor or requestor has many objectives, mark the high- priority goals to distinguish them from optional bells and whistles.

## Justification

Mention if the project is in direct support of organizational strategic plans, required by law (e.g. accessibility compliance), or required by your university (e.g. transitioning to a campus content management system). Depending on your library, projects endorsed or requested by the library director may also be considered to be required.

## Earliest start

List the earliest start date based on completion of related projects or needed participants. The earliest start date may even be 'immediately.'

## Proposed finish

List the date the requestor hopes to have this project completed and in use. The proposed finish date also is often 'immediately!'

## Latest finish

List the firm deadline. This date may be an exact date or an event such as 'end of summer.'

Although you might not require your colleagues to provide all this information on their own, you can post this list on your intranet (and point your colleagues to it) so everyone knows ahead of time what you will be collecting. Doing so helps your potential project requestors to think through their requests. You can also provide information in the same location about who to contact about a new project. If gathering information about new projects is out of your hands, encourage the person or group who does so to collect this same information.

Documenting this data serves many purposes. It ensures that you have enough information to decide when and if you will tackle the project. If you have more than one person managing web projects in your organization, it can help to identify connections between potential projects. The documents may help you compare projects when you are deciding priorities. They also serve to remind you about details if you do not start the project immediately. If you decide to move ahead with this project, this information will appear again in a project overview document as well as in more detailed documents that inform the project team.

# Deciding if a 'project' is actually a project

You might not think that differentiating tasks from projects is particularly important. The fact remains that not all requests submitted are really projects. Tasks, in contrast to projects, simply don't need as much project management attention. Ongoing maintenance tasks or other business-as-usual work also deserve different types of processes for planning and monitoring.

If you find yourself wondering if you really have a project, consider these definitions:

- 'A project is an outlay of resources with the intent of accomplishing a specific objective via an organized approach' (*Project Management for IT Professionals* 2005, 4).

- 'A Web project is a temporary endeavor that employs Internet technologies to achieve a specific objective by creating or enhancing a unique product' (Shelford and Remillard 2003, 50).

- 'A project is a temporary endeavor undertaken to create a unique product or service' (PMI Standards Committee 1996, 4).

- 'A project is usually a onetime activity with a well-defined set of desired end results' (Taylor 2004, 11).

Projects generally have a defined beginning and end—they are temporary and one-time. Projects are trying to produce a new or improved project or service. Generally, projects also involve two or more people, take at least two weeks of work, involve people from outside your own department, and include activities outside what you normally do (*Project Management for IT Professionals* 2005, 4). Figure 4.1 offers some side-by-side examples of tasks and projects.

Take a few moments to consider if the request you are reviewing really describes a project. If not, evaluate it as a new item for your task list or a new workflow.

**Figure 4.1** Examples of tasks and projects

| Tasks | Projects |
|---|---|
| Ongoing identification and repair of broken links | Cleanup initiative which identifies all external links to be kept on the site, moving them into a database to make future maintenance easier, and repairing broken ones in the process. |
| Adding a few new graphics picturing happy students to the library front page | Creation and implementation of a new comprehensive set of graphical elements used throughout the site and designed to reflect the library brand. |
| Daily monitoring of new content to ensure that it meets accessibility standards | Reviewing each web page using accessibility checking software and fixing all discovered errors with the goal of becoming 100% compliant within two years. |

# Prioritizing projects

Just as different libraries will rely on different people and groups to identify and investigate new projects, your library may also have one or more entities that approve projects. In many cases, deciding whether or not to undertake a project falls to the same person or group who gathered the information in the first place. You saw a list of the possibilities earlier in this chapter. This decision could also fall to:

- all possible web project managers together as a team
- a group of top administrators in your library
- the library dean or director.

Regardless of who does so, new projects need to be prioritized against others. Small libraries may not have as many people to propose new projects, but they also have fewer resources with which to accomplish projects. Medium and large libraries have more resources but also have more colleagues and users to support. Projects need to be prioritized in some way.

A first step in prioritizing is to review the justification recorded during the project information-gathering stage. You have a relatively easy decision if your project:

- is required to address a law
- is dictated by your university
- anticipates a major browser change which will render your pages incorrectly
- closes a security hole which hackers could exploit
- is requested by your supervisor
- is requested by your dean or director.

## Beyond the mission statement

 The more you can demonstrate how your web project supports the university's mission, the more support you'll be able to garner from your administration. The university's mission statement reveals part of the answer, but you'll want to flesh out how the mission affects reality by interviewing your library administrators and, if you can, colleagues across campus. Your organization might exist primarily to prepare students to enter the workforce—but the mission statement might not state this priority directly. Or, your organization might be more oriented toward preparing students for graduate school and research positions. The real mission of your organization will affect which web projects you prioritize, and will inform the requirements for each project.

**Figure 4.2**     Excerpt of library website goals from James Madison University Libraries

August 19, 2004

The goal of the James Madison University Libraries' website is to support the mission of the libraries.

**James Madison University Libraries' Mission Statement**

We connect students and faculty to ideas. We collect and deliver high quality information that reflects the richness of the curriculum and the many forms by which ideas are conveyed. We organize and preserve ideas for current and future generations of scholars. We teach members of our community to make intelligent use of information resources. We create an environment that promotes intellectual inquiry, exchange of ideas and discovery of knowledge. We collaborate with colleagues on campus and beyond to ensure open access to information. We participate actively in the intellectual life of the university. We support academic excellence by offering exceptional services that reflect the mission of James Madison University.

The website focuses on the needs of James Madison University students and faculty, both within the physical library spaces, elsewhere on campus, and off-campus. Specifically, the website provides services, collections, instruction, community, and promotion.

**Services**

The libraries' website provides online services to our primary users whenever possible, augmenting and at times replacing services offered within the libraries' physical walls. The website also provides information and guidance in the use of the services found in the traditional library spaces.

**Collections**

The libraries' website is the primary means of delivery for digital collections created both in-house and obtained from elsewhere. It is the primary finding aid for the physical collections. It provides intuitive access to the collections through logical organization and efficient search mechanisms. It provides opportunities for serendipitous discovery.

**Instruction**

The libraries' website educates our users to identify when information is needed and to locate, evaluate, and use it effectively. The website educates our users about procedures and policies for using the services and collections available to them at JMU Libraries. It also educates our users about current issues in scholarship, publishing, and access to information.

Armed with a deadline, you make sure that these projects get done. They take priority over all other projects. Most of the proposed projects, though, will not have such an obvious priority level. Or, many of them will have the same priority levels based on justification alone.

A next step in evaluating a proposed project is to compare it against what your library is already trying to accomplish. Many libraries have a strategic plan which articulates the library's mission, vision, and values along with top objectives and goals for a specified length of time. This plan may be the result of a collaborative process across the whole organization or a top-down mandate by administration. Either way, a proposed project directly supporting a goal found in that plan not only has the support of the requestor. It also has the support of your organization. Some libraries have also developed strategic plans, missions, and goals for their website (see example in figure 4.2). Not all projects need to speak directly to the specific goals in these strategic documents, but if the project doesn't even appear to match up with your library or website mission statement, it should begin to lose its urgency and fall to the bottom of your list of priorities or drop off the list altogether.

After reviewing the justification, description, and objectives, you will still need to prioritize those projects that have not moved to the top or the bottom of your list. Web design and software development companies have an advantage over internal web units when deciding whether or not to accept a job; they can rely heavily on a financial evaluation. At the least, they know how much they can charge for a particular job and they also are likely to track the number of hours worked on each job internally. Doing so allows them to analyze the cost benefit, return on investment, or payback period. Although that same company may also consider projects based on expanding their market or building their reputation, the financial numbers provide a quick means of comparing projects against one another.

## Financial evaluation methods

 If you are evaluating a project with financial aspects, you can use any of the following simple calculations. We've simplified the explanations here considerably, not accounting for inflation or opportunity cost. Find fuller explanations along with other financial evaluation methods in any standard finance resource. These three are described in similarly simple terms in Brandon's *Project Management for Modern Information Systems* (2006, 35).

## Cost benefit analysis or benefit cost ratio

Compares the cost of completing a project with the expected returns. A software developer may estimate that they will spend $200,000 in labor, servers, content, and promotion to create a new product. The company then expects to be able to sell that software outright to 200 libraries within five years, at $8,000 per library. Ignoring licensing revenues, the benefit is $1,600,000 for a cost of $200,000. The benefit-to-cost ratio is 8 to 1.

## Return on investment or average rate of return

Uses the same numbers, just expressed as the benefit minus cost divided by the cost. A return on investment for this same project, then, is ($1,600,000 − $200,000) / $200,000. The return on investment for this project is 700%.

## Payback period

Adds in the expected amount of time that the company can sell this product. If the software has a sellable life of five years, the company spent $200,000 to create this version, and they can earn $320,000 a year selling it, then the payback period is .625 of a year. The formula is investment cost divided by annual cash inflow.

Although most libraries do not ask their employees to track their time in billable hours like a design company, and few projects generate revenue, some parts of your projects might lend themselves to a financial analysis. For instance, replacing a licensed content management system with an open source solution has financial implications. You could estimate the staff time required of everyone on the project team and multiply by salary. You could then compare that to the savings you realize by no longer paying for the content management system.

Many of your projects, however, will have mostly abstract benefits. You may be creating an application that allows students to reserve group study rooms in the library, adding a popular new service. You may be implementing a federated search across different content silos, improving users' search experience. You may be creating a database of frequently asked questions, helping all your website visitors understand services and research options. You may be creating a repository for library statistics, used throughout the organization to evaluate services and purchases. These different projects may result in measurable changes—visits to the building and website, fewer basic questions at the reference desk, or increased use of statistics in the management of your library—but none of these returns show direct financial benefits.

Therefore, you will evaluate most of your projects using strategic rather than financial criteria. When faced with a list of possible projects or when considering how a new proposal fits into an existing list, you can score that project with a standard list of criteria against which all your projects will be judged. For each criteria, you or the person or group assigned to prioritize gives the project a score of 1 (poor score) to 10 (good score). Dan Brandon again offers excellent advice when he lists the following typical criteria (2006, 44):

- consistency with organizational mission and goals
- technical feasibility
- internal risk
- payback period
- degree of contracting/outsourcing
- development time
- impact on customer base
- impact on organization
- sociopolitical impact
- increase in organizational knowledge
- increase in organizational competitiveness.

This type of scoring lends itself well to a group evaluation of projects, averaging all responses together, and also helps to compare projects that are completely different from each other on the surface. However, for this system to work the evaluators need to be consistent and honest in their scoring.

## When decision-making is not transparent

Identifying project sponsors and project goals helps to make your own decision-making transparent to your colleagues. Working within an organization where others' decision-making is unclear, however, makes your job more difficult:

- People may expect *your* decision-making to follow the prevailing trends and you'll have to work extra hard to show otherwise.
- You may be blindsided by others' decisions.
- You may be executing projects that are based on unclear needs, not on the organization's mission.

You cannot change your organizational culture overnight. You can, however, control how you run your project. J. Davidson Frame (2003, 45) offers the following six-step process for approaching political problems if you are faced with a culture of hidden decision-making:

- *Assess the environment*: In most organizations, decisions are not made just at the top. Colleagues with power are spread throughout the organization. In your library, who has power to influence decisions? Do you lack buy-in from any of those decision leaders?
- *Identify the goals of others*: If you learn that an influential stakeholder disagrees with your decisions or project, what personal goals are at stake? If others encourage you to hide decision-making, what are they really trying to achieve?
- *Assess your own capabilities*: Are you good at difficult conversations and understanding views different from your own? If not, can you get advice or a representative to help you do so?
- *Define the problem*: What is the *real* conflict? How does the situation affect *your web project*?
- *Develop solutions*: What steps can you take to overcome poorly defined or changing goals from your project sponsor? Can you encourage project sponsors to be more open?
- *Test and refine the solutions.*

For example, suppose you are the web services librarian at your library. Your boss comes to you and tells you that the social sciences library wants to implement a specific brand of hosted wiki to replace their current website. Your team needs to create and support the stylesheets for the new site. You're probably thinking, 'Who decided to use a wiki? Why did they choose that brand? How will this affect the rest of the library organization's website? Why did no one ask me before things got this far?' Your boss will only say that this is the decision she was given by the library head.

Clearly, you will want to find out more information. Visit the librarians in the social sciences library, perhaps one at a time, to assess the environment. Identify their individual goals and those of the department head. Strive to understand the decisions made before the project came to you. Why a wiki rather than regular web pages? How would the wiki interact with other content on the site? Why this particular wiki brand versus another? Strive also to clarify who the project sponsor is and who needs to be involved in future decisions. As you learn about the goals of the project, consider whether in your opinion they were the best decisions. Consider your relationships with the librarians in this department. If you propose a different solution, would you have their support? Consider their decision-making power. Do you need their support? Developing solutions might mean clarifying the decision-making pathway, reviewing the actual decision, or finding strategies to deal with a decision you can't change.

What's important about this scenario is thinking through each step in Frame's approach. Suppose you jumped too quickly to 'developing solutions' without first clarifying goals. You might have started implementing templates for a wiki that then turned out to be unusable for the intended content. Or, suppose you immediately wrote to the whole social sciences library about why you thought their choice was bad, only to find out that the real decision-maker was an associate dean who wanted to use their site as a pilot test for wiki technology. By thinking through each step, you can avoid dangerous assumptions.

# Project overview

When a project request is confirmed as a project for you to undertake, identify and record expectations more formally through a project overview document (see figure 4.3.) A project overview will repeat or elaborate on much of the information found during the project request stage and may also include expected costs for software, hardware or outsourcing; your project team (by name or by skills); and a more detailed working timeline for major phases of the project. The act of creating this document ensures that you understand the goals of the project sponsor.

You can write a first draft of this document largely on your own, based on the information you gathered at the project request phase. In fact, you could use a project overview template as your initial project

**Figure 4.3**   Example project overview

---

**News application: project overview**

**Key people**

*Project sponsor*: marketing manager

*Key stakeholders*: reference, library administration, instruction, students, faculty, webmaster, public services director

*Other interested people (if any)*: campus web office

*Skills requested*: design (for public display and staff admin area), programming (backend database, authentication, getting content from admin to public display), project management, content coordinating

*Project team*: representatives from reference and instruction, student representative, webmaster, marketing manager, programmer with database expertise, project manager, someone with writing skills

**What and why**

*Brief description*: Design and create web application which allows us to publish news items in multiple places on our public website:

- distributed authorship—more than one person can enter and edit
- should be able to schedule news ahead of time
- users should be able to subscribe with RSS
- maybe allow our news to integrate with campus website.

*Project objectives*: The current News & Announcements page offers a quick and central spot to promote new services and collections and provide links to our various 'new' lists. This area is currently maintained with input from multiple people, funneled through the webmaster. It could be maintained more easily, leading to more frequent updates.

*Justification*: The dean of libraries has expressed an interest in making a more robust News & Announcements page. He'd also like us to promote more news throughout the site.

*Known costs*: none outside of current staff costs

**Working timeline**

- earliest start: right away
- proposed finish: May 2009
- latest finish: none.

---

request form, knowing that you will fill in some of the information only if you agree to do the project. Finalize the document with your project sponsor even before you gather your project team together. Some project managers will even require that the project sponsor should sign this document to confirm that it represents the project accurately. Depending on the formality of your organization, that signature step may be excessive. Whether you require a literal sign-off or not, you want to be sure that your project sponsor understands that the details are still vague and the resources, schedule, and features are still largely tentative. This document is the first expression of what you want to accomplish for your project sponsor. You do not know yet if you can accomplish everything that you've listed within the expressed deadline with the given resources. Be specific if you can be, but also accept that this is an early document in the process.

# Project specifications

The project overview contains only a rough description of your goal—not enough detail to really start work on any large project with confidence. Your next step as project manager is to assemble and begin working with your project team, and the next three chapters are all about doing exactly that. Your team will be researching possible solutions, engaging with users, and collecting input from colleagues in order to understand how best to accomplish the big picture goals listed in the project overview. Chapters 8 and 9, in fact, offer details about communicating with your colleagues and gathering user input.

The goal of all this work is to create project specifications: a detailed blueprint for your designers, developers, and writers. Creating the project specifications can be quite time consuming. In fact, Ashley Friedlein estimates that you should spend as much as 50% of a project's scheduled time and budget on clarifying needs and writing the project specifications (2001, 43). Scott Berkun recommends splitting a project timeline into thirds: 'Here's how the rule of thirds works. Break the available time into three parts—one for design, one for implementation, and one for testing' (2008, 27). Whether you are using half or a third of your timeline, you should spend a significant amount of your total project time in planning. Think of the adage 'measure twice, cut once.' By planning your work in detail up front, you prevent time-consuming mistakes once you begin to create. The reward is comprehensive project specifications that allow your team to estimate a timeline for completing the work, work towards the same vision, and be confident that the project sponsor approves of your plan.

As you research, your final plan will likely fall into three categories:

- *design issues*: look and feel, navigation, information architecture
- *programming*: interactive features, interoperability
- *content issues*: text and graphics to be included, needed help documentation.

You will read more about how these details can all be explained, and tips for working with the relevant members of the team, in chapter 10, 'Overall and design specifications,' chapter 11, 'Technical specifications,' and chapter 12, 'Web content specifications.'

# Introducing project management to your library

This chapter introduced the first of many formal project management concepts—the project sponsor, the project overview, project prioritization, and project specifications. Not everyone in your organization will immediately understand the importance of these concepts. In the authors' survey (Keach and Fagan 2008), ten of 65 web project managers mentioned that one of the top challenges in their library was a lack of project management techniques or a lack of understanding about why such techniques are needed. Your colleagues may never have seen a well-managed project, or perhaps they focus on the substance of projects, without paying much attention to how they get done. The level of understanding or at least appreciation for project management may affect your ability to obtain adequate resources to do the job right.

Building a record of success is the best way to increase your organization's appreciation of project management. Each project you manage successfully raises your reputation in your organization. In time, colleagues will come to you for advice on how to manage a project. The library administration may ask you to lead high-stakes projects, knowing that you will get the job done. You may be asked—or you may volunteer—to share what you know in staff training events. As your credibility as a project manager grows, you will find that your organization will gain an appreciation for the techniques you've demonstrated.

If web project management is entirely new to you or your organization, you'll probably want to start by introducing just a few techniques at a time. This book describes both formal and informal project management methods that we have found to be useful. Experiment with the ones that make the most sense to you first and gradually build your repertoire with new tools as you need them. With your colleagues, explain that you're open to reviewing their usefulness and thank them for using the methods you've chosen, even if they're not the most convenient for them:

- *To skeptics on your team*: 'I know you think technical specifications are just long-winded, useless documents. But I'd like to try them for this project, and see how they work out. We can discuss how well they worked afterwards.'

- *To your skeptical colleague*: 'I know you aren't sure why a project overview document is necessary for what seems like a small project. Yet I want to make sure that I understand your goals.'

- *To your skeptical project sponsor*: 'I know that we've never documented project sponsors before. I've read that identifying one is a good idea, particularly when managing projects which will likely have plenty of disagreement. Would you like to try it this time and see what happens?'

- *To your skeptical library administration*: 'I know assessment is increasingly important in libraries. I'm hoping that by tracking our return on investment for this project, I can help the library evaluate whether future projects like this are truly worth it for our users.'

# Conclusion

It's important for everyone to understand that although you've documented aspects of the project, the details are still vague and the resources, schedule, and features are largely tentative until your team does more research and creates the project specifications. The project overview document is the first expression of what you want to accomplish for your project sponsor. You do not know yet if you can accomplish everything that you've listed within the expressed deadline with the given resources. Be specific if you can be, but also accept that this is an early document in the process. Now that you have identified a project, understood where it fits in the priority list, committed to tackling it, and begun to think about the detailed project specifications, you should gather your project team so you can begin your research and clarify exactly how you will accomplish the project. Teams are so important to the web project that they are the subject of the next three chapters.

# References

Berkun, Scott (2008) *Making Things Happen: Mastering Project Management*. 2nd ed. Sebastopol, CA: O'Reilly.

Brandon, Dan (2006) *Project Management for Modern Information Systems*. Hershey, PA: IRM Press.

Frame, J. Davidson (2003) *Managing Projects in Organizations*. San Francisco, CA: Jossey-Bass.

Friedlein, Ashley (2001) *Web Project Management: Delivering Successful Commercial Web Sites*. New York: Morgan Kaufmann.

Keach, Jennifer, and Jody Condit Fagan (2008) *Survey of Web Project Managers in Academic Libraries*. Web survey conducted June 9 – July 1.

PMI Standards Committee (1996) *A Guide to the Project Management Body of Knowledge*. Newtown Square, PA: Project Management Institute.

*Project Management for IT Professionals* (2005) Mission, KS: CompuMaster.

Shelford, Thomas J., and Gregory A. Remillard (2003) *Real Web Project Management: Case Studies and Best Practices from the Trenches*. Boston: Addison-Wesley.

Taylor, James (2004) *Managing Information Technology Projects: Applying Project Management Strategies to Software, Hardware, and Integration Initiatives*. New York: American Management Association.

# 5

# The academic library web team

## Introduction

Teams, rather than one person, envision and execute most successful web projects. If you have strong graphic design skills along with technical know-how and solid writing abilities, you may be tempted to dream up and implement projects in isolation. Resist this urge! Even the simplest of projects benefits from fresh perspectives midstream. Consider how often you have written something and proofread it numerous times, only to find a glaring typographical error a month after you submitted it. Now consider the value of recruiting others to help not only with proofreading, but also with clarifying the objectives, information architecture, programming, database development, graphics, and testing. You not only gain help with identifying problems, but also create new solutions. The end result will be more polished and effective.

By establishing a team at the beginning of the project you also improve your chances of keeping to deadlines. You will be tempted to take on all work that matches your skills. By doing this, though, you will find yourself writing content and designing graphics at the same time, or testing the application, writing training materials, and marketing the end product all at the same time. As the project manager, you will also be checking progress reports, solving crises, and reporting to your stakeholders. By trying to do too much yourself, you short-change the quality of the project, the effectiveness of your project management, or both. Do your part to ensure quality in your end product and keep your project on track by keeping expectations for yourself realistic. Do this by recruiting talented colleagues for your team. Even if the size of your organization ensures that you are a one-person team, consider the ways in which you can solicit informal help from others throughout the process.

# Web committees and teams

Web groups within academic libraries tend to fall into one or more of three types:

- The *web project team* is a temporary group established to accomplish a specific project. Members include both technical and non-technical staff, with representation from throughout the library. This type of group may also include students, faculty members, and other end users. This chapter is primarily about the web project team.

- The *web technical team* is a group of technical and design staff created to implement projects and maintain the website. This type of group is based on expertise and job title and is typically a permanent work group or department involved with every web project. In large libraries, it may include multiple project managers, all directing projects at the same time. In many libraries, the technical web team forms the backbone of most web project teams. Individuals from this team may also serve on a web committee.

- Finally, the *web committee* is a group of representatives from throughout the library that meets regularly. The committee frequently includes design and technical staff. This type of committee may have both permanent and temporary members, typically assigned to the team for one to three years (Ragsdale 2001, 10). The scope of this committee differs sharply from library to library.

In the authors' survey of web project managers in academic libraries (Keach and Fagan 2008), of the 78 people who responded to a question about web project management groups, 77% reported that they use temporary web project teams formed on a project-by-project basis. These teams are often used in conjunction with one or more other groups, most frequently with both standing committees and departments, sometimes with just standing committees, and sometimes with just departments (see table 5.1). All together, 57% of those who responded to this question use temporary project teams in cohort with another web group.

Forty respondents provided information about the responsibilities of their standing committees. Some reported on more than one committee, for a total of 58 committees. Most of the respondents used just one committee at their institution, but 20% were at libraries using two web committees, and an additional 10% reported three or more web committees. The scope for these standing committees included a range of

| Table 5.1 | | Combinations of teams working on web projects in academic libraries | |

| Temporary project teams | Technical team/dept | Standing committee | Proportion of respondents (n=78) (%) |
|:---:|:---:|:---:|:---:|
| • | • | • | 23 |
| • | | • | 21 |
| • | | | 21 |
| • | • | | 13 |
| | | • | 13 |
| | • | • | 5 |
| | • | | 5 |

responsibilities (table 5.2). The authors grouped reported responsibilities into two broad categories—oversight/advice and hands-on—and found that 50% of the committees handled responsibilities in *both* categories for their library website. These dual-purpose web committees handle a

| Table 5.2 | | Scope of standing web committees |

| Scope of standing web committees | Category | Proportion reporting (n=58) (%) |
|:---|:---|:---:|
| Identifies new projects | Oversight/advice | 81 |
| Sets strategic directions | Oversight/advice | 64 |
| Designs usability tests | Oversight/advice | 64 |
| Prioritizes multiple projects | Oversight/advice | 62 |
| Conducts research & development | Oversight/advice | 62 |
| Approves website content and/or graphics | Oversight/advice | 53 |
| Enforces standards (style, accessibility) | Oversight/advice | 53 |
| Manages individual web projects | Hands-on | 48 |
| Web maintenance (broken links, etc.) | Hands-on | 45 |
| Writes website content | Hands-on | 45 |
| Creates website graphics | Hands-on | 33 |
| Final approval for completed projects | Oversight/advice | 31 |
| Programming | Hands-on | 29 |
| Teaches colleagues how to publish | Hands-on | 22 |

mixed bag of setting strategic direction, approving changes, offering advice, managing projects, writing content, creating graphics, and more. While some of these web committees take on most or all the above responsibilities, others have just one or two specific areas of responsibility in each broad category, for example, enforcing standards (oversight) and writing new content (hands-on).

Web committees that provide pure oversight and advice, without any hands-on responsibilities, accounted for just 29% of the 58 described standing groups. Some of these groups provided only high-level oversight: setting strategic directions and prioritizing possible projects. Others were responsible for more detailed oversight including approval of content and enforcement of standards. Still others were strictly advising bodies, performing research and assessment. Overall, few of the oversight and advice committees provided final approval for completed projects.

Involvement from across the organization was the most-cited factor for committee effectiveness. Respondents also mentioned tech-savvy membership and inclusion of the responsibility in the member's job description as reasons for effectiveness. Among the challenges of standing web committees were problems of authority and resources: the group may have great ideas, but no resources or authority to implement them.

These survey results suggest that academic libraries are using a combination of project teams, departments, and standing committees to get the work done, and no one combination of groups, responsibilities, or membership is the standard. The temporary web project team—formed to work on a specific project—is the topic of this chapter, although much of the information can be adapted to the other types of groups. You will read about the benefits of working within a team, suggestions for the skills your team members should have, and opinions about the size of your team.

# Skills for your team

Let the skills you need for your project lead you to your web project team members. In the book *Web Project Management*, Ashley Friedlein provides a list of 34 possible team members that a project may require (2001, 21). Friedlein's list of roles, found in figure 5.1, is a long one but he is quick to reassure that not all projects require all of his listed roles. In fact, one person may provide more than one skill in his comprehensive listing.

| Figure 5.1 | Friedlein's roles and responsibilities |
|---|---|

| | | |
|---|---|---|
| Client | Information Architect | Animator |
| Account Director | Art Director | 3D Modeler |
| Account Manager | Design Manager | Video/Audio Encoder |
| Account Executive | Designer | Webcast Specialist |
| Strategy Consultant | Interactive Designer | Content Deal Broker |
| Technical Consultant | Illustrator | Editor |
| Marketing Consultant | Data Architect | Copywriter |
| Project Director | Programming Manager | Journalist |
| Project Manager/Producer | Advanced Programmer | Researcher |
| Assistant Producer | Programmer | Community Manager |
| QA Tester | Database Administrator | Production Service Provider |
| Webmaster | Specialist Programming | |

*Source*: Friedlein 2001, 21

Whereas Friedlein's list reflects a resource-rich, commercial organization, the roles in figure 5.2 reflect common needs and realities for academic libraries. This list was inspired by Friedlein's, and with a close comparison between the two, you will find that the shorter list removes some roles entirely and consolidates others into single roles.

Before reading descriptions and details about each of these roles in the section that follows, consider that you may not need someone in all of these roles for every project. Nor will you need to have one person assigned to each role. In a small library, you may split the work up between just a few different talented team members. Project managers in all sizes of libraries struggle with having limited resources. To get some tips on how you can still accomplish projects without plentiful staff and money, see the callout 'Lack of staff resources or skills.'

| Figure 5.2 | Academic library web project team roles and responsibilities |
|---|---|

| | |
|---|---|
| Project Manager | Programmer |
| Project Sponsor | Database Programmer |
| End Users | Specialty Programmers |
| Webmaster | Content Editor |
| Library Application Manager | Video/Audio Content Editor |
| Graphic Designer | Testing Organizer |
| Interaction Designer | Marketing Coordinator |
| Information Architect | Training Coordinator |

## Lack of staff resources or skills

 Every library deals with problems of insufficient staff or financial resources at some time or another. Or, your library may not have allocated sufficient resources in the direction of web projects. You read about making the case for more direct support of web projects in chapter 2, 'The web project manager in academic libraries.' If those efforts prove to be unsuccessful, or your library really doesn't have the resources, what do you do?

- Work especially hard to set realistic scopes and timelines for your projects (see chapter 13, 'Planning the work').
- Pay attention to what other libraries are doing 'on the cheap.'
- Be ready to motivate your team. If you have negative thoughts about the level of funding, don't let these spread to your team. Focus on what you can achieve.
- Look for ways to partner across campus with faculty or staff. For example, the computing department may also want to do some usability tests. Perhaps they have money for participant incentives they could share in exchange for librarian facilitators.
- Seek out training opportunities for current staff.
- Look for grant or funding opportunities. Managing grant awards takes significant time above and beyond your project management role, so be sure that the opportunities you pursue have a chance of paying off enough dividends.

As a web project manager, your role includes defining the project solution to fit the available resources and skills. You may need to help your project sponsor adjust their vision so that it fits within the available resources.

# Web project team roles

## *Project sponsor*

You read about project sponsors in chapter 4, 'Defining your project.' Now that you are creating your project team, request that your project sponsor participates in the team. If you can include one or more sponsors on the team, they can approve decisions throughout the project without the need for separate meetings specifically for that purpose. A project sponsor from among the top-level administrators in your library may choose to be largely absent from team meetings, preferring instead to be involved only for pivotal decisions. As project manager, it will then be your role to keep that person informed of progress and to summarize dilemmas and possible solutions objectively when tough decisions arise.

For a more complicated project such as redesigning a branch library website, you could have the challenge of a large department as your project sponsor rather than one or two people. You should ask the department—either the whole group or through the department head—to suggest one or two individuals who can represent the entire department. These representatives then reconcile differences within the sponsor group.

## End users

In a situation where you are creating a web application or site used primarily by your colleagues, your end users are your colleagues. You could consider them internal end users. For example, you may be creating a database application used by a colleague to keep track of use statistics for research databases. Students and faculty will never see this database; you should concentrate solely on the needs of your colleagues. In most cases, though, you will have users in addition to your colleagues.

Any project involving the public website will have students and faculty as external end users. When creating your team, attempt to include one or more members of this user group for the valuable insights they can offer. Student employees within the library can be convenient and insightful participants, even though they may be biased by their library training and work experience. Make sure to get their supervisors' approval and be clear as to how much time they will be spending on your project. If you are unable to include them on the team itself, include them in selected activities such as co-design sessions and usability testing.

In addition to including actual external end users on your team, consider including colleagues who interact with external users frequently. Reference staff members help users to navigate the site and demonstrate research one-on-one. Instruction librarians teach groups of users how to get their work accomplished through the website.

## Library staff as both external and internal end users

 Library staff members can serve two user roles: as representatives of external end users and as internal end users. As opposed to a business website designed for shopping or promotion, a library website is used daily by those who work in the library. Library staff members need to research topics, identify specific facts, cite sources, and manipulate data in ways similar to advanced external users. As internal users, they may also use the website when teaching classes, search book titles in the catalog before ordering, and publicize job openings to potential applicants. They will also know about institutional goals that other users may not even consider. The library goal of educating students to be information literate, for instance, may not be on the list of priorities for a college student, but may be at the top of the list of goals for the library. In addition, many projects intended for your external end users also have an administrative interface for your internal end users to use. The benefits and challenges associated with this blurred line are explored in more detail in chapter 8, 'Planning for organizational communication' and chapter 9, 'Getting user input.'

Interlibrary loan staff members see the same mistakes repeated over and over as they process requests. These colleagues can offer anecdotal evidence of user behavior beyond the experiences brought to the team by the students and faculty members you recruit to participate.

If your library has a usability expert, consider inviting them to join the kickoff meeting. Alerting this person at the beginning of the project that you will need their help lets them integrate future testing into their schedule and become familiar with the goals of the project. If you do not have a usability person, consider asking someone to serve as your team's user input coordinator. Don't rule out usability activities just because of a short time-frame or limited expertise. You will discover simple options in chapter 9, 'Getting user input.' Just be sure that someone on your team is prepared to plan for user input.

## Webmaster

The person who handles day-to-day maintenance of your website will likely be a critical member of your team and may also serve as the project manager. This is the person who will tie the project into the rest of the website and ensure that the end product meets accessibility and branding standards. This person will have insight into relationships between the current project and existing content and file architecture. The webmaster will also be able to provide statistics gathered from the website. After the project moves from development to production, the webmaster is likely to assist with ongoing maintenance.

## Library application manager

In projects where you are working with library vendor systems such as the library catalog or an interlibrary loan application, you will also include the primary manager for those systems. This person may frequently be the project manager for a project involving 'their' system. With this person on your team, you add expertise in data storage, interaction with other systems, data standards, and vendor support. Much like the webmaster, the library application manager will be able to provide statistics from the system. When the project moves into production, the library application manager will likely be involved with ongoing maintenance and future projects involving these same systems.

## Graphic designer

Someone with graphic design skills should be on your team from the start. Everyone has an opinion about color choices, but it takes someone with design skill to come up with a clear layout, harmonious colors, and individual graphics such as buttons, logos, and photographs. This person will also consider page layout issues such as balancing white space with content. Early in the process, your graphic designer can begin to anticipate needs as well as participate in the design of rough drafts. Many academic libraries do not have a dedicated graphic designer, but you should still designate someone responsible for this role so that design choices are consistent with an overall plan rather than pieced together by committee. You will read more about working with designers in chapter 10, 'Overall and design specifications.'

## Interaction designer

If you expect users to interact with your creation, whether for a simple task such as filling out a form or a complex task such as playing an animated game, you will want someone to design what happens at each step of the way. Be sure to consider both external user and internal user interaction. For example, you may be designing a web application that seems non-interactive to students and faculty, but that library staff members manage with an administrative interface. In that case, the interaction designer will design the workflow for the administrative interface. The interaction designer may create storyboards or flowcharts of every possible sequence of events. On many teams, the graphic designer fills the role of interaction designer, too.

## Information architect

The information architect is focused on the organization and labeling of content for the project. This is the person who chunks content on individual pages, devises labels that users will understand, and designs navigation through multiple pages. Examples of deliverables that information architects create include blueprints of how different pages interact, wireframes laying out groupings of content on a page, content inventories, and lists of controlled vocabulary. Both designers and librarians can be natural fits for the role of information architect on your team.

---

### The field of information architecture

 Information architecture is a fairly recent field in web design, but is growing quickly. Conferences such as the American Society for Information Science & Technology's IA Summit bring together these experts from a variety of settings from all around the world. If you are not familiar with information architecture as a separate design discipline, consider reading the landmark *Information Architecture for the World Wide Web* (Morville and Rosenfeld 2006). If you would like to learn more about the distinctions between graphic design, interaction design, and information architecture (and more) read *The Elements of User Experience* (Garrett 2002). Both are well worth your time. See 'Recommended readings' at the end of this chapter.

---

# Programmer

For any web project that includes dynamic content—pulling content from another source into a web page or writing complex interactions—one or more programmers will provide critical input from the beginning, assist in writing specifications, and implement the final decisions. If you do not normally work with programmers, you will quickly find that individual programmers typically specialize in programming environments such as Microsoft ASP.NET or LAMP and in a particular programming language like Visual Basic, C#, or Perl. Your choices of solutions may be limited by the environments in which your available programmers work, unless you are able to consider outsourcing some of the programming work. Chapter 11, 'Technical specifications,' discusses these environments and programming requirements in more detail.

# Database programmer

Library websites frequently provide large amounts of similar data that lends itself to database-driven pages. Examples of projects that may use databases include interactive forms, staff directories, FAQ systems, news applications, research guides, and listings of research databases. Projects may also pull content from existing databases such as an online catalog. The database programmer will work with others on the team to clarify field elements and requirements, and then design and implement relational databases. This person will work with other programmers and the designer to tie back-end databases into the final web pages. The database programmer can also provide recommendations for regular backups and other maintenance issues. Databases are also discussed in chapter 11, 'Technical specifications.'

# Specialty programmers

Some projects require programming skills which are limited to just one application or need. A Flash programmer, for instance, attaches ActionScript programming to graphics to enable animations. Other programmers may specialize in developing multimedia applications and interacting with media players. If the library wishes to interact with university information systems, a programmer may need to learn a variant of SQL in order to make database connections, or even learn a programming language specific to a university system.

## Outsourcing skills for your web team

 Outsourcing some of your web team's work makes sense in quite a few situations. Discrete projects are one good example. If you are creating a stand-alone instructional game, for instance, you may choose to hire a programming firm with extensive Flash skills. If the game is a discrete product and will not require ongoing maintenance and changes, outsourcing might make sense even if you have Flash expertise in your library.

Usability testing is another opportunity for outsourcing. If you don't have usability expertise in your library, consider hiring a consultant to help you develop a testing protocol and analyze your results, while you provide the participants and facilitators.

## Content editor

The content editor creates new content, re-uses existing content, and enlists others to create content. In many cases, the person with the most expertise for the site content will already be on the team as the project sponsor. In other cases, one person will pull together the expertise of many others in the organization to piece together new content, or research and write content herself.

The content editor may also perform final checking, monitor adherence to style guides and controlled vocabulary, and recruit a proofreader to explore the finished product with fresh eyes, looking specifically for writing and linking errors. Web content is discussed in detail in chapter 12, 'Web content specifications.'

## Video/audio content editor

If your project incorporates video or audio, you will want a video/audio expert on the team. This person may reformat files for streaming, set up web cameras for live feeds, or arrange for videotaping presenters. This person will likely rely on the content editor to write scripts and identify speakers. More detail on working with video and audio can be found in chapter 12, 'Web content specifications.'

## Testing organizer

For any project that includes user interaction, you should also include a testing organizer to gather together surrogate users to test the performance. Often referred to as 'quality assurance' testing, this is separate from evaluating the usability of your project and is intended to find bugs, dead ends, and other errors. This testing should happen more than once in the process, and plenty of time should be allowed for it. The tester not only coordinates testers, but also ensures clear and consistent error reporting. After each round of testing, the programmers revisit the code to fix bugs and the tester then follows up and double-checks each issue. If you expect to develop major revisions to the system that will require re-testing, the testing organizer should develop a testing script or checklist to facilitate an organized and consistent approach. You will read more about technical testing in chapter 11, 'Technical specifications.'

## Marketing coordinator

Towards the end of the project, while the project manager, designers, programmers, and content authors are actively finishing off their checklists, the marketing coordinator plans the marketing push to both internal and external users. This person may work with existing marketing committees or staff within the library, or be responsible for all aspects of planning and implementing the promotion of the finished product. Marketing websites involves both new and traditional

---

### Marketing library web projects

 If your library has a person or committee dedicated to marketing, you might be able to enlist their help with marketing your web project. Or, you might need to forge your own path. Either way, be sure you take advantage of online marketing techniques. You can find tips online including the following:

- 'Marketing Your Organization's Web Site,' *http://www .coyotecommunications.com/webdevo/webmrkt.shtml*
- 'The Web Marketing Checklist: 32 Ways to Promote Your Web site,' *http://www.wilsonweb.com/articles/checklist.htm*

- 'Make Your Web Site Famous,' *http://www.entrepreneur.com/article/printthis/193476.html*
- Houghton-Jan, Sarah (2008) Twenty steps to marketing your library online. *Journal of Web Librarianship* 1 (4): 81.

marketing techniques (see callout 'Marketing library web projects'). In some cases, as discussed in chapter 14, 'Concluding your web project,' your team may not be responsible for marketing at all. If that is the case, skip this role for your team.

## Training coordinator

As the project draws to a close, a member of the team creates training materials for any administrative interfaces or interactive systems. This person may also conduct in-person training or create online tutorials, and assist the content editor in writing help documentation for external users. This role is easy to forget or shortchange after working on a lengthy project. Assigning someone to follow through on training will pave the way toward a positive reception of your project by your users.

## Project manager

Don't forget that you are a member of the project team. This entire book explains what you will be doing!

### Competing work

Most individuals on your team, including you, will have day-to-day work obligations to juggle alongside a role on your project team. In order to participate, non-librarian team members may have received explicit approval and support from their supervisors, or even have been assigned to the team by their supervisor. Librarian members of your team likely considered time commitment, current obligations, and long-term goals before agreeing to serve. Web-related staff probably didn't have a choice and also have regular duties such as managing updates to the website, troubleshooting display problems, and assisting web authors.

Regardless of how your team member entered your team, that person may be unwilling or unable to temporarily lighten their regular load. Libraries frequently operate on lean staffing and the consistent stream of users and materials means that most staff cannot put their regular job to the side. As the project manager, you cannot know or dictate how much time your team member actually has to spend on your project.

Your organization may undertake multiple major projects at the same time and highly desirable team members will be tapped for multiple projects. When they commit to your project, they may not know how much time their other projects will require. You may find that these team members can only commit to short bursts of time. Discuss project team obligations openly with your team members so they can make good decisions about participating or adjusting other workloads.

## Team size

By now, you may be wondering if you will need to rent a lecture room for your kickoff meeting. Despite the lengthy list of skills to look for in your team members, you want to create a team that is a manageable size. Experts disagree on what size that might be:

- Peter-Paul Koch writes: 'The total web team shouldn't consist of more than seven people. When working with six other people you can (barely) keep track of who's doing what and what you yourself can do to help him or her. When the team rises beyond seven, this becomes impossible' (2003, n.p.).

- Glenn M. Parker writes: 'Although optimal size will depend on the specific team mission, in general optimal team size is four to six members, with ten to twelve being the maximum for effectiveness' (1994, 156).

- Ashley Friedlein writes, 'The majority of projects require a team of about six to eight' (2001, 20).

- Jon R. Katzenbach and Douglas K. Smith write: 'Virtually all effective teams we have met, read or heard about, or been members of have ranged between 2 and 25 people' (2004, 10).

One reason the opinion on team size varies is because of the different types of teams. Some of the opinions about team size are based on the technical and design side of a team alone, not one that includes end users and project sponsors. Other size recommendations focus on permanent work groups rather than temporary project teams. Richard Whitehead, in *Leading a Software Development Team* (2001), suggests a range somewhere between two and fifteen but highlights an important distinction in how one sets the size of the team: 'it's the size of the "core" of the team that matters' (2001, 117). If you would like to explore the pros and cons of different team sizes in more detail, read *Cross-functional Teams: Working with Allies, Enemies and Other Strangers* by Glenn M. Parker (1994), which dedicates a brief and readable chapter to the topic. Parker uses published research to evaluate the arguments in favor of a large team.

For the team described in this book, you could easily gather eight or more members in your full team. The core will include technical and design staff members who have tasks throughout the life of the project, while you will sporadically engage others such as end users and trainers in the process. Many of your team members will do double duty on your team. If you have two programmers, one might proofread the other's work. Your graphic designer and interaction designer may be one and the same. An end user may create training documents. As the project manager, you may also be the information architect. Your project sponsor may lead the marketing plans. The list above, therefore, is not a list of people you need to recruit, but a list of roles that need to be assigned to the people that you have. Figure 5.3 lists some decision-making tips for creating your team to keep it small and efficient.

The approach we suggest in this book is to have a relatively small design and technical core team working side by side with internal and external end users. The core team will likely be working on this project full time throughout the project, while the rest of the team will be contributing regularly but less intensely. Depending on how many users your end product will affect, the complexity of your project, and the resources you have available to you, your team may exceed ten people. When that is the case, you will likely break them into smaller subteams for some of the work, and bring them all together for other aspects.

**Figure 5.3**   Decision-making tips for creating your team

| Scenario | Advice |
|---|---|
| If many different colleagues can provide a needed skill. (Example: content editor) | Then consider recruiting a colleague who brings multiple skills. Use this opportunity to recruit someone with the needed skill who has expressed frustration about being outside the process in the past. |
| If a small number of colleagues can provide the skill. (Example: graphic designer) | Then your skilled colleagues may be in high demand. Consider timing the project to fit within their schedules. |
| If no colleagues can provide the skill. (Example: Flash programmer) | Then consider outsourcing the skill to colleagues on campus. The campus IT department or marketing office may be able to assist with technical or design skills. Or:<br><br>• Consider outsourcing the skill to an outside provider.<br>• Ask academic departments at your institution if your needs match a class assignment or if they can recommend a student with the skills.<br>• If neither budget nor time allows these alternatives, rethink the project. If you expect to need this skill again, consider training or hiring for the skill. |

## Training and hiring according to needs

 The list of skills for your web project team goes beyond selecting members for your team. You can also use it to:

- identify training needs for existing staff
- write job ads for new employees
- advocate for additional staff.

# Conclusion

In an academic library, the web project team will likely contain more roles than people. That makes selecting team members critical for the web project manager. Think carefully about which people in your library will be able to contribute to the project and which skills your library may need to find outside its walls. The next chapter will discuss the dynamics of interaction between various personalities on your team, followed by a chapter on team communication. In these two chapters, you will learn how to lead your group of people toward working as a productive and efficient team.

# Recommended readings

Garrett, Jesse James (2002) *The Elements of User Experience*. Indianapolis, IN: Pearson Education.

Houghton-Jan, Sarah (2008) Twenty steps to marketing your library online. *Journal of Web Librarianship* 1 (4): 81.

Morville, Peter, and Louis Rosenfeld (2006) *Information Architecture for the World Wide Web*. 3rd ed. Sebastopol, CA: O'Reilly.

# References

Friedlein, Ashley (2001) *Web Project Management: Delivering Successful Commercial Web Sites*. New York: Morgan Kaufmann.

Katzenbach, Jon R., and Douglas K. Smith (2004) The discipline of teams. In *Harvard Business Review on Teams that Succeed*, 1–25. Boston, MA: Harvard Business School Publishing.

Keach, Jennifer, and Jody Condit Fagan (2008) *Survey of Web Project Managers in Academic Libraries*. Web survey conducted June 9 – July 1, 2008.

Koch, Peter-Paul (2003) The ideal web team (part 1). *Digital Web Magazine*. April 10, *http://www.digital-web.com/articles/the_ideal_web_team_part1/*.

Parker, Glenn M. (1994) *Cross-functional Teams: Working with Allies, Enemies, and Other Strangers*. Jossey-Bass Management Series. San Francisco, CA: Jossey-Bass.

Ragsdale, Kate W. (2001) *Staffing the Library Web Site*. Washington, DC: Association of Research Libraries.

Whitehead, Richard (2001) *Leading a Software Development Team: A Developer's Guide to Successfully Leading People and Projects*. New York: Addison-Wesley.

# 6

# Library web team dynamics

## Introduction

In the previous chapter, you learned about the individuals who should be members of your team. Once you've identified the members of this dream team, you must shepherd the team to success. Your team may combine individuals who have been on many teams together and others who have never worked together before. Some of your selected individuals may not even know each other.

Before you gather your team together for the first meeting, you should begin to anticipate the stages that teams go through as well as how different individuals work within a team. In this chapter, you will learn about common personality types within libraries and information technology and also discover strategies for working with the personality types you are likely to encounter on your team.

## Stages of team development

Bruce W. Tuckman first proposed in 1965 that teams progress through stages called forming, storming, norming, and performing. The literature still frequently cites his four-stage theory today. A fifth stage that Bruce W. Tuckman and Mary Ann Conover Jensen proposed in 1977—adjourning—is less frequently mentioned but included here:

- *Forming* is the stage at which your team members begin to learn what the group will be doing and how they will relate to others in the group. This time can be filled with both politeness and testing of the leader's authority (Tuckman 1965, 396; Bradbary and Garrett 2005, 19).

- *Storming* is the stage filled with interpersonal conflict and emotional responses. You may see personal agendas taking priority over the group's goals. Outside of meetings, individuals may avoid following through on tasks or otherwise work against the group (Tuckman 1965, 396; Bradbary and Garrett 2005, 19–20).

- *Norming* is the stage in which your team begins to coalesce. Individuals in the group begin to follow group standards so meetings begin to become productive. They also may share constructive criticism more freely (Tuckman 1965, 396; Bradbary and Garrett 2005, 20).

- *Performing* is the stage at which individuals in the group become enthusiastic about the task at hand. They may fill in for others' weaknesses in order to get the project completed successfully. Finally, the group is functioning like a team instead of a group of individuals (Tuckman 1965, 396).

- *Adjourning* is the stage during which your team members begin to disengage from the project and end their work together. Tuckman and Jensen added this stage to the model after noticing that other researchers reported teams go through a final stage of closure (Tuckman and Jensen 1977, 423).

You should expect your group of colleagues to progress through these stages until they are actively challenging each other with constructive criticism and great ideas.

Just because teams move through these phases does not mean that your group of individuals will necessarily become an effective and successful team. You may remember participating on a project team, for instance, where everyone always got along and no one ever disagreed. Tuckman's theory suggests that such a team never reached the point where it was really *performing*. Your goal for the team is to create something original and effective rather than perfectly agreeable.

The *storming* stage of this process can be more obviously challenging to you as the leader as well as others in the team. You may find that decisions you made during the *forming* stage are suddenly up for debate. Meetings may be stressful. Remind yourself and others that the conflict your team experiences can help team members learn about each other and eventually lead to great creativity. During this stage, though, watch for individuals who overstep bounds or respond to the conflict emotionally. If disagreement becomes personal or destructive during a meeting, consider taking a short break to allow your team members to disengage and depersonalize the disagreement. You'll learn about additional ground rules and suggestions that can help you weather the *storming* stage in the next chapter.

# Personality types

Each time you form a new team for a web project, you bring together colleagues who each have their own style of dealing with deadlines, conflict, tasks, and communication. These styles may be obvious—like a team member who consistently interrupts others—or subtle—like a team member who is unwilling to provide an estimated completion date. Initially, the differing styles on your team may be just interesting curiosities, but as you approach conflicts and deadlines you may find that these differences begin to get in the way of project success. Without understanding what underlies members' behaviors, your project may grind to a halt.

A personality inventory can improve how individuals on your team work together, which in turn increases the likelihood of success. The purpose of an inventory in the context of a team is two-fold: to gain insights into yourself and how you articulate your ideas, and to gain insights into how others think and communicate their ideas. The end result can be team members who better value each person's contributions, even when the style of making those contributions is different. Knowing that someone is shy about speaking up in a group is one thing; learning how to increase the odds that your 'introvert' will speak up when ready is another thing entirely. Not every project will require a formal personality assessment. As project manager, though, you can benefit from at least considering your team's personalities. Consider a more formal personality inventory for high-risk projects, large groups, long time-span projects, and permanent groups.

The Myers-Briggs Type Indicator® (MBTI®) is a popular personality inventory used within organizations as well as in counseling, and is the one about which you will find the most research. Introduced in 1942 by Isabel Briggs Myers and Katherine Cook Briggs, it is based on personality types described by C. G. Jung in 1921 (Myers 1998, 11). The assessment tool has been revised over the years, but the personality types it describes have remained constant.

The MBTI® considers four different scales:

- The Introversion–Extraversion scale considers where the person focuses their energy. The two ends of the scale are expressed as I and E.
- The Sensing–Intuition scale considers the ways in which a person collects information. The two ends of this scale are expressed as S and N.

- The Thinking–Feeling scale describes decision-making tendencies and the two ends of the scale are expressed as T and F.

- The Judging–Perceiving scale expresses the desires toward the outside world and is influenced by the two previous scales. The judging end of the scale, expressed with a J, prefers decisions and closure achieved through the decision-making preferences of either Thinking or Feeling. People at the perceiving end of the scale, expressed with a P, prefers flexibility based on their style of collecting information expressed in the Sensing–Intuition scale (Myers 1998, 6).

Combining all the scales together, the inventory produces a four-letter designation that points to preferences for everything from communication to careers to relationships. Someone with a ISTJ designation, for instance, shows preferences toward Introversion, Sensing, Thinking, and Judging. Find descriptions of each of these types in *Introduction to Type* (Myers 2000) or the *MBTI Manual* (Myers 1998).

The Keirsey Temperament theory, developed by David Keirsey and Marilyn Bates in 1978, uses the same letters and scales as the MBTI® but uses four temperaments instead of sixteen types. With fewer divisions, the Keirsey Temperament may be easier to apply simply because you are learning about fewer styles. Also, you can take the Keirsey Temperament Sorter, found in *Please Understand Me* (Keirsey and Bates 1978), without any help from a facilitator.

Most personality inventories can only be purchased and administered by a certified facilitator. Ask your campus human resources or training department if they can provide your team with an assessment workshop. Also check with psychology professors on your campus. They might incorporate assessment testing in their courses and be a certified facilitator. If your budget allows, consider investing in one of the range of assessment workshops and online assessments offered by business consultants. CPP, Inc. (*http://www.cpp.com/*), the publisher of the MBTI®, is one of the leaders in this field. If you will be investing in a workshop, consider inviting your whole organization to increase understanding throughout the organization (and save you time for your next project team).

## Alternatives to the MBTI®

The MBTI® is widely known and used but is not the only tool. Consultants and human resource offices may also offer complementary or alternative assessment tests. Ask what they offer and what they recommend for your situation. The list below is only a sample. The ones that require a facilitator are usually validated over time through research and are more reliable.

### *Require a facilitator*

DISC Profile™, *http://www.discprofile.com/*

Assesses communication styles in four scales: Dominance, Influence, Steadiness and Conscientiousness. This assessment is based on the psychological work of William Moulton Marston, starting in 1928.

The Fundamental Interpersonal Relations Orientation-Behavior Instrument™ (FIRO-B®), *https://www.cpp.com/products/firo-b/index.aspx*

Measures the level of interaction a person wants with others on three scales: Inclusion, Control, and Affection. This test is published by the same company as the MBTI® (CPP, Inc.) and is often administered with the MBTI®.

Interstrength® X-Styles Assessment, *http://www.16types.com/Request.jsp?pView=DynamicPage&Content=InterstrengthXStyles*

Based on the interaction styles described in *Understanding Yourself and Others®: An Introduction to Interaction Styles* (Berens 2000). This assessment identifies tendencies for interacting with others in four different styles: Chart-the-Course™, Behind-the-Scenes™, In-Charge™, and Get-Things-Going™.

Management Team Role-Indicator® (MTR-i™), *http://www.16types.com/Request.jsp?pView=DynamicPage&Content=MTR-i*

Focuses on roles on teams rather than personality type, identifying eight different roles: Sculptor, Curator, Explorer, Innovator, Conductor, Scientist, Coach, and Campaigner.

> ### Do not require a facilitator
>
> **Keirsey Temperament Sorter®**, *http://www.keirsey.com/*
>
> Uses the same scales as the MBTI® but sorts the sixteen types into four temperaments. You can use your results from a MBTI® test, or take the Keirsey Temperament Sorter, found in *Please Understand Me* (Keirsey and Bates 1978), without any help from a facilitator.
>
> **Personal DNA™**, *http://www.personaldna.com/*
>
> Fun, free online quiz, which rates the taker on 13 traits. Developed by ATTAP Technologies Inc., 'whose goal is to help fulfill the promise of the web by making useful stuff available to all.' This test may be interesting to web designers and programmers on your team if only for the variety of widgets used in responding to the questions.
>
> **The Platinum Rule®**, *http://www.platinumrule.com/*
>
> Book and assessment tool created by Tony Alessandra. The Platinum Rule® is a simplified classification that attempts to describe four different styles: Director, Socializer, Relater, and Thinker. You can take this assessment without a facilitator through books, workbooks, and online tests found through the website.

If the idea of learning more about yourself is appealing to you, you may be tempted to require your entire team to participate. You should not require it, though. The *MBTI® Manual* offers sound advice for any personality inventory; taking the inventory should be voluntary and the results belong to the individual (Myers 1998, 360). These two rules are good policy for any assessment test you may decide to use in team building. Provide an opportunity to take an assessment test, but do not require it. The *MBTI® Manual* suggests that members of the team who opt out can still learn about the types and about their colleagues by serving as observers during a group session. In addition, when the results come in, do not require that your colleagues share the results with the group. Instead, let them keep their results private (1998, 364).

## MBTI® types among librarians and programmers

Research studies of both librarians and programmers have identified MBTI® personality types that are common for these two professional areas. Learning about that research helps you to anticipate and prepare for some likely personalities on your team.

Scherdin (1994) set the benchmark for MBTI® types found within librarianship. Through a 1992 survey of 1,600 librarians sponsored by the Association for College and Research Libraries, she found the most common types to be ISTJ (17%) and INTJ (12%). See the callout, 'Common types for librarians and programmers,' below. The other types were represented, but not in such high percentages. She also discovered that the majority of her respondents were Introverted types (63%) and Intuitive types (59%). In contrast, the general population tends to be Extraverted types (65%) and Sensing types (68%) (1994, 132–3). Scherdin analyzed that same data again in 2002, focusing on just academic librarians, and still found a large percentage showing preference for ISTJ (16%) and INTJ (12%), as well as INTP (11%) types (2002, 243). A high occurrence of ISTJs and INTJs was found again by Agada (1998, n.p.) who studied students in library science programs.

Studies of the MBTI® type and information technology (IT) professionals—including programmers and systems administrators—suggest that they are similar to librarians. In a large study of 1,229 IT professionals, Lyons found larger numbers of ISTJs (22.6%), INTJs (15.5%), and INTPs (12.1%) than in the general population (1985, 108). Studies since then have been small, some testing just twenty employees within a particular company, but the ISTJ, INTJ and INTP types tend to recur commonly among IT professionals in those studies (Turley and Bieman 1995; Kaluzniacky 2004; Karn et al. 2007).

These results do not suggest that all librarians or all programmers are ISTJ, INTJ, or INTP types. It does suggest, however, that you will likely find a preponderance of these three types on your team. Kroeger, Thuesen,

## Common types for librarians and programmers

 *Introduction to Type* (Myers 2000, 13) offers these descriptions for these three types:

- *ISTJ*: Quiet, serious, earn success by thoroughness and dependability. Practical, matter-of-fact, realistic, and responsible. Decide logically what should be done and work toward it steadily, regardless of distractions. Take pleasure in making everything orderly and organized—their work, their home, their life. Value traditions and loyalty.

- *INTJ*: Have original minds and great drive for implementing their ideas and achieving their goals. Quickly see patterns in external events and develop long-range explanatory perspectives. When committed, organize a job and carry it through. Skeptical and independent, have high standards of competence and performance—for themselves and others.

- *INTP*: Seek to develop logical explanations for everything that interests them. Theoretical and abstract, interested more in ideas than in social interaction. Quiet, contained, flexible and adaptable. Have unusual ability to focus in depth to solve problems in their area of interest. Skeptical, sometimes critical, always analytical.

**Figure 6.1**   The Keirsey temperaments

| Keirsey temperament | MBTI® type |
| --- | --- |
| NF | ENFJ, INFJ, ENFP, INFP |
| NT | ENTJ, INTJ, ENTP, INTP |
| SJ | ESTJ, ISTJ, ESFJ, ISFJ |
| SP | ESFP, ISFP, ESTP, ISTP |

and Rutledge in *Type Talk at Work* encourage mapping the MBTI types to Keirsey temperaments (see figure 6.1) (2002, 51). Doing so highlights that librarians and programmers tend to frequently be NTs and SJs.

*Type Talk at Work* (Kroeger, Thuesen, and Rutledge 2002) and the *MBTI® Manual* (Myers 1998) both do excellent jobs of explaining how these different temperaments and types tend to approach work in any setting. In general, NTs theorize and think things through completely and want to know all the facts about a problem and then develop more than one possible solution. They tend to have high standards for themselves and others. They usually speak and write precisely and clearly, and value consistency. They can be impersonal and can overlook the day to day, and they can burn out when asked to focus on details. This Keirsey temperament has the nickname 'Rational' (Myers 1998, 61–2; Kroeger, Thuesen, and Rutledge 2002, 56–7).

SJs tend to be stable and structured. They organize, they are dependable, and they respect procedure and hierarchy. They can be more patient with systems and organizations than with other people. They can anticipate missteps based on their knowledge of the history of the organization. The temperament has the nickname 'Guardian' (Myers 1998, 59–60; Kroeger, Thuesen, and Rutledge 2002, 57–8).

The NFs, or 'Idealists,' affirm others and help them to get along. They tend to be persuasive. Others don't like to disagree with them because of their warmth (Myers 1998, 53–5; Kroeger, Thuesen, and Rutledge 2002, 57–8). Almost a quarter of the librarians studied, but few of the IT professionals, were NFs.

Finally, although a quarter of the general population is SP, or 'Artisan,' only a small percentage of the studied librarians and IT professionals were. The SP tends to be flexible and adaptable to the moment, without looking to the future. They tend to be strong in solving immediate and hands-on problems, and demonstrate practicality (Myers 1998, 60–1; Kroeger, Thuesen, and Rutledge 2002, 58–9). Both librarianship and information technology, incidentally, tend toward a philosophy of 'plan first and then act,' suggesting why this temperament is unusual within both environments.

## Gender in libraries and computing

 Women tend to outnumber men in librarianship, while men outnumber women in computing fields. This gender division holds true for computing specialization within libraries, too, with men more likely than women to work in technology positions within libraries (Ricigliano and Houston 2003, n.p.). Your teams will likely be a mix of library and computing staff along gender lines. The majority of women in the USA have a MBTI® preference for feeling rather than thinking, and so you may be tempted to make assumptions about communication styles based on gender. Scherdin's 2002 study, though, showed that the women in librarianship commonly prefer Thinking styles, more so than women in the general population (2002, 132). You may read about differences in communication style between men and women, but for the teams that you are likely to create within libraries, you would do well to focus on the overall personality rather than gender.

Consider how you can maximize strengths of the temperaments on your team. Your team will likely not all be NTs and SJs, but the majority of your team may be. Consider how the temperament types that differ from this majority, perhaps including your own, may have different perspectives from this majority bloc on your team. Kaluzniacky offers an in-depth discussion of the full list of MBTI® types just for IT professionals. Much of what he writes applies to librarians as well. What follows are tips focused on web projects, adapted from his book (2004, 10–11):

- Many of your team may be Introvert types, so look for the less common Extravert types and use them to best advantage. Your Extravert types will be obvious candidates for presentations to others outside the team and user training, but also consider them for working with stakeholders to identify possible features for your project.

- Your team will likely be split between Sensing and Intuitive types. Sensing types often excel at testing, scheduling, programming, and creating detailed documentation. Intuitive types often excel at creative solutions and big-picture planning.

- The Feeling types on your team will likely be in the minority. Use them to best advantage in leadership positions and for interacting with non-IT staff when gathering needs and input from users and colleagues. They are also good candidates for anticipating how well your project will be received by your organization. Leave structured deliverables to the Thinking types.

- Finally, you'll likely have fewer Perceiving types than Judging types. Tap your Perceiving types for work like brainstorming and modeling so that the Judging types can implement with precision and structure.

## Library administrators and the MBTI®

 When communicating with library administrators and supervisors, consider that their MBTI® types may be different from non-supervisory colleagues. Scherdin found that library administrators were more commonly Extravert and Intuitive types than other librarians, although more than half were still Introverted types (1994, 137). A study by John Tyson of 70 academic libraries in Virginia identified more Extravert and Judging types among library administrators (Tyson 1998, 45).

If you would like to get more advice on applying temperaments and types to the workplace and also introduce these concepts to your team and administrators, consider reading *Type Talk at Work* (Kroeger, Thuesen, and Rutledge 2002). This book is written for a general audience and offers tips on team building, problem solving, conflict resolution, goal setting, time management, stress management, and more, all based on MBTI® and Keirsey temperaments.

# Conclusion

Maximizing the contributions of each of your team members to complete the project successfully is part of your job as a project manager. Learning about the different types and temperaments on your team helps you to respect others and use natural tendencies to advantage. Even if you don't choose to incorporate these tools into your team building process, you should use these tools to learn about yourself. Understanding the lens through which you see the world will help you to become a better leader, communicator, and colleague.

# Recommended readings

Alessandra, Anthony J., and Michael J. O'Connor (1996) *The Platinum Rule: Discover the Four Basic Business Personalities—And How They Can Lead You to Success*. New York: Warner Books.

Berens, Linda V. (2000) *Understanding Yourself and Others®: An Introduction to Temperament*. 2nd ed. Huntington Beach, CA: Telos Publications.

Keirsey, David, and Marilyn Bates (1978) *Please Understand Me: An Essay on Temperament Styles*. Del Mar, CA: Promethean Nemesis Books.

Kroeger, Otto, Janet M. Thuesen, and Hile Rutledge (2002) *Type Talk at Work: How 16 Personality Types Determine Your Success on the Job*. Revised and updated ed. New York: Dell Publications.

# References

Agada, John (1998) Profiling librarians with the Myers-Briggs Type Indicator: Studies in self selection and type stability. *Education for Information* 16 (1): 57–69.

Bradbary, Dan, and David Garrett (2005) *Herding Chickens: Innovative Techniques for Project Management*. San Francisco: Harbor Light Press.

Kaluzniacky, Eugene (2004) *Managing Psychological Factors in Information Systems Work: An Orientation to Emotional Intelligence*. Hershey, PA: Information Science Publications.

Karn, John. S., Sharifah Syed-Abdullah, Anthony J. Cowling, and Mike Holcombe (2007) A study into the effects of personality type and methodology on cohesion in software engineering teams. *Behaviour & Information Technology* 26 (2): 99–111.

Keirsey, David, and Marilyn Bates (1978) *Please Understand Me: An Essay on Temperament Styles*. Del Mar, CA: Promethean Nemesis Books.

Kroeger, Otto, Janet M. Thuesen, and Hile Rutledge (2002) *Type Talk at Work: How 16 Personality Types Determine Your Success on the Job*. Revised and updated ed. New York: Dell Publications.

Lyons, Michael L. 1985. The DP psyche. *Datamation* 31, August 15: 103–105.

Myers, Isabel Briggs (2000) *Introduction to Type: A Guide to Understanding Your Results on the Myers-Briggs Type Indicator*. 6th ed. Oxford: Oxford Psychologists Press.

Myers, Isabel Briggs (1998) *MBTI Manual: A Guide to the Development and Use of the Myers-Briggs Type Indicator*. 3rd ed. Palo Alto, CA: Consulting Psychologists Press.

Ricigliano, Lori, and Renee Houston (2003) Men's work, women's work: The social shaping of technology in academic libraries. Paper presented at ACRL Eleventh National Conference, Charlotte, NC.

Scherdin, Mary Jane (2002) How well do we fit? Librarians and faculty in the academic setting. *Portal: Libraries & the Academy* 2 (2): 237–253.

Scherdin, Mary Jane (1994) Vive la différence: Exploring librarian personality types using the MBTI. In *Discovering Librarians: Profiles of a Profession*, 125–156. Chicago, IL: Association of College and Research Libraries, American Library Association.

Tuckman, Bruce W. (1965) Developmental sequence in small groups. *Psychological Bulletin* 63 (6): 384–399.

Tuckman, Bruce W., and Mary Ann Conover Jensen (1977) Stages of small group development revisited. *Group and Organizational Studies* 2: 419–427.

Turley, Richard T., and James M. Bieman (1995) Competencies of exceptional and nonexceptional software engineers. *Journal of Systems and Software* 28: 19–38.

Tyson, John C. (1988) A study of the personality type of academic library directors in the Commonwealth of Virginia using the Myers-Briggs Type Indicator. Doctor of Arts, Simmons College, Graduate School of Library and Information Science.

# 7

# Team communication

## Introduction

When you think of project management, you may first think of planning and scheduling. In academic libraries, however, a large part of your job is communication with your organization (discussed in chapter 8, 'Planning for organizational communication') and with your team. This obligation to keep your entire team engaged and informed throughout the process will take a surprising amount of time when you are doing it well, and it is one of the biggest challenges to leading a team. As you should surmise from the previous chapter about team dynamics, one style of communication will not fit everyone on your team or even make sense for all the different things you need to communicate. Instead, you should take advantage of a variety of meetings, workspaces, and written updates to keep everyone engaged.

## The kickoff meeting

Of all meetings that you have, the kickoff meeting is your first and best opportunity to prepare your team for success. You've spent considerable time with your project sponsor thinking through the goals of the project. You've identified needed skills and enlisted top-notch members for your team. Your team members, however, will each arrive with a different level of knowledge and enthusiasm about the project. The kickoff is where you introduce everyone on the team to the project (and if necessary, to each other) so you can officially start. You also get a chance to set the tone for the entire project lifecycle. Refreshments might be in order; if it's a huge project, ask your library administration if the organization can provide coffee or snacks.

Participants should walk away from this meeting with answers to the following questions:

- What is this project trying to accomplish?
- Who is on the team and why?
- How much work is this going to entail?
- Will we succeed?
- Am I glad I am working on this project?

The following sections will spell out these items in greater detail.

---

### Invite the boss

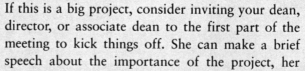

If this is a big project, consider inviting your dean, director, or associate dean to the first part of the meeting to kick things off. She can make a brief speech about the importance of the project, her confidence in the team, and her willingness to commit necessary resources to the project. After her comments, she can excuse herself gracefully or observe as you continue with the content of the meeting.

This high-profile individual may enjoy the opportunity to see this talented group gathered in one place and to learn more about the project specifics. Your team will benefit from knowing your project has blessings from the highest level.

---

## What is this project trying to accomplish?

Sharing the objectives of the project is a perfect way to begin your kickoff meeting. It gives everyone the same starting point. Your objectives have been handed down to you (or confirmed) by the project sponsor. Let everyone know who the project sponsor is and what they want. Announce that part of the team's work is to review and revise objectives, albeit with your project sponsor's signoff. Be prepared to communicate which decisions are already a done deal, and which are negotiable. Consider using a formal project overview, described in chapter 4, 'Defining your project,' to save time and to ensure you consistently describe the project over time.

Your team members also may bring personal objectives to the project or be concerned about how the finished project will impact their regular work. Suppose your team is implementing a next-generation library catalog interface. The cataloging librarian may have concerns about how well the new interface will showcase the hard work his team has put into enhancing catalog records. The instruction coordinator may be thinking about how her team members will be able to revise web tutorials and handouts in time for the next semester. Your web programmer may be disgruntled because the library didn't go with her recommendation and instead selected an alternate product written in a language in which she has less expertise. You may have your own goals of wanting to try out new project management ideas to see if they work, or to set the stage for a future web project. These secondary objectives aren't necessarily bad, but you save yourself some confusion if you can learn about these personal objectives earlier rather than later.

By sharing objectives at the kickoff meeting, you and your team members will have the opportunity to detect and rectify some early areas of conflict. Be cautious of objectives that are:

- politically motivated
- out of project scope
- unrealistic
- in direct competition with stated objectives.

Stay open-minded toward objectives that are:

- mistakenly missing from your original list of objectives
- great ideas that hadn't occurred to anyone else yet
- natural tie-ins that easily fold into the project.

This first meeting may be too early to ask your team members to reveal all their objectives and motivations. They may have not yet reflected on the project enough to spontaneously volunteer additional objectives. They may not yet know each other well enough to offer additional objectives which could be seen as self-serving. One option for getting hidden objectives on the table is to assign homework at the end of the kickoff meeting where you ask your new team members to review the project goals and to share any new or revised objectives at the next meeting, or beforehand directly to you. At that next meeting, examine each suggestion as a group. Add any new primary and secondary objectives to the project overview document and request approval from the project sponsor.

## Who is on the team and why?

Ideally, you selected everyone on this team to support the skills needed for this project. You may have instead inherited a group from someone else or be working with a group of volunteers or assigned representatives. No matter how the group was formed, as you begin to share the objectives of the project, every person in the room will start to wonder just what their role on the project will be. It's up to you to discover what each person brings to the project and ensure that everyone else knows, too. Give your voice a break during your kickoff meeting by giving everyone else a chance to introduce themselves and share what they believe they bring to the project. Doing so allows your team members to call attention to their skills without appearing to brag, and can help a team member to understand how they fit. Having them introduce themselves also allows you to find some hidden skills. If someone is unclear as to why they are on the team, you have an opportunity to chime in.

### An activity for sharing skills

With a group of people who already know each other, you may have no trouble getting everyone to describe what they think they will contribute. If your new team members don't know each other, you may end up with just a name and title followed by an uncomfortable silence. This likely comes as no surprise to you if you are working within a library or information technology unit. As you read in chapter 6, 'Library web team dynamics,' many members of your team may find speaking spontaneously in a group uncomfortable.

Use a variation on a standard 'introduce each other' exercise to allow your team members to work through what they'll say before they are asked to speak:

- Pair up your team members and distribute the list of roles for a web project team found in chapter 5, 'The academic library web team.' Remember to include yourself in this activity.

- Ask each pair to interview each other. What do you normally do at work and what do you feel you bring to this project? Encourage discussion in the safe one-on-one interviews, especially if someone isn't sure what they bring.

- After the one-on-one interviews, ask each person to provide a brief introduction of the other person to the group.

- Follow up with a group discussion: what skills are you missing? How will you fill in these gaps?

## How much work is this going to entail?

You may call on some of the same people from project to project—and hopefully the same people will agree to work with you again—but you will frequently involve staff who have never worked on a web project before. They may be surprised by:

- the amount of time it takes to clarify project specifications

- the ways in which technological realities can alter the end product

- the importance of systematic and thorough testing.

These aspects of web projects are hidden from most of your colleagues until they work on a web project. As a project manager, you need to lead each group through the process anew. The kickoff meeting is a good time to share an overview timeline (figure 7.1) including the major phases of the project. Even if that timeline is largely guesswork, you will help the team understand when their skills will be needed most. Your timeline will also let them know when you anticipate the entire project will be done. If you eventually find that you are unable to meet that proposed deadline, you should still let your team members end their commitment to your project team and return to their other work. Give them the option to continue if they are interested and able, but respect their time by allowing them to make and keep other commitments.

**Figure 7.1**    Example overview timeline

Overview timeline: room scheduler project

February: Kickoff meeting
February–April: Clarify project specifications
April–May: Write design, technical, and content specifications
June–July: Programming, design, content
August: Testing, bug fixing
August–September: Training and promotion
October: Review project

## Working with team members or colleagues who are stretched too thin

 At certain times each year, your team members and colleagues will have too much work to do. You'd like to be able to expect more from them, but they really can't give any more. If you're forming a new team, you'll want to address this issue as you choose team members, and you'll want to talk explicitly about workload expectations with them and perhaps even their supervisors. You may need to revise your team's timeline or scope depending on how much your team members can offer and how much you need a particular person on your team.

Here are some strategies for reducing the load:

- Allow the team to help set realistic deadlines.
- Consider re-scoping the project according to workload.
- Talk with your project sponsor, library administration, or team members' supervisors about possibly relieving the member from other duties.

Whether or not you can reduce the amount of work, you can simplify your team members' commitment to the project:

- Be specific with your questions. Don't ask 'What do you think?' Ask them to vote on A or B, offering comments if they would like.
- Be considerate of their time by sending out agendas before meetings and only meeting if you have a reason to meet.
- Maintain a project website to which they can refer if they lose track of e-mails and meeting times.

With your team and with colleagues, always express profound empathy for the fact that they are juggling multiple responsibilities. Be effusive in your praise for their hard work and contributions toward the project.

## Will we succeed?

In an academic library, you will have both eternal optimists who overestimate the team's ability to succeed and confirmed pessimists certain that old barriers will once again block progress. Part of your job in the kickoff meeting is to bring realism to both perspectives. You must believe this team can complete the project successfully, but you must also prepare your team for obstacles that will get in your way. Some of those obstacles will be interpersonal, as you learn to work together as a team. Others will be external to the team, as you deal with limited resources in time and money. This is your first chance not only to generate enthusiasm, but also to acknowledge the challenges ahead of you.

## Activity for identifying challenges

In your kickoff meeting, open the floor for the pessimists to share their guesses as to obstacles. Then, as a group, brainstorm some strategies to mitigate those barriers.

| Obstacles | Strategies |
|---|---|
| We are all overworked | Recruit additional help? Outsource some tasks? |
| Lots of people care about the outcome | Each of us shares ideas with colleagues and brings input back to team |
| No student users on our team | Tap student assistants for specific meetings/exercises |
| Team members aren't in the same building | Set up a brainstorming wiki or blog; alternate meetings between buildings |

## Am I glad I am working on this project?

Obviously, you want the answer to be yes. In an academic library, however, team members may come with legitimate worries about the project, some of which you will work to alleviate during this meeting. How much time will you ask of them? Will the project be successful? What will it be like to work with the other members of the team? You may personally be worried about the magnitude of the project, the deadlines, and the responsibility of coordinating so many people. Acknowledge your nervousness if that's your style, but remember to also show your enthusiasm for this project and your team members' participation.

Members of your new team may look for any number of factors that will make them glad to participate. They may want to:

- think the project at hand is important and will have an impact
- feel like they are important to the project's success
- like the other people on the group
- want to be known for working on a successful team
- want to know that they are making users' lives easier
- have a break from their regular work.

You cannot reassure your team members that you will meet all of these desires, but you can maximize the chance that your team members walk away from this first meeting looking forward to the next meeting. Run your kickoff meeting with all the good meeting practices you will learn in this chapter and include the points in this section in your agenda. Doing so sets the stage for all the meetings to come.

A final note about kickoff meetings: although you will be eager to call the kickoff meeting as soon as you've identified your team, resist holding your kickoff meeting until you have committed your own time to the project. Pulling your team together, getting them excited, and then ignoring them while you get your schedule in order adds up to a disastrous start for a project. Doing so breaks an implicit commitment to your team of your time. Doing so also encourages them to revoke their commitment in return.

# Getting started with the research

Researching the competition and the literature is a good early activity for everyone on your team. Distributing this work helps to bring your team members up to speed on possible solutions for your project and also engages them in active work right away. As web project manager, it is your responsibility to ensure that the team's work is well informed. Looking at other websites can reveal successes, failures, possible secondary features, and visual examples that can be used in discussions with stakeholders.

When looking at other sites, remind the team that your library may have significantly different financial and staff resources compared to your 'competitors.' Colleagues will undoubtedly ask why your website is not more like some other library website. Different resources, student populations, and missions all affect what different institutions can and will provide. As a start, find out from your library administration if your library has identified a peer group of libraries or if your university has a peer group of universities. Explore their websites to see if they offer a potential model for you to emulate (or not). You should also explore non-peer-group libraries' websites; designated peers may not be true peers in resources dedicated to library web projects. As you explore beyond your institutional peers, you may find that you develop a reliable list of web project peers with comparable resources to your own. Libraries with the same vendor's integrated library system, for instance, may serve as excellent peers for some projects. Libraries with a similar number of staff focused on web projects are also good starting points. Start a list of all of these peer institutions with details about why they are on your peer list. You may find yourself returning to these library websites each time you research the competition.

A real benefit of working on library websites, as opposed to commercial websites, is that other libraries are usually eager to share information to help you in your project. If you find your team drawn to a particular library website as a model of what you'd like to achieve, contact that library to ask how their solution works for them and their users, what kind of work went on behind the scenes, how long it took them to develop, and how much time they spend on maintenance. You may be surprised to discover that they don't like what they are doing and are about to change. If they have reasons for that anticipated change, you'll be happy to know this rather than blindly following their old solution as your model.

As you research competitors, your team may identify several already-created solutions which will meet your needs. To compare different commercial products, speak to other libraries about their experiences, invite sales representatives to provide demonstrations, and look for product reviews in the literature. You may also identify homegrown solutions or open source applications. Encourage your team to learn more about products even if they seem to be too expensive or too challenging to support. By investigating all types of solutions, you will gain valuable insights into possible features and design options.

You should also spend time researching the literature, especially if your project is centered on a specific tool rather than just a redesign. Library journals publish frequent articles about instruction tutorials, library catalog features, content repositories, federated searches, and other specific tools and projects. Whether the literature you find is primary research, case studies, or reviews, whatever you can learn from others will help you to eliminate your own missteps.

# Routine team meetings

You should communicate with both your whole team and portions of your team in routine meetings throughout the project. These meetings will be the primary way that you gather input and decisions from your project team. Your meetings also keep everyone engaged in the project and give your team a chance to ask questions.

In your kickoff meeting, discuss the frequency of meetings as a group. How often you meet depends on your project timeline and intensity as well as your team members' other work. Formal weekly meetings with everyone in attendance may be too frequent if you are also trying to maintain other work. With five work days between meetings, you would have little time to accomplish your action items. Meeting less frequently than once a month, however, would mean your team spends many weeks not thinking about your project at all. Generally, you will be choosing biweekly or monthly meeting times.

Immediately after the kickoff meeting, you should book upcoming meeting times for the duration of the project. Doing so is your request to your team members to keep those times free. It also creates a regular series of deadlines which force you to move forward. You may not know yet exactly what you'll be doing at each meeting, but you can use those meeting times as deadlines for action items and as milestones. Finally, you can always cancel or shorten the meeting if you believe your team's time would be spent more efficiently working independently or in small groups. If you do completely cancel a meeting, send your team an update of progress made since the previous meeting so they stay informed. Using a shared calendar system simplifies scheduling immensely (see callout 'Saving time with a shared calendar').

We have all sat through meetings with no agenda, no purpose, and no end in sight. As the project manager, you have a golden opportunity to provide direction for each meeting. The reward for running an efficient meeting goes beyond getting work done on your project. Your team members will spread the news that you run a good meeting. Building that positive reputation makes recruiting your next project team that much easier. In other words, sticking to a few good-meeting basics pays off with big dividends.

## *Respect your team members' time*

Trust that your team members have others things to do instead of meeting. Those who have added this project onto their regular duties

## Saving time with a shared calendar

If your library or campus does not use a shared online calendar, explore Google's or Yahoo's calendar tools as alternatives. Some members of your project team will already have extensive time commitments on their schedules, such as reference desk shifts, instruction classes, other meetings, conferences, and vacations. Looking at everyone's schedule in the convenience of your own office lets you identify and schedule meetings outside of meeting time and without an endless stream of e-mails or phone calls.

Shared online calendars also allow all attendees to see who is invited and who intends to come to the meeting. Use the shared notes area to post the agenda so everyone can check it at any time. And, you can typically e-mail all attendees easily for meeting reminders, updated agendas, and follow-up minutes using the same application.

have work piling up while they are away from their desks. Core members of your team—those who are spending almost all of their time on your project—are eager to get back to coding the features that the team agreed upon at the last meeting. Respect their time by treating their time as important as yours:

- Schedule meetings at least one week in advance, or reserve a regular time for the team to meet. Doing so allows your attendees to plan their week in advance.

- Send out an agenda one to two days before the meeting. The act of creating an agenda helps you to confirm that you have a reason to meet. If you find that your entire agenda is informational, consider saving everyone's time by sending that information electronically to your team instead of meeting. Ask others to do the same.

- Send out any advance reading at least two days before the meeting. Not everyone will review the material. You will often find, though, that doing so gives the introverts on your team time to think through the information beforehand, increasing the odds that they contribute during the meeting.

- Start meetings on time, even if some members are not yet present. Starting late rewards those who arrive late. You want to reward those who are on time.

- End meetings on time, even if you need to carry over discussions to the next meeting. If you have trouble with this rule, set a timer to go off ten minutes before the scheduled end of the meeting or assign a time keeper.
- End the meeting early if you are done early.

Following through on your commitments to your team members is another way of respecting your team members' time. For example, if you tell them that you will provide weekly updates, do so. If you find that your commitments were unrealistic, review and revise them as a team.

---

## Time management

If you do not have a good handle on how you manage your tasks and your time—and many of us do not— make use of one of the endless assortment of books that offer advice. No one theory works for everyone, so you may need to experiment to find the solution that fits your work style and work environment. One practice the authors recommend is to anticipate the amount of time you will need to focus on this project during a typical week and then block it off in your calendar for the duration of the project timeline to prevent over-committing to other meetings and tasks. Similarly, you might ask your team members to identify how much time they can realistically spend on the project in a typical week and then commit to it by blocking time on their calendars, too. Some popular time and task management books are listed in the recommended readings at the end of this chapter.

---

## Write a good agenda

Management books offer a relatively short list of rules for writing an agenda. With so much consistency in the advice, the surprise is that many meetings do not follow these rules. Even if your library is not in the habit of preparing agendas, lead the way by writing a good agenda for your meeting. Agendas also help the person taking minutes to organize their notes.

Your agenda should include:

- location and date
- start time and end time

- list of attendees
- list of agenda items
- time allotted for each item
- leader of discussion for each item.

The rule you may find most difficult is listing the time allotted for each agenda item. If you typically keep meetings short and on-track, then you might consider this piece of information optional. One way to find out if you do keep meetings on-track is to ask your project team if they would like time limits for each item. If everyone clamors for time limits, then you may not be keeping your meetings as on track as you thought.

## Communicate clearly

In chapter 6 you learned that members of your team may communicate differently based on their personality types. During and after the meeting, use different strategies to help everyone understand the tasks at hand:

- Explain reasons for different meeting activities, particularly the 'soft' ones like team building. You will find that you are more likely to get the MBTI® Sensing types on board if they understand the purpose of the activity.

- During the meeting, make it clear if the purpose of an agenda item is to brainstorm creative and possibly even unrealistic solutions to a problem. You will help the Judging types hold their tongue rather than critique every idea as impractical. That gives space for the Perceiving and Intuitive types to work within their strengths of generating ideas.

- Signal when an agenda item is focused on delegating action items for execution outside the meeting. Doing so helps the Perceiving and Intuitive types to hold on to their creative and tangential ideas until a more appropriate time.

- When your team makes a difficult decision during a meeting, provide a mechanism for offering additional thoughts after the meeting but within a deadline. Send e-mails asking for more thoughts or visit your team members' offices. Doing so gives time for the Introvert types to contemplate without the distractions of the others in the meeting.

- Leave about five minutes at the end of your meeting to review decisions and action items from the meeting, satisfying the Sensing and Judging types' desire for step-by-step instruction and closure.

- Allow yourself ten minutes or so of informal hallway time after the meeting. You may find that the Feeling types continue to socialize after the business is done, while Introverts may have held information back from the group that they are now eager to share with you.

- Record topics of conversation, decisions, and action items clearly in minutes, and share them soon after with the group after the meeting. This step helps everyone on your team regardless of personality type.

If you would like to read more about communication and the MBTI® personality types, consider reading the informative and concise 'Dealing with conflict' section of the *MBTI Manual* (Myers 1998, 335–39).

## Share the note-taking wealth

Rotate the responsibility of taking minutes through your team alphabetically or by using some other arbitrary order to spread the work around and allow everyone to contribute. Doing so has a hidden benefit, too. Comparing what someone else *thinks* you said to what you *meant* to say can teach you about your own communication weaknesses. If everyone misunderstands the facts you shared, perhaps you need to pay more attention to how you are sharing those facts. Request that the minute-taker submit the minutes to you for review so you can add URLs, include updates, or make corrections.

## *Establish ground rules*

In the previous chapter about team dynamics, you read about the often-stressful stage of 'storming' that effective teams go through. Lay the ground rules before those tensions arise so you successfully weather the storm. Ground rules can be common sense, courtesy rules:

- no interrupting
- no shouting
- no ridiculing
- let everyone speak
- respectfully disagree.

They can also clarify vague areas such as the use of laptops or mobile devices during meetings, the appropriateness of food and drink at a meeting, and the confidentiality of proceedings. You should lead your team through establishing these rules early and your team should agree on them unanimously. Ask for everyone's help in keeping to these rules.

---

### Empathic listening

In *The Seven Habits of Highly Effective People*, Stephen Covey defines empathic listening as being open to changing your mind while you are listening (2004, 239–41). This worthy and challenging goal is crucial when working on projects that prompt debates within your organization. Within an academic library, for instance, a passionate debate might run along these lines:

> Librarian A: 'How will a student ever learn what the word "periodical" means if we don't use it on our site?'

> Librarian B: 'Many students don't know what the word "periodical" means, so we shouldn't use it on our site.'

Prepare yourself and your team for inevitable disagreements by suggesting empathic listening as one of the ground rules. Try to listen to the opposing viewpoint as if you were listening to it for the first time and you hadn't already made up your mind. If you find your meeting devolving into line-in-the-sand entrenchment, consider taking a short break to allow everyone to disengage and reflect on the opposing viewpoint. When you regroup, try to lead the team through understanding both points of view objectively.

---

# One-on-one meetings

As project manager, you will hold one-on-one meetings with team members and others in the organization. Here are some things you'll want to consider:

- Before the meeting, think carefully about your goals for the meeting. Why are you making the time to meet with the person? The reason could be different than the stated purpose. For example, the meeting topic might be 'progress update' but your true goal might be to provide encouragement and praise.

- During the meeting, stay open to the possibility that the other person might have their own goals for the meeting. One good strategy is to begin the meeting reviewing what you think you're discussing, and ask sincerely if they have other topics they were hoping to address.

- Take good notes, especially if the other person does not seem to be doing so.

- Schedule ten to fifteen minutes of your time after the meeting to address immediate action items.

- Send the person a quick e-mail after the meeting to summarize action items and thank them for the meeting.

When you meet one-on-one with some members of your team but not others, you risk excluding members of your team from decision-making and updates. Minimize this possibility by alerting the rest of the team to any decisions made outside the large meetings and including one-on-one meeting summaries with the other meeting minutes for future reference.

# Virtual and physical workspaces

The team we describe in this book is likely cross-departmental and the members are unlikely to have offices near each other. As project manager, you should establish one or more workspaces in which your team members can interact with each other outside of planned meetings. These workspaces provide a home for working documents for everyone's reference and can also serve as one avenue of communicating with those outside the team. Whether virtual or physical, you can create active, dynamic spaces that energize your team.

## *Project rooms*

Grab any opportunity to establish a physical project room. Glenn M. Parker, in *Cross-functional Teams* (1994, 175), makes a strong case for the importance of physical proximity for team members:

> Although there is probably no way to accurately measure it, the opportunity to interact with your teammates on an informal, daily basis contributes to team effectiveness because it breaks down the barriers between strangers, helps overcome past relationship problems, and facilitates the growth of new partnerships.

Although a project room does not provide the level of interaction your team would get from a cluster of nearby offices, a project room is a step in that direction.

Consider underutilized rooms in the basement, a corner of the break room, or shared suite areas. Your project room, in fact, doesn't even have to be just yours. It could be a library meeting room in which you are allowed to keep materials from your project. The only real requirements for your project room are that it has internet access and enough space for three or more people to meet.

Some things you can do with a project room:

- Hold regularly-scheduled meetings.

- Meet with your core team members on short notice to brainstorm a solution to a thorny problem.

- Hang up story boards, timelines, flow charts, and other artifacts created during the project.

- Post your project charge and meeting rules of conduct.

- Hang up printouts of other websites that inspire your team.

- Escape from the distractions of personal offices to focus on the project.

- Invite everyone in your organization to stop by anytime to offer suggestions. Be sure to include a message board or suggestion box.

---

## Water cooler project room

Here's a variation of the project room idea: hang information about your project on a bulletin board or wall space near the water cooler, coffee pot, mailboxes, elevator entrance, vending machine, or other place where your colleagues already gather. Post attractive documentation from your project to share with your colleagues and provide space for them to offer their suggestions. Include a listing of everyone on your project team.

Suggest stand up, one-on-one, or three-person meetings with your team members in this spot while grabbing a quick cup of coffee, engaging other colleagues if they happen to be around and interested. By doing this, you keep your process open to colleagues and stay in touch with them, too. You may find that project team members who join your impromptu side meetings will also be more engaged in the whole process.

## Project websites

Regardless of whether or not you create a physical workspace for your project team, your team needs a virtual workspace. Some organizations simply use shared network drives, but it's also helpful to have a website. Unlike shared file space, websites can provide important context for the various documents which your team will create and need to refer to throughout the project cycle. Your project site might include:

- a list of project members and e-mail addresses
- a timeline
- regular updates
- minutes of meetings
- screenshots of applications and pages
- formal documentation
- results of usability studies
- examples of similar projects
- in-process mockups
- testing versions.

Give everyone on the team access and tools to publish to the site with Adobe Dreamweaver, Adobe Contribute, Microsoft Expression Web, or another HTML editor.

## Instant messaging

Depending on the size and nature of your group, instant messaging (IM) can be an excellent tool. AOL, Yahoo, Google, and MSN are all examples of IM networks; tools like Meebo and Trillian allow you to use IM with all IM networks (see callout 'Instant messaging software'). Using IM can help a group of people feel like they are working side by side even if they are on different campuses. Using IM, you can see at a glance if your colleague is available and then ask quick questions. If you aren't already using IM to communicate with your technical team, they may appreciate it as a tool they can use to fire off quick questions that will allow them to move forward in coding or design. During a project launch week, it can be invaluable for coordinating the rapid messages that can ensue.

---

## Instant messaging software

 The following instant messaging networks offer both downloadable clients and web-only interfaces:

- AOL Instant Messenger (AIM), *http://www.aim.com/*
- Yahoo! Messenger, *http://messenger.yahoo.com/*
- Google Talk, *http://www.google.com/talk/*
- Windows Live Messenger, *http://download.live.com/messenger*

Although they offer sophisticated features such as video chat, simple text messaging will usually suffice.

The following cross-network instant messaging tools allow you to log in to all the above accounts simultaneously so you can send and receive messages from any IM network:

- Meebo, *http://www.meebo.com/*
- Trillian, *http://www.ceruleanstudios.com/*

---

# Wikis

Exemplified by Wikipedia (*http://www.wikipedia.org*), a wiki is one of the most flexible tools listed here. Use a wiki for updates, minutes, documents, or anything else you would post to a traditional website. The benefits of wikis include the ease of publishing and built-in tools to show the most recently added pages, a history of edits, and the ability to upload and attach files. Examples include MediaWiki (*http://www.mediawiki.org*) and PBworks (*http://pbworks.com*).

# Blogs

Although people commonly think of blogs as tools for one author, you can actually give everyone on your team permission to publish to a blog, either with separate accounts or one shared login for the whole group. Team members will find the custom of displaying information in a chronological order to be particularly valuable, and they can post comments without feeling that they are intruding on the main content, as they might in a wiki. Examples include Blogger (*http://www.blogger.com*) and WordPress (*http://wordpress.org*).

### Discussion boards

Also called threaded discussions and forums, discussion boards allow any number of simultaneous asynchronous conversations. Unlike e-mail, all the posts get collected together for easy future reference and everyone can see all the messages. Examples include Google Groups (*http://www .groups.google.com*), Yahoo! Groups (*http://groups.yahoo.com*), and YetAnotherForum (*http://www.yetanotherforum.net*).

### Suites

Sometimes called portals, suites combine more than one tool together into an integrated online work environment. Basecamp (*http://www .basecamphq.com/*), created by 37signals, provides a suite of tools just for managing projects. Generic examples such as Google Sites (*http://sites .google.com*), Drupal (*http://www.drupal.org*), and DotNetNuke (*http:// www.dotnetnuke.com*) can provide some of the same functionality. Even course management software such as Blackboard (*http://www.blackboard .com*) and Sakai (*http://sakaiproject.org*) falls into this broad category.

## Staying up to date

Just providing a physical or virtual space is not enough; you also need to encourage its use. Regardless of which tool you use and how much encouragement you provide to the team to participate, the majority of the updates and information posted will come from the person who is assigned to do so. Maintaining the information on the project webpage is a natural task for you as the project manager because you will be the most informed about progress from day to day. If posting regular updates does not speak to your strengths, you might:

- schedule a recurring meeting on your calendar for posting updates
- distribute the work by giving everyone rights
- assign the task to someone else on the team.

Regardless, make sure that someone is maintaining online information. Even if they don't tell you, your team members may check it regularly to recall what was supposed to happen when, what was decided at the last meeting, or to share information with others in the organization. If nothing else, you may want a reminder of how this project played out when you later contemplate a similar project.

# Conclusion

Preparing foundational activities for the kickoff meeting and adhering to good practices for routine meetings and work spaces sets initial expectations about workload, commitments, and communication practices. When the pressure of an approaching deadline bears down on you, you may forget to send regular updates or worse, be tempted to try to do it all yourself. Closing off communication with your team, though, is one of the biggest mistakes you can make during a project. Similarly, when meetings seem to produce disagreements rather than harmony, you may be tempted to give up on them. By setting up regular communication structures from the start of your project—before the pressures really start—you inform the entire team about what needs to be done and increase the odds that the whole team works together to the finish line.

# Recommended readings

Allen, David (2001) *Getting Things Done: The Art of Stress-free Productivity*. New York: Penguin.

Covey, Stephen R. (2004) *The Seven Habits of Highly Effective People: Restoring the Character Ethic*. New York: Free Press.

Garton, Colleen, and Kevin Wegryn (2006) *Managing Without Walls*. Lewisville, TX: MC Press.

Lencioni, Patrick (2002) *The Five Dysfunctions of a Team: A Leadership Fable*. San Francisco: Jossey-Bass.

Levine, Stuart (2006) *Cut to the Chase—And 99 Other Rules to Liberate Yourself and Gain Back the Gift of Time*. New York: Currency Doubleday.

Miller, Brian Cole (2007) *More Quick Team-building Activities for Busy Managers*. New York: AMACOM/American Management Association.

Parker, Glenn M., and Robert Hoffman (2006) *Meeting Excellence: 33 Tools to Lead Meetings That Get Results*. San Francisco, CA: Jossey-Bass.

# References

Covey, Stephen R. (2004) *The Seven Habits of Highly Effective People: Restoring the Character Ethic.* New York: Free Press.

Myers, Isabel Briggs (1998) *MBTI Manual: A Guide to the Development and Use of the Myers-Briggs Type Indicator.* 3rd ed. Palo Alto, CA: Consulting Psychologists Press.

Parker, Glenn M. (1994) *Cross-functional Teams: Working With Allies, Enemies, and Other Strangers.* Jossey-Bass Management Series. San Francisco: Jossey-Bass.

# 8

# Planning for organizational communication

## Introduction

Good communication with the web project team is important in any environment. Good communication about web projects with the rest of the organization is especially critical in academic libraries. Two issues create this need. First, the library's website may not be the most important part of a library, but it is one of the more visible. Some may feel that the web gets too much attention, yet are also sensitive to even small changes on the library web. Second, academic libraries have many functions, and staff may find it challenging to stay current about all aspects of the organization. Moreover, this diversity of interest within the organization means different colleagues will be keenly interested in different projects. These two issues mean that while most people in the library have an interest in web projects, they may have trouble staying abreast of what's happening.

Some of your colleagues may have surprisingly strong emotions related to web projects, even for projects outside their area. This atmosphere means that a simple communication mistake can create a large reaction. As the project manager, this reaction is likely to land in your office! By creating a communication plan at the outset and considering some organizational communication strategies in advance, we hope to help you avoid unnecessary stress and at the same time serve as a model for good communication practices within an organization.

Therefore, this chapter discusses three aspects of communicating with your colleagues. First, you will learn about developing a communication plan. Then, you will read about ways to get input about your project from your colleagues. Finally, this chapter concludes with considerations about organizational communication in general.

# Developing a communication plan

If your organization has a lively staff intranet, active listservs, blogs, and wikis, and effective committee structures, your job as a web project manager will be much easier. If not, however, your problem is not to fix your organization's communication. Focus instead on developing an organizational communication plan that will support your project. If your project communication is successful, you may have a real impact on your larger organization's interest in communicating effectively, but that's not your primary goal—your priority should be the success of your project.

The previous chapter talked about communicating with your team. In this chapter, you'll read about communicating with the rest of the organization:

- developing a communication plan
- gathering input from colleagues
- handling organizational communication issues
- using technology in organizational communication
- forming consensus.

In chapter 13, 'Planning the work,' we will focus on planning the project itself—who will do which specific tasks and when. In academic libraries, it is just as important to plan for organizational communication about your project. Careful communication and regular updates will not only increase the support for the project itself, but will also showcase the success of project management techniques.

## *Drafting the overall communication plan*

Here are some nuts-and-bolts questions you should ask yourself before the project begins:

- Who will want updates about the project's progress?
- How often will you communicate updates?
- Who will assemble the updates?
- Which pieces of your planning documentation can you use as material for your updates?
- What method will you use to provide updates?

For example, suppose you are managing a project to implement LibraryThing for Libraries in your online catalog at the request of the associate dean for public services (the project sponsor). You're working with a small project team and expect to also involve reference and instruction librarians as stakeholders. The project sponsor, your project team, and the reference and instruction librarians will all expect a different level of updates. You might choose to send updates to your project team weekly but to the reference and instruction colleagues every two weeks. Due to his other responsibilities, you may only be updating your project sponsor once per month. Even if some of your updates report little progress, you'll ensure that you are 'on top of things' by scheduling the frequency of updates in advance.

As project manager, it's your responsibility to plan for communication about the project. You'll likely want to be the one who sends major updates so that people see you in the role of project manager. That does not necessarily mean you need to *write* the updates yourself. You can:

- write an outline and have members of your team fill in status details and URLs
- ask members of your team to be responsible for updating a central project website
- write an update and have your team review it for accuracy and completeness
- enlist the help of one team member tapped as marketing coordinator.

Now is also a good time to think about how other pieces of your planning documentation can support this function. For instance, the project overview described in chapter 4, 'Defining your project,' is an excellent summary document for many different audiences. By revising the project overview when you make changes to primary objectives or the timeline, you have a ready-made introduction to the project. In chapters 10, 11, and 12, you will learn about flow diagrams, wireframes, site maps, and use-case scenarios that can help you think through options and then record decisions for the team. As the project proceeds, they also become excellent tools to communicate with a broader audience. Look at all the documentation you've created as a potential way of communicating with those outside the team.

The academic library environment will also influence what methods you use to communicate updates. In today's academic libraries, e-mail is still the most commonly shared communication tool. Even if you are using a blog, website, or other tool for project tracking and status reports, you will likely need to send e-mails that point to the official location of updates. You may also want to highlight major milestones or dates using e-mail. Once you have an idea about how you'll regularly update your colleagues about the project, consider carefully how you will gather input from concerned stakeholders within your organization.

---

### Communications related to project launch

The final chapter of this book discusses launch-related communications in detail. Early in the project, though, is a good time to at least outline a rough plan for the final communications related to your web project. Knowing you'll revisit these ideas later, take some time to consider:

- What launch-related communications do you think will be necessary? Will there be training sessions needing announcements and reminders? Will there be an opportunity to preview the project before launch?

- Who should receive launch-related communications? Who will be affected by this launch? Think about both internal and external audiences.

- Who should send which launch-related communications? Does your project sponsor or library administration want to be involved?

- When should each announcement happen?

---

## Gathering input from colleagues

Chapter 9, 'Getting user input,' offers many methods for gathering input from others. You can use many of those same methods to gather input from your stakeholder colleagues. As you have created a project team from within your organization, each team member will bring some insight to the project during regular meetings and work. As a team, discuss how and when to get additional input from colleagues outside the project team.

Almost every technique listed in chapter 9 can also be used to get input from colleagues, either at the same time or in separate sessions:

- personas
- card sorts

- reviewing mockups
- bug testing
- surveys
- focus groups
- interviews
- usability testing.

In addition to these methods, you might connect with your colleagues through departmental meetings or library-wide meetings where you share progress, discuss issues, and accept comments.

You should be careful to explain your intended use of colleagues' input. Clearly communicate that their input is just one piece of your team's research. This helps to clarify you are asking for insights and input, not a vote. Explain that you are combining their suggestions and advice with all the other information you have gathered to make the best decisions. Consider sharing details with them about which suggestions you incorporated into the project and which ones you did not, along with some explanation. Make sure they understand that the project sponsor is the final authority on lists of features, the look and feel, and the functionality of the project.

To a certain degree, you should take cues from your project sponsor about how much you should be engaging the rest of the organization on this project. The size of the project may be so small or the scope so focused that only a small number of stakeholders will even be interested. When you are leading a high-profile project such as a complete website redesign, many of your colleagues will have an interest in being involved. You should still discuss the input-solicitation process with your project sponsor.

If the process of getting input seems too time-consuming to you, your team, or your project sponsor, consider the following reasons why you should engage your colleagues:

- You gain valuable information by asking for input from your colleagues. Even if your project team is large, team members can't possibly know everything.
- You are the public face of this project. If you share and solicit information openly, you will gain a positive reputation that will help the next project you lead.
- You may find that you need to tap colleagues outside of the project team to write content, help with testing, and otherwise give their time.

Asking their opinions from the start increases the odds that they are happy to help you later.

- Previews of work-in-progress can decrease anxiety about the eventual transition to a changed or new site. Disgruntled colleagues can lead to slow or uneven adoption of changes, regardless of how well your team executed the project.

- Involving the whole organization calls positive attention to those on your team. This may be especially meaningful for team members who do not usually work on high-profile projects. You can increase the pride they feel in working on your project if others are informed regularly of the team's work.

You read in chapter 4 about the difficulty of managing a project within an organization where decision-making is not transparent. You can make sure you are not contributing to an environment of hidden decision-making by engaging all the stakeholders.

# Organizational communication issues in academic libraries

Private web development companies and academic library web teams work with clients in different ways. If you were the project manager in a design firm hired by a library, your relationship with that library would be linked entirely to the project. The library would be your customer, not your workplace. If you work in an academic library, however, you were likely a member of the organization before the project, during the project, and after the project. Therefore your role as project manager is conflated with your other roles in the organization. Good communication with colleagues is therefore critical not only for a given project, but also for long term relationships. This section will discuss some of the key areas of organizational communication as it relates to web project management.

## *The use of technology in organizational communication in academic libraries*

Depending on which activities you plan for, you'll probably want to make some choices about technology. Which activities will you want to conduct face-to-face and which can be done just as well (or better) virtually? A small project with simple announcements might be supported just by e-mail or a simple blog. A project exploring radical changes to the library website will probably require face-to-face meetings with the organization in order to explain the extent of the change and increase the chances for buy-in. Large projects will require numerous channels of communication. The callout 'Using Web 2.0 for organizational communication' offers some advice about using new tools for your communication plan. If you want to read more about this area we recommend the book *Information and Communication Technology in Organizations* (Bouwman et al. 2005).

---

### Using Web 2.0 for organizational communication

Your project team may have decided to use a blog, wiki, or other form of Web 2.0 communication for work. It might make sense to them for others in the organization to simply subscribe to the group's RSS feed if they want updates! But just because the technology allows for alerts doesn't mean that your colleagues have integrated RSS feeds into their lives. Using Web 2.0 effectively for organizational communication may be technically simple, but socially complex. If you do decide to go ahead with a Web 2.0 tool for communication, you might find these tips helpful:

- Begin with the end in mind. What would it look like if your Web 2.0 communication plan worked? What would each person in your organization have to do in order for it to be effective?

- Don't ask people to do new things with new technologies. If your library is considering using chat reference for the first time, and the reference librarians aren't bloggers, don't use a blog to begin discussion.

- Consider using both a Web 2.0 channel and a Web 1.0 channel. For example, offer complete information on the team blog, and periodically use e-mail to alert stakeholders about updates.

If you're determined that only people who subscribe to your feed or visit the project blog will be updated, then communicate these expectations clearly.

---

## The challenge of forming consensus

Web projects in academic libraries can have many internal stakeholders. In private sector jobs, employees don't typically think of the company website as 'belonging' to them. In libraries, employees have strong feelings of ownership. Any changes to the library catalog, for example, will be of interest to reference, instruction, cataloging, government documents—just about everybody! Additionally, library staff use the website in many roles: a subject specialist may use the catalog to develop library collections, teach students, and do personal research. Web projects carry this burden more heavily than other library areas because websites are so highly visible and many sections of the library website are used directly by library staff in their work. In addition, most librarians have at least minimal expertise with authoring web pages. Many of your colleagues will feel like they are experts on the topic of web design.

Due to all these internal interests, consensus-building will be a major part of your role as web project manager. You will likely bear several responsibilities in this area, including communicating clearly when requesting input, discussing issues when colleagues disagree, and balancing internal and external user needs.

Remember that by identifying a project sponsor, you will do much to lift this burden from your shoulders. You aren't exempt from soliciting input, but the project sponsor becomes the one who shoulders—or at least shares—the burden of contentious issues and controversial decisions. As you weigh input from your colleagues, share the conflicts openly with your project sponsor.

The following sub-sections discuss several areas to consider about creating an environment where consensus can be built.

## Communicating clearly when requesting input

You read about purposeful efforts to gather input from colleagues earlier in this chapter. How you ask for that input and demonstrate your use of it contributes to the amount of input you receive, when you receive it, and long term goodwill. Here's a typical scenario in an academic library: you send out a library-wide e-mail with hyperlinks to the library's new journal finder web page and you encourage your colleagues to visit the link and send you comments. You get a handful of e-mails with both kudos and suggestions for improvement. One person writes to say they think it should be called 'Periodical Finder,' not 'Journal Finder,' but no one else does. You make adjustments based on both your colleagues' majority opinions and user input. You launch the site on time, one week before the semester starts. Immediately, you receive three e-mails from people who hadn't chosen to provide input earlier but are now concerned about various aspects of the completed project. You also get a frustrated e-mail from 'Periodical Finder' demanding to know why the name wasn't changed, since 'everyone else' supported this change. What happened?!?!

This story illustrates that people in this organization had different expectations relating to their input. Some colleagues expected you to implement every suggestion. Others may have expected additional opportunities for input. Some colleagues may not have even noticed your request. When requesting input, then, be clear about what you're going to do, do it, and then when you've done it, illustrate that you kept to the plan. If responses show a sharp division of opinion, take the issue to your project sponsor for a decision. You may never fully satisfy everyone's expectations.

This example also illustrates the need for repeated communication using different techniques, especially if you perceive the project to be of high interest. Although your project is a top priority for you, your e-mail may have arrived in some colleagues' in-boxes at the same time as many other requests. Other colleagues may not have understood the anticipated changes when explained by e-mail, but would have had opinions when shown the project in person. Others may have benefited from being able to respond to others' opinions, such as the change in name. A single communication about this upcoming change just may not have been enough.

Early in the project, identify when you'll be showing everyone the team's progress, when you'll ask for input, and when you plan to launch the project. Announce as much information as you can right away. Returning to our journal finder example:

> Dear Colleagues, I am pleased to announce that the Web Team has begun work on our new Journal Finder web page as previously announced by Jane Smith, our project sponsor! We plan to have a rough mockup for you to look at in March, and will be asking for your input by April 1st so we can make decisions for revision by April 15th. This schedule will allow us to launch the site in May. For more information about this project, please visit the project page.

In your communication plan, sketch in several tasks and dates:

- Just before March, send a reminder that the mockup is coming—maybe with more specific dates and deadlines.

- During March, send at least one reminder that all input is due by April 1st so that you can launch the site in May.

- When April 1st arrives, send a 'thanks for your input, we're moving ahead!' e-mail. Consider including one of your previous e-mails in the text of that e-mail just to demonstrate you're following the plan.

You'll want to use this technique again when you show the final results, and when the project launches. Finally, if you're keeping a project web page for communicating with your colleagues, you'll want to include the URL for this page in all your e-mails. Be sure the project web page is up to date and illustrates how you've followed the plan for input. One option is to list out all the input you've received in a table, with notes about how your team responded to the various suggestions.

## Discussing issues when colleagues disagree

If you are serving as a web project manager in an academic library, you will be involved in numerous conversations involving disagreement. Whether you are discussing options one-on-one with your project sponsor, working within your project team, or receiving input from your colleagues, you may find that you are presenting an opposing viewpoint. Or you may find yourself mediating between two opposing viewpoints with no strong opinion of your own. Although your project sponsor will provide the deciding vote on issues with disagreement, you will want to plan activities that identify those issues, facilitate open communication, and work toward consensus.

Three of the habits that Stephen Covey presents in *The Seven Habits of Highly Effective People* are highly relevant to communicating about opposing viewpoints. The first, 'Think Win–Win,' suggests it is important to form an attitude where people can believe *both* parties can achieve their goals (2004, 207). When you are on one side of the disagreement, an important component of this dynamic is to have *courage*: the willingness and inner strength to speak your thoughts and feelings. The other is to have *consideration*: the willingness and inner strength to listen to others' thoughts and feelings with respect (2004, 217). In other words, it's important to think through both what would be a 'win' for you as well as what would be a 'win' for the person with whom you have conflict.

Then, you can work towards solutions where both parties can see a winning situation.

A related principle from Covey is 'Seek first to understand, then to be understood' (2004, 239–41). Most of us listen so that we may then reply. Covey suggests that we should listen only with the intent to understand what the other person is saying. This 'empathic listening' is a major paradigm shift for most people. It is easy for web project managers to assume that we understand the solution to a given problem—after all, we usually know the most about the overall project. But if we listen with that attitude, we miss out in the insights that our colleagues offer. If you are not truly listening with an open mind, colleagues will see through your façade. Sincerity shows.

The final relevant Covey principle we'll mention here is just one word: 'Synergize' (2004, 262–63). When trying to resolve a dispute, often people only see the divergent paths. If things are going well, perhaps the group will form a compromise where some parties concede some points and gain others. Covey urges people to think of a 'third way'— not a midpoint between all divergent viewpoints, but instead, a new solution no one has thought of before.

We have borrowed heavily from three of Stephen Covey's principles in this section. We strongly encourage you to read at least these three chapters in *The Seven Habits of Highly Effective People* in order to support your work as a web project manager. If you can make time for the entire book, though, it will be well worth your time.

## Case study of an activity to build consensus

 One of the database-driven areas of the authors' library's website provided lists of information resources categorized by the type of information they contained: articles, images, video, etc. These database-driven lists were too long, and sometimes there were odd items in the list. Librarians had different opinions about what these 'types' should be called and which ones were important enough to be listed on the front page of this area. The project manager (one of your authors) planned a series of meetings:

- At the first meeting, the librarians performed a card sort using four sets of index cards with all the possible 'types of information' and blank cards for new suggestions. The librarians broke up into four groups of three to four people each and decided which types of information were most important to them. Each group also offered new suggestions for vocabulary. Before the second meeting, the participants received typed-up results of this exercise to see what everyone else had done.

- At the second meeting, the group discussed the remaining areas of disagreement. The project manager used comments from this discussion to make final decisions. Because people saw first-hand how divergent their colleagues' opinions were, they better understood that someone just had to decide among the options.

- At the third meeting, the project manager presented the final 'information types' that would appear on the front page and wrapped up the discussion. Through e-mail, librarians volunteered to maintain one or more of the new 'information type' pages.

Not only did this process result in volunteerism and intelligently designed pages, it demonstrated the complexities of the problem to everyone in the group. If the web project manager or even a small team had made an executive decision about which 'types' were most important, people would have remained dissatisfied about how the decisions had been made and whether their input was *really* given consideration. This way, even though the web project manager made the final decision, everyone saw how many different points of view there were and how hard it was to decide.

## Conclusion

Developing a communication plan will help you remember to update your organization regularly about the project at hand. By gathering input from your colleagues, your team has the opportunity to strengthen both the project and the process. As web project manager, it will fall to you to identify competing interests of internal and external stakeholders. Your colleagues may tell you that they want to include news announcements and enticing graphics about research databases. Your users may tell you that they aren't interested in promotional content on the library front page. Your job is to understand both perspectives and explore ways to reach 'win–win' between them. By cultivating good habits and planning for organizational communication, you may even set a model for others in your organization to follow.

# Recommended readings

Bouwman, Harry, Bart van den Hooff, Lidwien van de Wijngaert, and Jan A. G. M. van Dijk (2005) *Information and Communication Technology in Organizations: Adoption, Implementation, Use and Effects.* Thousand Oaks, CA: Sage.

Covey, Stephen R. (2004) *The Seven Habits of Highly Effective People: Restoring the Character Ethic.* New York: Free Press.

Flynn, Nancy, and Tom Flynn (2003) *Writing Effective E-mail.* Fifty Minute Series. Rev. ed. Menlo Park, CA: Crisp Learning.

Keyton, Joann (2004) *Communication and Organizational Culture: A Key to Understanding Work Experiences.* Thousand Oaks, CA: Sage.

Kliem, Ralph L. (2007) *Effective Communications for Project Management.* Boca Raton: Auerbach.

# References

Bouwman, Harry, Bart van den Hooff, Lidwien van de Wijngaert, and Jan A. G. M. van Dijk (2005) *Information and Communication Technology in Organizations: Adoption, Implementation, Use and Effects.* Thousand Oaks, CA: Sage.

Covey, Stephen R. (2004) *The Seven Habits of Highly Effective People: Restoring the Character Ethic.* New York: Free Press.

# 9

# Getting user input

## Introduction

While commercial website developers do not face the same organizational challenges as academic libraries, they must work much harder to gather precious input from their target user groups. Comparatively, academic libraries have relatively easy and free access to the input of their primary users. This input is rich with opportunities for the web project team. User input can help you be sure a project meets clear user needs.

As web project manager, you do not need to be the organization's usability testing expert, survey developer, or statistician. However, you need to understand the available methods and the possibilities and limitations offered by each. You need to make sure the methods will fit into the project's timeline. You can also promote ethical standards, good methodology, and healthy skepticism. Especially in an academic library, the importance of critical and ethical evaluation of user input should be made a part of the organizational culture. Although gathering, analyzing, and interpreting user input may be done by others, the web project manager's role is to ensure this important task is accomplished.

## Who are your users?

Identify target user groups as early as possible in the project. Although the primary user groups of most academic library web projects will be students and faculty, many projects will have numerous secondary user groups, including campus staff, visitors, and community users. You read about librarians and library staff members as colleagues in chapter 8, 'Planning for organizational communication.' They may also be an important user group for your particular project. Secondary groups might also include distinct populations such as international populations or students returning to school after other careers.

Identify both primary and secondary user groups for each project, but be sure to focus on the primary users. For example, if you are developing a web tutorial for incoming freshmen, transfer students or incoming graduate students may also use it. You may be tempted to try to design a system that meets all potential user groups' needs. Focus instead on the primary group—in this case, incoming freshmen—and spend the most time considering their input on the project. If a significant number of graduate students end up 'making do' with the tutorial, perhaps you can plan a second project for their needs.

Individual units of the library are likely to have different perspectives on 'who our users are.' The web project manager's job is to identify all the user groups for a given project, confirm those groups with the project sponsor, and make sure that the project is informed by all the necessary user groups. In your neutral role, you have the obligation to think from the perspective of the project itself, rather than a particular unit's or individual's goals. Your job is to make sure not only that a key user group is not forgotten, overlooked, or ignored, but also that the project does not try to be all things to all people.

## When should you get user input?

You should begin to get user input as soon as you have written the project overview (see chapter 4), but before you write the specifications (see chapters 10–12). As described in chapter 5, 'The academic library web team,' consider including representative users on your project team or inviting them to specific meetings so you can regularly check your assumptions. You can also informally brainstorm with student employees or faculty colleagues about potential features for the project. Ask users not only about the features your project sponsor requested, but also new ones that come to mind. If you have an existing interface or system that you're revising or replacing, you can use that as a basis for discussion. Some of the users' ideas may not be practical for the immediate project and some may never be practical, but capture the ideas as you receive them so you can refer back to them again. You should look for every opportunity to get feedback from your users.

Since they spent time and energy with you, it's generally a good idea to send the users information about the outcome of their contribution. Tell them how their input affected the project, if and when you think they'll be able to be involved again, and when you think the project will be available for use. Send them a link to the new site when the project is complete.

## Participation incentives

 A common problem academic libraries face is providing adequate participation incentives to users. Cash, of course, is a good draw. But what if you do not have funds available or their use is restricted by university policy? Here are some alternative incentive options:

- If you have a privately owned bookstore or dining service, check with your institution's business office to see if they provide the institution with a supply of complimentary gift certificates. This is not an unusual arrangement.

- If you have funds but cannot give participants cash by law or regulation, consider purchasing food or small gift items such as USB flash drives.

- If you have only a small amount of funds, consider a raffle where only one participant takes the prize.

- At some institutions, a 'get out of a library fine' card could be an option—but of course you'd need to check with your circulation department!

- In the academic environment, many participants will offer their opinions for free. Talk up the value of participants' expertise and explain clearly how their participation will make a real difference.

- Another option is to form an 'advisory board' that is on-call for a year's time, perhaps paying members one incentive for the year's participation.

# Whose responsibility is it to get user input?

As a web project manager, your responsibility is to plan for user input as part of the process, but you do not necessarily need to oversee individual activities. Your project sponsor, for instance, may have already done some user research before she approached you with this project. In all cases, other members of your project team can help. They can schedule brainstorming meetings with users, send follow-up e-mails, or develop interface mockups to show user groups. Be sure to consider potential partners in other departments, too. Perhaps a psychologist, sociologist, or anthropologist would be interested in helping with the statistics on a user behavior study and perhaps even co-writing an article for publication. As described in chapter 4, consider appointing a member of your project team as the user input coordinator. He can review all relevant user research already done, plan additional activities, and if necessary form a subcommittee to do the work. Just check in to be sure he develops a plan that will gather input effectively, and keep an eye on the execution of the plan. Make sure the group is delivering on their good intentions.

# Using existing research and information

In many cases, you may not have to conduct an extensive effort to gather information about user needs. One of the benefits of working on web projects in academic libraries is that colleagues in other libraries are generally willing to share their experiences with users, formally and informally. Members of the project team should search the library literature for related projects or situations. After identifying what others may have done on a similar project, you can contact the author for more information. They may be willing to provide additional details, updates on the project, or advice that they did not include in the article.

## Existing information about user needs for web interfaces

 With its increased emphasis on providing information online, the US federal government has invested in some significant efforts to study user behavior. One excellent resource it has developed is *Research-based Web Design and Usability Guidelines* (US Dept of Health and Human Services 2006), a book that codifies research findings on specific topics related to web interfaces. The book reports on both the importance of the topic as well as the strength of the evidence.

For recent case studies on how libraries have been investigating user needs, simply search 'usability' or 'user study' in your local library literature database. Evaluate their methods and conclusions carefully; although many libraries work hard to follow current usability practices, not all will serve as the best model for you to follow.

# Using web statistics

Web logs can provide important, objective information about users. Every time a user enters your site, clicks on links, and leaves your site, they are providing you with input. How did they find your site? What choices did they make while within your site? Where did they go when they leave? These are just a few of the questions you can answer about users by analyzing web statistics.

Every web server's administrator has access to web statistics via the server log files. Unless you are serving in that capacity yourself, you may need to ask for these explicitly and possibly also ask for help with implementing log analysis software. Interpreting web statistics is something even experts can have trouble with. Think carefully about what you want to know about your users and choose appropriate metrics from the software you've chosen. When you're ready to learn more, we hope you or your library's webmaster will check out a book on this topic since this area is worthy of further exploration (see 'Recommended readings' at the end of this chapter).

## Web statistics software

 The following products offer a variety of options for gathering and analyzing web statistics:

- **AWStats** (*http://awstats.sourceforge.net/*), free log analysis software; written in Perl; supports many server log formats. See also their comparison chart: *http://awstats.sourceforge.net/docs/awstats_compare.html*.

- **Google Analytics** (*http://www.google.com/analytics/*): this is not a server log analysis tool, but instead tracks clicks on your site after you paste a few lines of code into the web page for which you want statistics. The 'site overlay' tool shows your web page annotated with the percentage of users clicking on various links. To track use of Javascript or other special interactive page elements, you'll need to insert tracking codes as specified in the Google Analytics documentation section, 'How Do I Track Dynamic Sites?'

- **Urchin Software** from Google (*http://www.google.com/urchin/*), for purchase. Created by Google and sold by authorized resellers,

Urchin looks and acts more like log analysis software than Google Analytics. Urchin can analyze multiple server logs.

- **The Webalizer** (*http://www.webalizer.com/*), free log analysis software; written in C; supports standard Common Logfile Format server logs.

- **WebTrends Analytics** (*http://www.webtrends.com/Products/ Analytics.aspx*), for purchase. This is one of many examples of software with 'suites' of products that support web tracking and analysis.

## Segmenting your users with web statistics

Web statistics software frequently lets you segment your users by geography or browser version, but these are of limited use for most libraries. With additional user input methods or some additional time, you may be able to segment your users by age, academic level, status (student, faculty, staff, visitor), academic department, or other traditional academic organizational groups. If your library has a sign-in for users, it may be fairly easy for you to track useful subgroups of users, defined either by the user login or matched up to a central database. If you don't, however, you can observe different segments of users by criteria found in your log files. These won't necessarily be the same groups you are using for other purposes, but they might still be interesting as you identify:

- what sites they came in from
- what file(s) they accessed or downloaded
- what pages they landed on first in your site.

Suppose you notice a significant number of entry hits on the library home page coming from the library's special collections page. You might look at this segment to see what these users do after they arrive. Which pages do they visit most frequently?

## Which statistics to track?

Choose which web statistics to gather and analyze based on your website goals. Although it's probably interesting that your website traffic is increasing by 10% each year, that doesn't tell you whether your users are finding what they need. For example, increased visits could mean that users aren't finding what they need until they visit many pages on your site. Don't try to analyze all your web logs. Just pay attention to the performance metrics you've decided to track. You can always look special topics up on an ad hoc basis. Here are a few suggestions for statistics that may inform an entire project redesign:

- *Navigation report*: this shows you the order in which visitors click through pages on your website and how long they stay on each page. This is an ideal report to segment by user group, if possible.

- *Landing pages*: this is important to track because you do not always control where users enter the site. Suppose 20% of your users enter your library website through the 'About the Libraries' page. You might want to make sure this page looks great, and you might want to check out what makes it so attractive—does it have metadata making it appear high in search engine rank? Perhaps you can tweak your home page to use some of the same strategies. Don't automatically try to discourage users from entering on this secondary page. Instead, think about what you can do to get them to where they want to go *from* this page to other parts of your site.

- *Page load times*: in a quick glance, you can see which pages on your site are taking the longest to load. A sudden increase in page load times for a given page might indicate a web application that is overloaded with data or is suffering performance issues.

- *Visits and time on page*: track these for any section of your website for which you are doing a redesign or marketing campaign. For example, if you're overhauling the front page for the e-journal portal, you'd want to see if usage was increasing or decreasing, and whether users were getting off the page more quickly than they were before (which is good for an e-journal portal!).

- *Pages by popularity*: whether you are revising a particular section of your site or the entire site, review the top pages by number of hits for any surprises. You may find particular pages which are surprisingly popular. Is this due to accidents of navigation? Or are they more useful than you thought?

- *Keyword statistics*: although libraries do not usually pay search engines for keywords to make their sites rank higher, these statistics can still prove interesting. Rushton, Kelehan, and Strong at Binghamton University worked on a search engine optimization strategy and managed to improve their website's ranking for certain keywords (2008).

Each of these metrics can inform decisions for your project and help you evaluate its success after you are done.

## Using conversion rates in libraries

Visitor conversion is another area libraries should investigate. Commercial websites' goals focus on converting visitors into customers who make a purchase. Libraries' conversion rates might not be about dollars, but about sense: how many of our *visitors* are converted to *users*? That is, how many visitors to the library website actually use a service or a resource? At Western Michigan University, Michael Whang conducted a banner ad campaign on the library website and found that using conversion rates to measure performance not only helped provide additional e-metrics to evaluate specific services, but could also be used to 'make a very convincing case for academic libraries trying to prove their value and return on investment' (2007, 106). In *Web Analytics for Dummies*, Pedro Sostre and Jennifer LeClaire (2007) emphasized the importance of comparing your conversion statistics to one another (benchmarking) rather than trying to achieve a certain percentage.

# Methods for gathering user input

Analyzing web statistics and reviewing the literature are not replacements for learning from real, live, local users, but they can help point you to the questions to ask. You may have tried your best to create a web interface that responds to what all the published research and past statistics are showing, but you won't know how well it delivers until a real user tries it out. We

---

### User input at the organizational level

 Your library's administration may conduct regular surveys or prepare regular reports that involve gathering, analyzing, and interpreting user input. It is the web project manager's job to be familiar with what information might be relevant and to bring that information to bear on the current project. You may also see opportunities for modifying future organizational information-gathering efforts. For example, many academic libraries participate in the LibQUAL+ survey (*http://www.libqual.org/*). In addition to requesting information from your administration, be sure to provide them with an executive summary of new information you discover.

could fill multiple books with suggestions for working with users. Instead, we've included a 'Recommended readings' section about studying user behavior at the end of this chapter and will cover only a selection of possible methods that seem especially practical for today's academic libraries.

## Using personas to visualize your user groups

One technique to make your user groups more real to stakeholders and the project team is to create personas. We first read about creating personas in Christina Wodtke's *Information Architecture* (2003, 165–88). On the surface, this technique may sound like a hokey management gimmick, but some information architects swear by the practice. The idea is that instead of designing for some generic, vague 'user,' designers create fictional characters that stand in for real users. The personas are created based on interviews with users, demographic data, and a little bit of imagination. The more realistic your personas are, the better. Good personas beg to be made happy with interfaces and features that will satisfy them. Alan Cooper, the author of *The Inmates Are Running the Asylum* (1999), also discusses the use of personas. He suggests that while designers don't need to make each persona *exceptionally* happy, interfaces need to avoid making any persona *unhappy* (1999, 144).

Using personas is a good way to involve others in your organization. Consider getting a group of library staff together to create personas of your most likely users. Give them some demographics and a general outline, but get them to contribute most of the personality descriptions from their own experiences. Small groups of two to three colleagues creating each persona work well. You can even include student employees or other members of your primary user group to participate and help keep the personas realistic. Sarah Bordac and Jean Rainwater suggest another way to define user personas is to categorize reference questions from chat reference transcripts, interview public service staff, and make direct observations of users (2008, 116). Figure 9.1 shows an example persona constructed by library staff at the authors' institution.

## Card sort

A card sort is an activity where labels, navigation elements, or terminology representing page content are written individually on cards, and users are asked to sort them into similar or even hierarchical groups.

**Figure 9.1** Example persona

*Personal name*: Dan Nole

*Age*: 26

*Home at JMU*: The Village dorms

*Quotes*: 'Laugh now, cry later.'; 'I want to be where the music is.'

*Personal background*: From Northern Virginia, Dan is the middle child in his family, with an older sister and a younger brother. His parents pay his tuition. Dan did well enough in high school to get into JMU but didn't apply himself and had to work for a few years before going to college. He likes to party and he's in a band. The lead singer of his favorite band, Sublime, shares his last name (but with a different spelling), but that's just a coincidence. He's relatively computer literate and downloads music from iTunes regularly. He's thinking about making music his career, but he doesn't know where he fits in yet. His major is undecided for now and he's a freshman.

*Goals*: This first year at JMU, one of his teachers asked him to do a presentation on a topic (he chose independent rock music labels). He searched on Google and found some good information. He also visited the library the day before the assignment was due and found an article and a book because his teacher required it. He also uses the library to keep up with *Rolling Stone* and *Billboard* magazines.

If he can't be on stage in a band, he wants to be behind the stage making it happen. To meet that goal he has to get good grades within his major once he picks one. He eventually wants to find a job that will let him pursue his real interest—music.

*Photo credits*: Karen Meadows, photographer. Alex Meadows, model. Used with permission.

An *open sort* is where you allow users to make their own groups, whereas a *closed sort* provides fixed categories. You can follow a card sort with a discussion with users about why they placed cards in a particular pile. If a web project involves a large group of library staff as primary stakeholders or user group, consider card sorting as a small group activity. Then, bring the discoveries back to the larger group to help them reach consensus. Angi Falks and Nancy Hyland (2000) provide detailed instructions for conducting and evaluating this technique in an academic library setting.

## Co-design sessions with users

A co-design session is a fun and productive activity you can do with users. You invite a group of users to help you design the final product. You explain the goals to the group, provide white boards and markers, and then let imaginations run wild. The objective is not to ask your users to do the design work for your designer. Instead, you gain a better understanding of how your users think about the content and the interactions. By concluding the co-design session with each participant explaining their choices to the larger group, you learn what your users really want, regardless of the technology and design limitations.

## Reviewing mockups with users

If your project involves web programming, then user input is especially critical. In addition to getting input prior to drafting programming specifications, you'll want to be sure to show them wireframes or mockups of the interface design before any programming has been done. Looking at a mocked-up web interface, even on paper, can jog fresh thoughts and possibly identify missing features. You don't want your web programmers to finish coding a database-driven web form only to find you forgot a critical data field.

## Bug testing with users

Involving users in the bug testing of your web project can also be helpful. Not only are you gaining extra eyes to find bugs, your users can offer last-minute suggestions. Many of their suggestions may be easy fixes, such as changing text labels to avoid jargon. Difficult-to-accommodate suggestions can be saved for later on a wishlist. Although asynchronous bug testing is possible, scheduling one time with many users can help find bugs that only occur when multiple users are acting simultaneously. Either way, you'll want to be sure to have a bug testing script (see *http://sites.google.com/site/pm4web/Home/book*) for them to follow and have a bug-tracking system ready to go (see chapter 11).

## User surveys

Surveys are frequently used in academic librarianship. They are an easy and efficient way to gather information, and if using the internet, they can be created, distributed, and analyzed quickly and easily. Writing survey questions is challenging, however. Good survey research requires paying attention to things such as sample size, question wording, and choice of scale. There are several short and highly useful books on survey research listed in the recommended readings at the end of this chapter.

One of the big problems with survey research is nonresponse. Floyd Fowler explains how nonresponse can bias survey results (2002, 39–46). If you have a 30% response rate, it is likely that your respondents are either heavy library users or have strong opinions about the library. You may be finding nothing about the behavior or opinions of non-library users or typical users. A 30% response rate may seem fairly high—surely enough to be useful. But, consider tables 9.1 and 9.2. With a 90% response rate, as shown in table 9.1, you can be fairly certain your population is evenly divided on the issue: if the 90 responses you get are split 50–50, even if the 10 non-responders would have all answered 'Yes,' this would only change the results to a 45–55% split. With a 30% response, as in table 9.2, you have a situation where it appears that the population is evenly divided—but it's entirely possible that 85% of the population would say 'Yes' and only 15% would say 'No.'

**Table 9.1** Survey of 100 people, with 90% response rate

|  | Total responses | Non respondents | Range of total responses possible |
|---|---|---|---|
| Yes | 45 | 0–10 | 45–55 |
| No | 45 | 0–10 | 45–55 |

**Table 9.2** Survey of 100 people, with 30% response rate

|  | Total responses | Non respondents | Range of total responses possible |
|---|---|---|---|
| Yes | 15 | 0–70 | 15–85 |
| No | 15 | 0–70 | 15–85 |

Here are several suggestions for reducing nonresponse to surveys, inspired by Fowler:

- Offer an incentive for participation (see callout earlier in this chapter).
- Make the task easy; use as few questions as possible.

- Send multiple invitations and reminders to complete the survey.

- Use more than one mode to contact participants. For example, you could e-mail an invitation and also announce the survey during instruction classes.

Offer alternative modes of response for those who do not respond initially (2002, 50).

If you do a survey and get only a 30% response rate, the information is not useless. It can suggest a direction and inspire follow-up techniques. And, you will definitely learn something that will help you conduct a better survey next time! But it would be inaccurate, not to mention unethical, to use your survey results as evidence that a given proposition is generalizable to the larger population. Get user input, use what you find, but acknowledge the limitations of your research.

## Focus groups

Facilitated groups of five to ten people can help you define problems, clarify objectives, and propose solutions. Focus groups are an excellent way to show internal groups that your team is interested in listening to what they have to say. David Morgan (1997, 8–15) lists the main advantages of focus groups:

- Compared with participant observation, focus groups allow the researcher 'to observe a large amount of interaction on a topic in a limited period of time'.

- Focus groups can provide information about attitudes and decision-making that observation could fail to detect.

- Focus groups offer concentrated observations on the researcher's interests.

- Focus groups allow for valuable comparisons made by the people in the group discussions.

The disadvantages include:

- Focus groups are even less of a natural setting than participant observation.

- Focus groups are limited to verbal behavior and self-reported data.

- Focus groups require a qualified moderator.

- Focus groups may provide less detail about a given participant's opinions and experiences.

In an academic library, some focus group participants may not be able to offer many insights on your website due to lack of familiarity. For example, if you show a focus group a portion of your website they've never seen before, discussion might be difficult. You could instead send them a link in advance and note that their participation requires them to spend fifteen minutes exploring the site before the meeting. Previewing the site gives them more familiarity—and likely more interest—in the topic. Or, you could instead use the focus group time to ask them more general questions about their needs, ignoring the specifics of the website.

Morgan offers several 'rules of thumb' as a point of departure for focus group research design:

- Use participants who have traits in common. For example, it might not be effective to have a mixed group of students and faculty unless your project is a site facilitating their interaction.

- Have six to ten participants per group—and be sure to err on the side of scheduling too many participants, since no-shows can be common.

- Have three to five groups per project. The idea behind this is to stop collecting data 'when the moderator can accurately anticipate what will be said next in a group' (1997, 43). Conducting only one group, says Morgan, is a bad idea because 'it is impossible to tell when the discussion reflects either the unusual composition of that group or the dynamics of that unique set of participants.' Even two groups are much safer, since if they differ, you would know that you need to keep studying.

- Use a moderator to conduct a relatively structured interview (1997, 32).

- Avoid recruiting participants from one source—for example, library student workers—if you are trying to understand a larger group. Although focus groups do not produce generalizable data, it is still important for researchers to minimize sample bias.

Spend some time in advance thinking about how you will analyze your focus group data. You're probably interested in learning about the reasons for people's reactions, not just the reactions themselves. This means you'll need to allot time for asking people follow-up questions, which reduces the number of initial questions you can ask. Focus groups take time but can offer valuable information. If you are eager to learn more about analyzing focus group data, consult *Focus Groups*, by David W. Stewart, Prem N. Shamdasani, and Dennis W. Rook (2007, 115).

## Interviews

Interviews are similar in concept to focus groups, except you visit with people one-on-one. Although this may seem more time consuming, there are some advantages: you do not have to find a time and place that accommodates everyone; you can speak with people in their natural environment; and you may learn more about real habits as people may be more forthcoming when not speaking in front of a group. This could be an excellent technique to use with faculty, for example, who may not wish to admit ignorance within a focus group setting. Seidman (2006, 42) notes some of the potential pitfalls of contacting and selecting participants for interviews. For example, sometimes the people to whom you have the easiest access are not good interview subjects, including people you supervise, students you teach, friends, and even acquaintances.

## Ethnographic studies

Although ethnographic methods are not new, their use in academic libraries is more recent. Nancy Fried Foster and Susan Gibbons, editors of *Studying Students* (2007), present several examples of ethnographic tools and techniques used to understand undergraduate students and their use of information. In addition to interviews and co-design sessions, they employed photo surveys and mapping diaries to learn about students' current work habits. An anthropologist guided several library subteams through these research methods.

## Usability testing

Usability testing is a process of evaluation and measurement of user performance on a specific application or website. It can involve the use of recording software (see callout 'Usability testing software') which allows you to unobtrusively gather information about the user's activities. A simple process might look like this:

- Create scenario with specific tasks for user to perform.
- Observe users as they complete the tasks.
- Measure user performance on the tasks, including success and time spent on task.
- Analyze results.

What usability testing gets you is a list of *possible* usability issues. As discussed in a later section, you cannot know how generalizable the results of a usability test are unless you are able to test large numbers of users.

One of the specific challenges to usability testing in academic libraries is that the most convenient facilitators (library staff members) usually have a lot invested in the interfaces being tested. It is hard for staff to interact with participants in an unbiased way, or to analyze and report objectively. This is called the 'evaluator effect' (US Dept of Health and Human Services 2006, 195). Libraries with at least a small budget could consider outsourcing at least part of the work of usability tests. Usability consultants are often willing to provide just facilitation services and help with report analysis, while your team can do the work of soliciting participants and providing the lab and incentives.

The recommended readings at the end of this chapter include several good books that provide complete explanations of how to conduct a usability test.

---

## Usability testing software

 Morae, by TechSmith, Inc., *http://www.techsmith.com/morae.asp*

Morae is a two-part piece of software. The Morae Recorder will record all user activity on a computer, including on a website. It captures desktop activity, audio, camera video, and a complete chronicle of system events, all synchronized into a single file. The Morae Manager allows the usability tester to process the recording, make clips, bookmarks, and code results. Although you can calculate some usability metrics, you'll have to do some work by hand.

**Bailey's Usability Testing Environment (UTE), by Mind Design Systems, Inc.,** *https://www.mindd.com/*

This two-part tool assists with quantitative usability evaluation of websites and web applications. The UTE Manager allows a tester to set up scenarios and survey questions, then after testing, to compile the test results into a customized report and summary. The UTE Runner presents participants with test scenarios and survey questions while tracking the actions of the subject throughout the test including clicks, keystrokes, and scrolling. Whereas Morae provides you a capture tool for audio and video, the UTE will walk

---

a user through the tasks and track both time on task and task success. This software is available for free to agencies in the US federal government and can be purchased separately or in software bundles with Morae.

## What about inspection evaluations?

You may have heard of inspection evaluations (also called 'heuristic evaluations' or 'expert reviews') used in place of usability testing (Nielsen 1994). In this method, a usability expert reviews a website using a checklist of usability issues and identifies potential problems according to his or her best judgment. Even with experienced usability professionals, research has shown that this method generates both false positives (problems that are not actually problems) and also misses real issues (US Dept of Health and Human Services 2006, 194). Use such methods at your own risk.

### Working with specific user groups

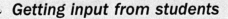 #### Getting input from students

- *Opportunities*: Students are one of the easiest user groups to work with. Most colleges have lots of them. They generally like to offer their opinions.
- *Challenges*: Getting a representative sample from your student population can be difficult. For example, it is tempting to grab some users from the reference area. While this is perhaps better than nothing, you won't be learning about students who don't choose to come into the library.
- *Tips for working with students*: Avoid stressful times of the semester, like exam week. Be prepared to meet with students after regular business hours.

#### Getting input from faculty

- *Opportunities*: When asked directly for input, faculty are generally candid.
- *Challenges*: Faculty are busy people. Faculty in different disciplines will have different perspectives, so be sure to identify participants from several disparate departments.

- *Tips for working with faculty*: If your library has subject librarians or departmental liaisons, enlist their help for soliciting feedback. Faculty are more likely to respond to someone they know than a blast e-mail from a stranger. Consider visiting faculty in their offices to get a feel for the environment in which they work.

## Getting input from librarians and library staff

- *Opportunities*: Library staff members generally have lots of opinions based on frequent use of websites. Because they are your colleagues, their opinions are easy to solicit and you can visit them in their own offices to watch them work.

- *Challenges*: Your colleagues can be both internal users of your web project and observers of how external users use your web project.

- *Tips for working with librarians and library staff*: If library staff members are a primary user group for which you are designing, solicit their input just like you would an external user group. Be careful to distinguish input they offer about how *they* use the site versus how they observe *others* use the site.

## Getting user input from visitors and public users

- *Opportunities*: Since many visitors are from outside academia, their perspectives are often fresh and unique. You can learn some surprising things that people are doing with your website.

- *Challenges*: Unlike students and faculty, who share many reasons for visiting your library's website, visitors may bring diverse needs to your user groups. For example, you could find that older users are making heavy use of a genealogy bibliography that was originally written for a freshman honors class, and they're frustrated with the small font size that the students find convenient.

- *Tips for working with visitors and public users*: Be purposeful with your choice of incentives for this group. The dining services vouchers you got for students and faculty may not be as attractive for visitors.

# Ethical issues

Ethical issues are not yours to meet alone, but you may be best-placed to watch out for potential trouble areas. This section will discuss the importance of verifying validity and generalizability of research as well as the implications of involving human subjects in your work.

## *Valid and generalizable results*

As web project manager, you may receive many reports about user behavior. 'We've been noticing that users have a hard time using the new federated search software,' says the head of reference. 'I took a survey of the business students in my instruction class, and they prefer the advanced search, so we should change the default search to advanced,' says a business librarian. This type of input is good because it raises research questions. But how much evidence is sufficient to make a decision? What types of evidence about user behavior can you rely on?

There are two important characteristics to consider about social science research design: validity and generalizability. *Validity* is whether the methodology will provide valid results. As William M. K. Trochim (2006) states:

> Virtually all social research involves measurement or observation. And, whenever we measure or observe we are concerned with whether we are measuring what we intend to measure or with how our observations are influenced by the circumstances in which they are made.

When we talk about the validity of research, therefore, we are talking about the quality of different parts of our research methodology. For example, if you are timing participants' completion of a task that involves using research databases, and some of the research databases are faster than others, then your time measurements will not be *valid* for comparing user performance. A way around this, of course, is to make sure participants are using the *same* research database and performing similar searches. Although your entire team can be on the watch for problematic methodology, it is your job to make sure this question is considered.

*Generalizability* is how representative your test's results are of your actual population. Jakob Nielsen (2000) is often paraphrased to say that usability testing only needs to be done with five users in order to find most usability issues. However, this should not be interpreted to mean that the experience of those five users is *representative* of the entire user population. While those five users may identify most of the issues one would encounter from using the interface, you will not be able to determine from this data what percentage of your user population would encounter that issue. Nielsen proposes that twenty participants are necessary to be able to make statements about how your results can be generalized (2006, n.p.). Even these twenty participants need to be selected carefully to ensure they represent your target audience. Other researchers say this number is even too few, suggesting 35 are necessary (Bailey 2006, 18).

You don't need to use only methods that will result in generalizable findings. Getting a list of usability problems from five or so users will still benefit any web project. As Nielsen (2006, n.p.) concludes, 'the first several usability studies you perform should be qualitative. Only after your organization has progressed in maturity with respect to integrating usability into the design lifecycle and you're routinely performing usability studies should you start including a few quant [sic] studies in the mix.' Just be sure to watch for statements like 'Most of our users can't find the drop-down menu' if you've only tested five users. As web project manager, you need to be on the lookout for the relative validity and generalizability of your methods.

## *Involving human subjects in your work*

Before you speak with your first user, pause for a moment to review your institution's policies about the use of human subjects in research. You may not consider gathering input for your project to be 'research,' but your institution may see things differently. If the website or printed policies are not clear, e-mail the appropriate department about your project to see if it qualifies. The name of this department will vary. Look for 'Institutional Review Board,' 'Human Subjects Review Board,' or 'Office of Research.'

At the authors' institution, both surveys and usability tests require prior review and approval by the institutional review board. All collaborators must take an online training session every three years if they will be working with human subjects. The participants must sign consent forms describing potential risks, their ability to opt out, and how the information will be stored.

You or others on your team may see this as a potential roadblock to your project. Filling out forms and waiting for feedback is certainly time-consuming. Would anyone really notice if you didn't get approval from your local board? Do you really need to bother? Although you would probably get away with avoiding your local review board, you really should take the time to investigate and follow the applicable procedures. Why should you take the time to do this?

- First, the 'right thing to do' is not as obvious as one might think. For example, one time the authors were planning to videotape participants and planned to tell them that videotaping was optional. But we had not provided an obvious way for participants to 'opt out' of the video. On review of our proposal, our institutional review board suggested we default to *not* videotaping participants *unless* they checked a box on the consent form. This increased the comfort of our participants and put their needs and wishes first. In another case, we had not thought to specify for the destruction of the CDs on which we had recorded participant videos, which of course is important to participants—would you want a video of your behavior to be left lying around in public trash?

- Second, your institution may be legally liable to ensure that all research, including unpublished, informal research, is conducted according to government or organizational regulations (see callout 'Ethical frameworks').

- Third, the review board may suggest changes that will actually improve your methodology and result in more successful research.

- Finally, even though you may not be thinking about publishing research based on your findings, you or one of your collaborators may later wish to do so. Most scholarly journals will require that you have gained human subjects research approval.

Institutional review boards have a storied history. As early as 1971 in the USA, the US Department of Health, Education, and Welfare began to require their creation. Infamous examples of abusive research, such as the Tuskegee Syphilis Study (Centers for Disease Control and Prevention 2008), may seem far away from the research you plan to do, but the inherent ethical issues underlie any research project with human subjects.

**Ethical frameworks**

**United Kingdom**

*Research Ethics Framework*, Economic and Social Research Council, *http://www.esrc.ac.uk/ESRCInfoCentre/Images/ ESRC_Re_Ethics_Frame_tcm6-11291.pdf*

*Research Excellence Framework (REF)*, Higher Education Funding Council for England, *http://www.hefce.ac.uk/Research/ref/*

**United States**

*Research Involving Human Subjects,* National Institutes of Health, *http://grants.nih.gov/grants/policy/hs/*
US Federal Regulation Standards 45 CFR 46, *http://www .nihtraining.com/ohsrsite/guidelines/45cfr46.html*

# Organizing, analyzing, and reporting effectively on user input

If you plan to gather user input for all or most projects, and we hope that you do, take some time to think about how you will organize, analyze, and report on the user input you gather. Spending some time on this area will benefit your organization, your project team, your users, and if you choose to publish, the rest of the library community.

Objective analysis and effective reporting on how you've been incorporating user input can set an example for the rest of your organization. If other departments have not been gathering user input, perhaps you will inspire them to try. You can also build trust within your organization about how user-centered your project teams are. Think about who else in your organization might be interested in your findings, even if they have not yet been involved in the project, and send them a summary and link to your report. This can expand organizational support for your project as well as provide useful information across the organization. This is also a good opportunity to report to your library administration. They will undoubtedly be impressed by your team's effort to connect with users.

Organizing the results also makes it easier for you and your project team to refer back to lessons learned from users on earlier projects. By providing user input reports on a staff intranet, future project teams will

**Figure 9.2** Excerpt from an intranet page

# JMU LIBRARIES DIGITAL SERVICES

**Research Resources Evaluation Activities, 06-07**

- 06-07 Timeline (proposed)
- Questions to be answered
- Proposed activities
- Wishlist – categorized

**06-07 Timeline (proposed)**

**November, 2006:**
- Review April 06 Research Databases Survey results. Also review R2 stats such as hit count, rating.
- Terminology / GFTG discussion with Lynn
- Draft usability testing plan

**December 1, 2006:** Meeting with liaisons and others interested in R2.
Powerpoint: Access to Library Research (survey results)
Handout: Usability Testing Plans

**December, 2006** (tentative): Survey selected students / faculty about the new R2 pages.
[hoping for at least 50 student and faculty respondents]

be able to learn from your work. Just make sure you've followed any commitments you made to keep user information anonymous, private, and secure. Figure 9.2 shows an example from the authors' intranet listing user input-gathering efforts for a web project entitled 'Research Resources.'

Whether your users are internal or external to the library organization, providing them with the results from your input-gathering effort demonstrates the time providing input was well spent. Consider sending a short summary with a link to the full report. You might wish to wait to report to users until at least the major decisions have been made, or even after launch, so they can see the impact of their input in a concrete way.

# Conclusion

By putting effort into research design, librarians have the opportunity to increase the effectiveness of their methods for gathering user input. Take the time to define your user groups to better inform your web projects.

Purposefully gather input about your users' needs and plan time for these activities in your project timeline. The numerous methods listed in this chapter may seem overwhelming, so think of this as a menu of options from which you might choose one or two for a given project. When you gather input, be sure to follow good research practices and promote honesty in the use of the findings. Making sure to observe your institution's human subject protocols will help you avoid many pitfalls, so don't skip this step. Finally, if your user input-gathering effort was substantial, consider publishing your findings so the rest of the library community can benefit. By spending time focusing on user input, you will be sure that your web projects are as effective as they can be.

# Recommended readings

## Web statistics

Sostre, Pedro, and Jennifer LeClaire (2007) *Web Analytics for Dummies*. Hoboken, NJ: Wiley.

Whang, Michael (2007) Measuring the success of the academic library website using banner advertisements and web conversion rates: A case study. *Journal of Web Librarianship* 1 (1): 93–108.

## User surveys

Fowler, Floyd J. (2002) *Survey Research Methods*. Applied Social Research Methods Series. 3rd ed. Thousand Oaks, CA: Sage Publications.

Fowler, Floyd J. (1995) *Improving Survey Questions: Design and Evaluation*. Applied Social Research Methods Series. Thousand Oaks, CA: Sage Publications.

## Focus groups and interviewing

Greenbaum, Thomas L. (2000) *Moderating Focus Groups: A Practical Guide for Group Facilitation*. Thousand Oaks, CA: Sage Publications.

Morgan, David L. (1997) *Focus Groups as Qualitative Research*. Qualitative Research Methods Series. 2nd ed. Thousand Oaks, CA: Sage Publications.

Seidman, Irving (2006) *Interviewing as Qualitative Research: A Guide for Researchers in Education and the Social Sciences.* 3rd ed. New York: Teachers College Press.

Stewart, David W., Prem N. Shamdasani, and Dennis W. Rook (2007) *Focus Groups: Theory and Practice.* Applied Social Research Methods Series. 2nd ed. Thousand Oaks, CA: Sage Publications.

## Usability testing

Krug, Steve (2006) *Don't Make Me Think! A Common Sense Approach to Web Usability.* 2nd ed. Berkeley, CA: New Riders.

Nielsen, Jakob, and Hoa Loranger (2006) *Prioritizing Web Usability.* Berkeley, CA: New Riders.

Spool, Jared M. (1999) *Web Site Usability: A Designer's Guide.* San Francisco: Morgan Kaufmann Publishers.

Tullis, Tom, and Bill Albert (2008) *Measuring the User Experience: Collecting, Analyzing, and Presenting Usability Metrics.* Burlington, MA: Elsevier, Inc.

# References

Bailey, Robert (2006) Applying usability metrics. Conference paper presented at Usability Metrics: How to Measure Performance and Progress, Washington, DC.

Bordac, Sarah, and Jean Rainwater (2008) User-centered design in practice: The Brown University experience. *Journal of Web Librarianship* 2 (2): 109–138.

Centers for Disease Control and Prevention (2008) *US Public Health Service Syphilis Study at Tuskegee, http://www.cdc.gov/tuskegee.*

Cooper, Alan (1999) *The Inmates Are Running the Asylum.* Indianapolis, IN: Sams.

Falks, Angi, and Nancy Hyland (2000) Gaining user insight: A case study illustrating the card sort technique. *College & Research Libraries* 61 (4): 349–357.

Foster, Nancy Fried, and Susan Gibbons, eds. (2007) *Studying Students: The Undergraduate Research Project at the University of Rochester.* Chicago: Association of College and Research Libraries, *http://www .ala.org/ala/mgrps/divs/acrl/publications/digital/Foster-Gibbons_ cmpd.pdf.*

Fowler, Floyd J. (2002) *Survey Research Methods*. Applied Social Research Methods Series. 3rd ed. Thousand Oaks, CA: Sage Publications.

Morgan, David L. (1997) *Focus Groups as Qualitative Research*. Qualitative Research Methods Series. 2nd ed. Thousand Oaks, CA: Sage Publications.

Nielsen, Jakob (2006) *Quantitative Studies: How Many Users to Test?*, *http://www.useit.com/alertbox/quantitative_testing.html*.

Nielsen, Jakob (2000) *Why You Only Need to Test with 5 Users*, *http://www.useit.com/alertbox/20000319.html*.

Nielsen, Jakob (1994) *Usability Inspection Methods*. New York: John Wiley & Sons, Inc.

Rushton, Erin E., Martha Daisy Kelehan, and Marcy A. Strong (2008) Searching for a new way to reach patrons: A search engine optimization pilot project at Binghamton University Libraries. *Journal of Web Librarianship* 2 (4): 525–547.

Seidman, Irving (2006) *Interviewing as Qualitative Research: A Guide for Researchers in Education and the Social Sciences*. 3rd ed. New York: Teachers College Press.

Sostre, Pedro, and Jennifer LeClaire (2007) *Web Analytics for Dummies*. Hoboken, NJ: Wiley.

Stewart, David W., Prem N. Shamdasani, and Dennis W. Rook (2007) *Focus Groups: Theory and Practice*. Applied Social Research Methods Series. 2nd ed. Thousand Oaks, CA: Sage Publications.

Trochim, William M. K. (2006) *Introduction to Validity*, *http://www.socialresearchmethods.net/kb/introval.php*.

US Department of Health and Human Services (2006) *Research-based Web Design and Usability Guidelines*, *http://www.usability.gov/pdfs/guidelines.html*.

Whang, Michael (2007) Measuring the success of the academic library website using banner advertisements and web conversion rates: A case study. *Journal of Web Librarianship* 1 (1): 93.

Wodtke, Christina (2003) *Information Architecture: Blueprints for the Web*. Boston: New Riders.

# 10

# Overall and design specifications

## Introduction

The last two chapters focused on communication and interaction with your stakeholders, and briefly covered researching the competition and the literature. The next three chapters will discuss how to translate the project needs you identified into specifications for design, programming, and content. These overall project specifications are typically lengthy and may even be composed of a series of documents. They are the equivalent to the blueprint for a building, except that both laypeople and technical staff will be reading them. Without them, you can't know what resources you need or how much time the project will take, nor can you communicate fully with your project sponsor to be sure that you are accomplishing what they want. Take your time to make the project specifications as comprehensive as possible.

The next three chapters present overall specifications and then three separate aspects—design, technical, and content—and include tips for working with team members in each area. In this chapter and the next two, choose which pieces of documentation are best-suited to your project. If you are new to project management and these chapters seem overwhelming, pick just one or two ideas to try for your next web project.

## Overall project specifications

Some elements of project specifications do not fit neatly into the divisions of design, technical, or content areas; instead, they relate to the entire project. Include the following pieces of information in your overall specifications:

- project overview (discussed in chapter 4)
- project team members' names and contact information (discussed in chapter 5)

- feature list (discussed in this chapter)
- exit and success criteria (discussed in this chapter)
- project schedule and timeline (to be discussed in chapter 13).

Also, be sure to include the date, author, and project website URL on all project documents, perhaps in a document template, header, or footer. For more details on best practices for a project website, refer to chapter 7, 'Team communication.'

## Feature list

One of your research goals is to identify the features which will satisfy your project sponsor's needs. When you first started brainstorming on the project, you likely started with a long list of possible features. As you continued to research, some of the features dropped off the list as unrealistic or not desired by users. In the process, you may have also added new features. The resulting feature list may be all over the place: specific tasks that users should be able to accomplish, design suggestions about look and feel, information architecture issues about navigation and content organization, and technical issues of interoperability.

To gain a better understanding of the options, attempt to cluster the items into design, technical, and content suggestions. Bring this list to your project team with a goal of prioritizing. Which of these new features are likely to be of value based on the research you've done so far? Do any of them contradict each other? Will any be particularly time-consuming to implement?

For each feature, identify whether it is:

- *required*: requested by the project sponsor—these are the drop-dead features
- *secondary*: does not contradict any of the required features and is important to include
- *optional*: may be useful to a small number of people
- *not desired*: contradicts required features or has little apparent value.

With your expanded list of features well-organized and your research in hand, now meet with your project sponsor. You should explain each feature to the sponsor along with some notes on the origin of the suggestion. Encourage the project sponsor to correct the team's work by reprioritizing the features as required, secondary, optional, or not desired.

The resulting list will be your team's marching orders and included in your overall specifications. You will describe them in more detail in the design, technical, and content specifications.

## Exit and success criteria

With a clear idea of the necessary features, you can now document criteria that will help you know if your team is successful in meeting the project goals. Within your list of success criteria, consider marking some items as exit criteria—indicators of when your project work is done. Scott Berkun describes exit criteria in *Making Things Happen*: 'without exit criteria the team must depend on their subjective opinions for what "good enough" means for a project, which is an enormous waste of time. Everyone will have different opinions about what good enough is' (2008, 305). Take the guesswork out of the end of the project by listing specific deliverables, preferably with some measure of quality. Examples include not only lists of required features, but also metrics such as the number of non-critical bugs allowed, results of usability tests, increased system response time, and accuracy levels. Berkun wisely suggests establishing exit criteria not just for the end of the project, but also for milestones throughout the project timeline (2008, 304–5).

Whereas exit criteria are focused on the duration of the project, the rest of the success criteria frequently cannot be measured until well after the project has ended. For example, during your research of a website redesign, you may have discovered that your e-mail reference users were asking basic questions about how to request book loans from other libraries. Therefore, one success criterion might be reducing the percentage of questions submitted to e-mail reference asking basic questions about interlibrary loan. Success for this criterion can only be measured after an entire semester passes. Similar types of success criteria include increasing traffic to particular content on the site, more user time spent on the site, and more return visitors (all measured by website statistics software); fewer failed searches (as evaluated by search logs); or improved user satisfaction in the site (as measured in annual user surveys). All of these examples are specific and measurable, but you can't measure them until well after the project is over.

In addition to exit and success criteria, you can list features that the team and project sponsor have rejected as not desirable or as only optional (Berkun 2008, 304). This last part of the list is particularly important if colleagues have varied opinions about what exactly the project is trying to achieve. You may have documented exceptions in your project overview and in every discussion of the project to date, but it doesn't hurt to repeat the exceptions once again.

## Accessibility

Your overall specifications are an excellent place to capture your decisions related to accessibility standards, which will inform design, technical, and content decisions. If your library's website already has policies and procedures in place, you can reference those and simply note any special circumstances relating to the project at hand.

The World Wide Web Consortium's Web Accessibility Initiative (WAI) makes recommendations for everything from creating accessible content to providing accessibility features in web authoring tools. The WAI published the second version of the Web Content Access Guidelines (WCAG 2.0) in December 2008 (*http://www.w3.org/TR/WCAG20/*). 'WCAG 2.0 at a Glance' (*http://www.w3.org/WAI/WCAG20/glance/*), produced by the WAI, provides a quick summary of how to make pages perceivable, operable, understandable, and robust (see figure 10.1).

The WAI also provides 'How to Meet WCAG 2.0' (*http://www.w3 .org/WAI/WCAG20/quickref/*), a customizable guide where you can select your compliance targets and produce a document to include directly in your technical specifications. You can also list specific decisions related to accessibility in a chart (see figure 10.2).

Countries around the world have adopted the recommendations of the World Wide Web Consortium (W3C) either as guidelines or as mandated by law. The WAI provides a convenient international listing with links to standards including the European Union, the UK, and the USA (*http://www.w3.org/WAI/Policy/*). Check with your university's web office as well as with relevant government agencies to identify the level of required conformance with the WCAG.

Library websites provide information to your known community of students, faculty, and staff as well as the larger community beyond your campus. Even if you don't know of a user with disabilities, it's just good sense to design for all your potential users. As project manager, you can show your commitment to users by incorporating accessibility testing into all your projects. Use human evaluation to review each page and interaction, and use software to identify coding errors. See the callout 'Accessibility testing' for software options.

**Figure 10.1** WCAG 2.0 at a Glance

WEB ACCESSIBILITY QUICKTIPS

# WCAG 2.0 at a Glance

**Perceivable**
- Provide **text alternatives** for non-text content.
- Provide **captions and alternatives** for audio and video content.
- Make content **adaptable;** and make it **available** to assistive technologies.
- Use **sufficient contrast** to make things easy to see and hear.

**Operable**
- Make all functionality **keyboard accessible.**
- Give users **enough time** to read and use content.
- Do not use content that causes **seizures.**
- Help users **navigate and find** content.

**Understandable**
- Make text **readable and understandable.**
- Make content appear and operate in **predictable** ways.
- Help users **avoid and correct mistakes.**

**Robust**
- Maximize **compatibility** with current and future technologies.

This page provides a summary of Web Content Accessibility Guidelines (WCAG 2.0) that are online at www.w3.org/TR/WCAG20/; however **it is paraphrased and it is not a definitive version**

Please see the following key resources for learning and using WCAG 2.0:
- WCAG Overview www.w3.org/WAI/intro/wcag
- **How to Meet WCAG 2.0: A customizable quick reference to WCAG 2.0 requirements (Success Criteria) and techniques** www.w3.org/WAI/WCAG20/quickref/

Online at a **www.w3.org/WAI/WCAG20/glance/**                  Content Version: 17 October 2008
Editors: Shawn Lawton Henry and Wayne Dick.      Copyright © 2008 W3C® (MIT, ERCIM, Keio), All Rights Reserved.

## *Supported browsers and operating systems*

The W3C also urges designers to create websites to be compatible across web browsers and operating systems. Consult with your designers and

**Figure 10.2** Excerpt from an overall style guide including accessibility decisions

| Advice | Why | How |
|---|---|---|
| All images should have descriptive ALT tags. | This is text that shows up when the user hovers over a graphic. Screen-reading software, for users with vision disabilities, reads the ALT tag. | Adobe Contribute should ask you for text when you publish a new image. If not, right-click on an image and select Image Properties. Insert text in Description field. |
| When using Flash, provide a non-Flash version. | For users with disabilities. | Consider linking to a text version or reserving Flash for non-critical information. |

developers to create a checklist for which browsers and operating systems you'll test. You can use website logs to determine which browsers and operating systems your library website visitors are using. You'll also want to check for new and upcoming releases of browser software, which can have a serious impact on the appearance and functionality of your website. Be sure to budget time for checking your project; addressing such issues can be very time-consuming for designers and developers.

## Accessibility testing

The W3C has an excellent website providing guidance for accessibility testing as well as a descriptive list of tools to help with the process: *http://www.w3.org/WAI/eval/Overview.html*. One particular company, HiSoftware (*http://www.hisoftware.com/*), offers the following suite of accessibility products:

- **Cynthia Says:** free web accessibility validation tool, which can check a single web page for compliance with Section 508 or WCAG standards. Cynthia Says is also available through several toolbars and add-ons such as the web developer toolbars for Firefox and Internet Explorer. This software cannot check multiple web pages at a time.

- **AccVerify:** the enterprise software version of Cynthia Says which can validate entire websites and generate site-wide reports on accessibility compliance.

- **AccRepair:** an enhancement for AccVerify which walks you through fixing non-compliant code across web pages.

- **Hi-Caption:** an enterprise validation tool that lets you add captioning and generate transcripts for multimedia files such as Flash, WMV, QuickTime, and RealMedia.

Most web authoring and multimedia software also have built-in accessibility validation tools. For instance, Dreamweaver CS3 incorporates Cynthia Says into its reporting tools. Flash offers development support for creating accessible ActionScript and captioning video.

Remember that testing for accessibility requires a combination of automated tools and human evaluation.

With the project overview, feature list, exit and success criteria, accessibility standards, and supported browsers and operating systems providing an overall view of the project, you can now turn your attention to the specifics of design, technical, and content areas. This chapter will continue with a discussion of design specifications and will be followed by separate chapters on technical and content specifications. Separating these areas into separate chapters is somewhat artificial; each area is interwoven with the other two. Yet each section of the specifications has a critical role. Design specifications prevent programmers and authors from having to design while coding or writing text. Both technical and content decisions inform your team about design solutions. Different team members will typically spend more time in one area than others, only referring to the other two sections as needed to clarify questions. In fact, some projects will require more emphasis in one of these areas and may have little need for the others.

# Design specifications

Identifying and articulating what the end product will eventually look like and how your users will experience it is an important early step whether you are building your own application, implementing a ready-made solution, or redesigning even a single web page. The design choices that are eventually documented in the design specifications actually start as soon as you begin to research your goals and features. Translating your research into the design specifications can happen both within and outside of meetings, collaboratively, and individually. Your designers should start early with the simplest iterations to share ideas with the team, users, project sponsor, and colleagues. As research progresses and the team begins to narrow down the features, the designer begins to clarify the design specifications. As the technical and content work begins, designers should select color palettes, overall style, specific navigation and labels, and final page layouts. The goal for the design specifications is to provide enough detail to allow programmers and content editors to begin their parts while the designer continues to work. Be aware that programmers may not want to begin development until they see a design, while designers may not want to produce a design until they have content. In fact, all three areas—design, programming, and content—need to happen in parallel to meet most schedules. As web project manager, find out what your team members expect, and be prepared to negotiate solutions.

Get started on the visual design and markup early in your process. The most important reason is to ensure the visual mockups, flowcharts, and other representations actually meet the web project teams' expectations and meet the user needs you identified during your research. For those outside your project team, rough drafts of how the end product will look with the requested features are easier to understand than textual lists. This understanding is critical for getting input from your project sponsor, users, and colleagues. Your project will dictate which types of documentation discussed in the following sections make the most sense.

## Other websites

If a portion of a website other than your own is similar to your end goal, consider referring to it not only to get stakeholder input but also to document your decisions in the specifications document. Doing so is especially effective when trying to describe complex user interactions that can't easily be described in simple graphics. Also, the more refined your design ideas are when you show them to your stakeholders, the more mistakenly certain your stakeholders will be that it is too late for them to suggest changes. In fact, depending on how much your mockups differ from what they are envisioning, you can create genuine angst by demonstrating a too-polished mockup. You can sidestep this confusion by showing someone else's completed work as a model that you might emulate. Be sure to be clear that the other website is only being used as a model.

## Design patterns

Design patterns provide template-like solutions to common problems. Within the web world, this can mean a library of code snippets for reusable elements like drop-down menus, breadcrumb navigation, or a calendar picker. The idea of using design patterns to assist in software design was popularized by *Design Patterns* (Gamma et al. 1995). The book specified 23 core patterns that programmers could use as solutions to commonly occurring problems. Jennifer Tidwell (1999) adapted this concept for use by interaction designers. As web project manager, you may be able to save your designer's time by suggesting the use of design patterns, or at least using a design pattern as a basis for discussion. See the callout 'Design pattern collections available on the web'.

---

### Design pattern collections available on the web

 Patterns in Interaction Design, *http://www.welie.com/patterns/index.php*

User Interface Design Pattern Library, *http://ui-patterns.com/*

Yahoo! Developer Network Design Pattern Library, *http://developer.yahoo.com/ypatterns/index.php*

---

## Use-case scenarios

Use-case scenarios tell the story of a user encountering your website or application. The story might be told using text, a storyboard (see figure 10.3), or a short movie. You can explain why your user came to your site to begin with, how they interacted with the site to get what they needed, and what they did afterwards. You could have scenarios for each of your primary users or scenarios for the most important features.

To make a storyboard, you can use pencil and paper, Microsoft Word, PowerPoint, or whatever tool you have at hand. The important thing is that you are not spending time on graphic design, color, fonts, or even a high degree of neatness. Storyboards should focus on the elements required on the page and how the pages fit into the overall navigation. If your visual use-case scenario is rough enough, input will be more focused on the overall structure and plan for the site.

165

**Figure 10.3** Example of a use-case scenario using a storyboard

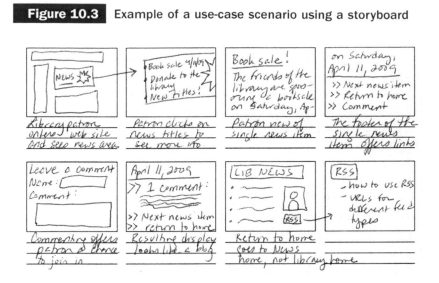

## Wireframe mockups

Wireframe mockups look like web pages without graphics, font styles, or color (see figure 10.4). They are an especially effective way to communicate what might happen on any given page and what that page generally looks like without unneeded distractions. Your designer should complete these before any programming is done, and your team should test them with users. Not only do they document page layout, which will

**Figure 10.4** Example of a wireframe mockup

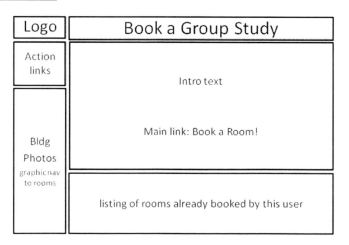

assist the content editors, but they also guide the creation of stylesheets which the programmer and content editors will use.

The act of creating and referencing these different visual designs—other websites, design patterns, use-case scenarios, and wireframes—helps you to think your project through. You get an extra chance to review goals and consider how your users accomplish their work within your project. You review each feature and consider how to deliver them to your user. In the process, you may discover that you are trying to fit too many features into one project. Or, you may discover that some of your optional features have natural homes side-by-side with the required features.

## Design style guide

In addition to illustrating design decisions visually, your design specifications should also document design decisions based on information architecture and graphic and design standards. Your decisions in each of these areas may come from best practices espoused by others, through your own user testing, from standard guidelines, or from conventions your designers established locally. Regardless of how the decisions are made, document them in your design specifications so you and your team don't forget to follow them.

## Information architecture

In your role as web project manager, you should ensure that your team pays attention to the information architecture decisions in your project. Information architecture is closely related to content, but we've discussed it in this chapter because it is also a design concept. In many ways, information architecture is also closely related to librarianship. If you are a librarian, many of the concepts described in this section may seem like common sense.

Principles of information architecture as applied to the web are spelled out in detail in Christina Wodtke's *Information Architecture* (2003). We've applied some of her principles to academic libraries:

- *Design for wayfinding*: Ensure your users know where they are on the site and where the content they need is located. Effective wayfinding can be difficult for library websites because we frequently lead our users to research databases and other external sites, and then want the user to return to our site to find full text or help with citing their sources.

- *Be consistent and document website standards*: Keep track of naming conventions with a simple thesaurus for your site. Refer to your library catalog and journal portal consistently across the website and in your projects. Lead the discussion with your stakeholders about whether to refer to journals, magazines, and newspapers as 'periodicals,' 'journals,' or 'articles.'

- *Provide preventative error support*: Design forms to minimize mistakes. For example, at the authors' institution, students are assigned an eight-character 'e-ID' used to log in to systems, but students often think of their e-ID as their full e-mail address. Library web forms asking for the e-ID add '@jmu.edu' in text after the input box to prevent a common mistake.

- *Rely on recognition rather than recall*: This may mean putting more links on a page rather than hiding links under drop-down menus.

- *Provide for varying skill levels*: Wodtke argues that new website visitors are only beginners for a very short amount of time. Most users are intermediate; they've learned how to accomplish their common tasks and now want to perform them as quickly as possible. Libraries must often choose between explanations (what is a peer reviewed journal?) and direct connections (a searchable database of the library's peer reviewed journals). Most users will need the latter more often than the former.

- *Provide meaningful and contextual help and documentation*: Wodtke advises, 'Don't just say Help—be helpful' (2003, 53). Plan for content that will be most helpful behind the 'help' link. Provide help whenever the user is unsuccessful. On 'no results' screens for the library catalog, for example, offer the information desk phone number as well as search tips.

Information architecture principles can appear to be common sense, but many common assumptions about information on the web are actually subject to much debate by information architects: 'users don't read;' 'users don't scroll.' As web project manager, be sure to question assumptions and gather the most recent research you can about how information architecture issues affect user behavior. A quick place to check is *Research-based Web Design and Usability Guidelines* (US Dept of Health and Human Services 2006), which lists common, research-based web 'rules' including some related to information architecture. As discussed in chapter 9, test any unclear assumptions with actual users. As you make decisions that affect multiple areas of your project, be sure to document them in your design specifications (figure 10.5).

**Figure 10.5** Excerpt of a design style guide

| Design advice | Why | How |
|---|---|---|
| When prompting users to enter their e-ID, add '@jmu.edu' in text after the input box. | Prevents the user from mistakenly entering @jmu.edu themselves. | Add text immediately after the input box element. |
| *Page titles should be descriptive of the page content.* Where appropriate, match the title at the very top of the browser with that which appears on the page itself. | Descriptive titles help users pick relevant hits out of search results. | In Adobe Contribute, add or change the title of a new or existing page by clicking on Edit and then Page Properties (upper right corner). |

## Graphic and brand standards

Your design specifications may list graphic standards specific to your current project as well as standards which are already in place for the library website as a whole. Even if your university does not enforce a consistent template or stylesheet, your university may have rules about the official logos, colors, placement, and size. In addition to your university's logo, you may want to include other university graphics and photos. For example, the university may already have a photograph of your building or students studying in your library. You should confirm that you have permission from both the subjects and the photographer before using any photos in your web projects. If you choose to take photographs of individuals yourself, you should still check university guidelines and your local laws to understand requirements for obtaining consent of identifiable individuals in the photographs. Alternately, explore image libraries that already come with this clearance. Document these policies in your design specifications so that everyone on the project team is clear about the rules and expectations.

Your design specifications may also include both information about branding guidelines for this particular project and references to relevant style guides that pertain to the website overall. Common elements included in a design style guide include color swatches with corresponding screenshots, RGB codes, and CMYK codes; font names; and notes on directory structure (Shelford and Remillard 2003, 207). Your designer should also create and specify the location of the following shared design files used for the project including:

- *Stylesheets*: These are used to define the font characteristics of components of each page such as title, headers, and body text. When designing according to accessibility guidelines, stylesheets also define the layout of blocks of text instead of using cells within a table to control layout.

- *Included files*: Designers can insert an 'include' code into a web page that inserts the contents of a second file. These *included* files can be used to provide elements to be repeated on many pages. Your designer might create included files for the header, footer, and navigation so that she can make updates to these common elements in one place.

- *Web templates*: Your designer might create one or more templates to be used for each page of a website. These templates might include stylesheets and included files, or could be completely controlled by a content management system.

- *Graphics to be used throughout the project*: Put them all in one logical directory and specify each one within the design, technical, and content specifications.

Some of these shared elements may be the same as for the rest of the library website. Your designer will continue to work on a complete style guide for this project as the work progresses. Recording the known details in one document will ensure that all developers on the team can find them easily and will reduce the need to make corrections. Note that you'll read more about the content issues related to style guides in chapter 12, 'Web content specifications.'

---

## Separating design from programming with stylesheets

Although stylesheets are important for any web project, they can be especially useful when creating a web interface with programming behind it. Properly designed stylesheets will allow you to change the visual appearance of your project website without altering programming code. Another payoff comes when you consider accessibility. By using stylesheets to control appearance instead of using tables and HTML, you create a site that users with vision disabilities can still use with software designed to read the text out loud.

Your library's stylesheet expert may be your graphic designer, your webmaster, your programmer, or even you! W3Schools provides an excellent suite of tutorials at *http://www.w3schools .com/css* and also offers a validation tool for standards compliance at *http://jigsaw.w3.org/css-validator*. Check the 'Recommended readings' section at the end of this chapter for more information on stylesheets.

# Working with designers

All aspects of design—graphic design, interaction design, experience design, and information architecture—are fraught with the challenge of disagreement. Non-designers frequently have strong opinions about design choices based on their personal experience, and librarians and other library staff are no exception to this trend. In fact, *you* may also assume that you know good design decisions versus poor design decisions without having an ounce of formal design training or skill. Also, many librarians have natural instincts toward information architecture honed by a work environment driven by the classification and retrieval of information. Many of your colleagues within the library also spend more time looking at websites in the course of their work than those in other professions. You should base your design specifications on a combination of all your research—not just input from colleagues. All this adds up to making design choices contentious within your library.

As the project manager, you have ideally chosen the designer working on your team based on skill. Your job is not to design. Rather, your job is to be sure that the design is influenced by constructive input and feedback. Designers can be quite receptive to design review sessions. It is then up to the designer to make the design decisions, just as it is up to the programmer to make coding decisions. As project manager, part of your job is to publicly defend the design decisions that your team made after the research and approval process. Don't rule out suggestions that might make good design decisions even better, but don't try to please everyone in your organization either. You should question, encourage, and assist—you can even sketch sometimes—but trust in the design skills of your designer. Design is a skill best left to the designers rather than the whole organization.

# Conclusion

You are documenting the decisions made for your project in the specifications documents for two purposes: to inform the work of the team and to get confirmation from the project sponsor that your plans are heading in the right direction. Ensure that the project sponsor understands each decision documented in the design specifications, even if it means creating different styles of documents to illustrate the decisions in different ways. If possible, involve your project sponsor in design discussions along with the rest of the team so she isn't surprised by decisions that appear in the project specifications. Although the project sponsor will still have chances to review and approve your work as the project proceeds, an accurate and understandable design specifications document is critical for the creation of the technical and content specifications, as well as the planning and scheduling that will follow. Get it right now, and you are well on your way to your project sponsor signing off on the project at the end.

# Recommended readings

Alexander, Ian (2002) *Writing Better Requirements*. Boston: Addison-Wesley.

Bowers, Michael (2007) *Pro CSS and HTML Design Patterns*. Berkeley, CA: Apress.

Holzner, Steven (2006) *Design Patterns for Dummies*. Hoboken, NJ: J. Wiley & Sons.

Meyer, Eric A. (2007) *CSS: The Definitive Guide*. Sebastopol, CA: O'Reilly.

Meyer, Eric A. (2004) *More Eric Meyer on CSS*. Indianapolis: New Riders.

Meyer, Eric A. (2003) *Eric Meyer on CSS: Mastering the Language of Web Design*. Indianapolis: New Riders.

Tidwell, Jenifer (2005) *Designing Interfaces: Patterns for Effective Interaction Design*. Sebastopol, CA: O'Reilly Media.

# References

Berkun, Scott (2008) *Making Things Happen: Mastering Project Management*. 2nd ed. Sebastopol, CA: O'Reilly.

Gamma, Erich, Richard Helm, Ralph Johnson, and John Vlissides (1995) *Design Patterns: Elements of Reusable Object-oriented Software*. Reading, MA: Addison-Wesley.

Shelford, Thomas J., and Gregory A. Remillard (2003) *Real Web Project Management: Case Studies and Best Practices from the Trenches*. Boston: Addison-Wesley.

Tidwell, Jenifer (1999) Common ground: A pattern language for human-computer interface design, *http://www.mit.edu/~jtidwell/interaction_patterns.html*.

US Department of Health and Human Services (2006) *Research-based Web Design and Usability Guidelines*, *http://www.usability.gov/pdfs/guidelines.html*.

Wodtke, Christina (2003) *Information Architecture: Blueprints for the Web*. Boston: New Riders.

# 11

# Technical specifications

## Introduction

This chapter focuses on writing three types of technical specifications: technical requirements, programming specifications, and database specifications. Whether you plan to buy or build a solution, this chapter covers what you need to know about the various tasks handled by the technical staff on your team. For applications you create, write detailed programming specifications and document decisions related to databases, coding, and testing. If your library is investigating commercial systems for purchase, you will need to document the technical decisions that the purchased system allows you to make.

If your project is purely a design and content project, you may not think you need technical specifications. But consider how even a simple form that sends an e-mail involves some technical decisions behind the scenes. Should hidden variables, time of day, or user information be included in the e-mail in addition to the user's input? Does the form need to be secure? Most web projects within academic libraries will follow some technical standards regarding security, and even projects consisting primarily of design and content issues should still have at least minimal technical requirements.

If you are doing double-duty as a programmer and a project manager, you should still create the documentation described in this chapter to keep yourself straight and to record decisions. Also, you'll need to plan your day carefully. Consider designating large chunks of time to each activity and make it clear to others when your door will be open and closed.

## Evaluating options

When your project is a new application rather than a redesign, you have many options to consider. Libraries without sufficient money will need to choose a free solution. Libraries without technical staff may need to choose a free Web 2.0 tool. Libraries that have both financial and technical resources have two additional options: purchasing a turnkey system or building an application from scratch. Each of these options has pros and cons, as shown in figure 11.1.

Generally, if you can use an existing solution rather than building your own, you should. Each custom application that your team builds will need support over time. With each new browser version, new server update, and new programming standard, your technical staff will need to review and possibly update your homegrown applications.

**Figure 11.1**  Comparison of turnkey, open source, freely hosted, and homegrown applications

| Option | Pro | Con |
|---|---|---|
| Turnkey system | • vendor provides updates and improvements<br>• ready-made<br>• no technical skills needed<br>• customer communities | • expensive<br>• cannot always integrate into rest of website<br>• what you see is what you get—no more, no less |
| Open source application | • ready-made<br>• usually can customize<br>• usually can integrate with rest of website<br>• no cash outlay<br>• customer communities<br>• creator and other users provide updates and improvements | • need technical skills<br>• expensive in staff time<br>• support not always available |
| Free hosted applications | • ready-made<br>• sometimes can customize<br>• no cash outlay<br>• few technical skills needed<br>• customer communities | • limited customization<br>• cannot always integrate with rest of website |
| Homegrown applications | • features and customization only limited by available skills<br>• no cash outlay | • time-consuming to create<br>• need to write and test updates regularly<br>• time-consuming to specify<br>• expensive in staff time |

Begin by evaluating the various options: commercial, open source, and free hosted applications. Put your required feature list in an evaluation grid with the options you are considering along the top. Evaluating these different options might include reviewing the maker's website, speaking to other libraries, inviting a vendor to provide a demonstration, downloading evaluation copies, or reading reviews.

If no solution gives you all the required features, reconsider your feature list. Is there one feature that is not provided by any solution? Or, is there one tool that is perfect except for one feature? Maybe your expectations are too high. Evaluate the lacking features with your project sponsor. Are those features really required or could they be moved to a different project? If no combination of third-party solutions satisfies all your confirmed features, then consider building an application.

While much of this chapter does describe specifications that could be used to build a system, many of the details are also relevant if you are implementing a third-party, turnkey solution. You should create technical specifications that describe how the third-party system will technically integrate with the rest of your website, if at all. You should document how the system can be and should be customized. You'll want to carefully document relevant terms of use and privacy statements to ensure they agree with your own expectations. You should implement a testing script and a bug-tracking system. You will still need to find a way to keep track of communications and documentation from the vendor or creator. The principles in this chapter also apply to Web 2.0 tools such as blogs, wikis, and social networking sites, as well as open source and commercial software.

# Technical requirements

The technical requirements document for a given web project specifies decisions such as the web server, hardware, software, security requirements, and network requirements. The technical requirements can also include a technical style guide, similar to those for design and content (see figure 11.2). Decisions about requirements may be based on both accessibility standards and the needs of your project's target users. For instance, if your project is specifically for faculty, you should list requirements for file sizes, supported browsers, and supported operating systems based on what you know about your faculty. A project designed for students may differ in requirements, specifying the desire to access

**Figure 11.2** Excerpt from a technical style guide

| Technical advice | Why | How |
| --- | --- | --- |
| Web pages should be saved with the .aspx extension.<br><br>Good: mypage.aspx<br>Bad: mypage.html, mypage.asp<br><br>There are some exceptions to this rule on the site. If you think you might have an exception, ask. | To allow use of current and future .NET applications like displaying and/or linking to news, features, FAQs. | Adobe Contribute will suggest a .aspx extension. If you change the file name, be sure to keep .aspx at the end. |
| Files names should not include spaces.<br><br>Good: mypage.aspx, my_page.aspx<br><br>Bad: my page.aspx | Browsers display those spaces with %20 in the address bar. This makes it hard for others to figure out the URL. | Remove spaces or replace with underscores (_). |

content through mobile devices. In an academic library, the technical requirements may not vary much from one project to another, so you might be able to create a standard list of technical requirements to refer to for each project.

Your programmers should also give security requirements careful thought. Most organizations have security rules to follow when using personal information such as social security numbers in the USA or national insurance numbers in the UK. Your university likely also has special rules to follow when using student information such as passwords, course enrollment, academic level, and home address. You will need to respect that level of security not only when you implement your final project, but also when you are testing. Also, if you are allowing users to interact with your content through forms and other submission mechanisms, you may be exposing your servers to security risks in new ways. Get guidance from your campus web office to ensure you aren't exposing the entire campus to security risks. Once you determine your security needs, record decisions within the technical requirements document so that the entire development team can follow the same standards.

## Application flow diagrams

To provide technical staff with a big-picture view of the overall flow, you can use an application flow diagram, which uses boxes to represent web pages or actions and arrows to represent a flow through a series of pages or an application. A flow diagram is especially useful for understanding each step in the user experience. The diagrams can also illustrate needed files, behind-the-scenes technologies, and interactions between systems. A diagram like the one shown in figure 11.3 points out questions right away: what happens if the user is not successful in logging in? Should they go to a campus help page or just go back to 'welcome' to try again? What happens if their search is not successful?

Note that both descriptive names and filenames for the pages of the application are given, and the programmer can see the different interactions at a glance. You will provide further details about each page and interaction in the programming specifications and database specifications, which are discussed in the next sections.

---

**Unified Modeling Language (UML)**

 If you have ever wondered if there are standards for boxes-and-arrows diagrams, you might want to check out UML, a graphical notation for expressing designs. UML is a standard language of visual representation that goes well beyond simple flowcharts and diagrams. *UML Distilled*, by Martin Fowler and Kendall Scott (2000), is an excellent introduction not just to the notation of UML, but also to the development processes accompanying its use.

---

# Programming specifications

No matter what language your programmers work in, they will have to translate your design documents and feature requirements into terse, logical code. Their job will be much easier if you have written programming specifications that describe precisely what they should create. They will have fewer questions and make fewer guesses if they have sufficient detail, and you will have more control over the web project. Writing detailed technical documents has a benefit for you, too: you get the chance to rethink just what your project will look like and what it will be doing. For example, as you're working through specifications for a web form, you will

**Figure 11.3** Example of an application flow diagram for a typical login form

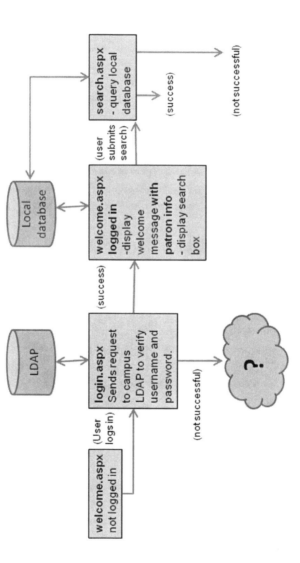

have to decide the specific text for each button. Following good usability practice, you may originally have wanted to design the submit button to say something like 'Calculate My Library Fines.' However, this wording would make the button much too large. So you decide to replace the button with an icon that functions as a submit button. Now you'll need to communicate with the designer to make sure that icon graphic gets created, and you'll need to reference the graphic file in the programming specifications. If you hadn't thought this detail through when writing the specifications, you would be scrambling later to develop a graphic.

In contrast to your technical requirements document, which is likely to be fairly short, your programming specifications document will probably be quite lengthy. Writing these specifications can be tedious, but it doesn't have to be difficult. For example, figure 11.4 shows a very simple authentication form.

**Figure 11.4**   A simple web form: login_entry.aspx

The programming specifications for that web form might look like figure 11.5.

**Figure 11.5**   Programming specifications for 'login_entry.aspx'

| Element | Properties | Functionality |
|---|---|---|
| JMU e-mail ID | Input box, 8 characters long<br><br>class = 'input_standard' | After the user types in this box and either tabs to or clicks in the next, a Javascript should check to be sure the entry is 8 characters, the valid length for this type of ID. |
| Password | Input box, 16 characters long<br>class = 'input_standard' | As user types password, display visual password protection (\*\*\*\*). |
| Login | Submit button with text value 'Login' class = 'submit_standard' | Submits the form to login.aspx. If login is successful, user is taken to workshops.aspx.<br>If login is unsuccessful, display the message 'Trouble logging in? E-mail us' (link to mailto:lib@college.edu). |

In this example, 'Element' describes what part of the page you're talking about. 'Properties' defines the attributes of each page element. 'Functionality' defines what should happen when the user interacts with the element. In this example, you want the form to check and see if the user has entered a valid ID in the field labeled JMU e-mail ID, which you know should be eight characters. Specifically, you want the form to do this as soon as the user moves to the next field.

Something to note about this example is that it depends on a stylesheet and so it's easy to refer to the appropriate class for each element. If you weren't using stylesheets, you'd define the visual appearance of each element as well, such as font size, font weight, font face, or color. This is yet another reason stylesheets are useful. If you decide to change the style of your web form, it would be very easy to do, because it would not require your programmer to rewrite her code!

A tiny detail in the specifications that can prove to be important later is the filename given to an application. Depending on the programming environment, the filenames may appear in the browser location bar. If so, you'll want to define them early to be sure that they are as user-friendly as possible. The programmers may refer to specific filenames within their code, and, left to their own convenience, you may end up with wordy names like 'HelpRequestFormFirstPage_2.html' rather than something simple to type like 'help.html.'

# Database specifications

For projects that involve databases, you should specify database design considerations along with the other technical specifications. Imagine you are planning a website where librarians submit a web form to report on their activities at professional conferences. The design specifications indicate that the results should display on a web page in the order of the date they were entered. The design specifications also state that users can search and display entries by the date of the conference or by the last-modified date. The team member creating the database needs these details in one document. Specifically, the database must capture all dates associated with the entry: the dates of the conference, the entry creation date, and the last modified date. This document should also include specifics about how date entries should be retrieved and sorted. While the decisions may have been made in the design phase, the programmer should also find these details in the technical specifications.

Understanding some basics about database design will help you work more effectively with programmers. In relational database design, there are three types of relationships: one-to-one, one-to-many, and many-to-many. Imagine a database where librarians need to be related to academic subjects:

- *One-to-one*: Each librarian has only one subject area. Jean is the liaison to history, and that's it.

- *One-to-many*: Each librarian serves as a liaison to one or more subject areas, but no subject area has more than one librarian. In other words, *one* librarian can serve *many* subjects. Jean is the only liaison to history and the only liaison to philosophy. In an unlikely variant, perhaps each subject has two librarians, but no librarian has more than one subject. This would also be a one-to-many relationship. *One* subject is served by *many* liaisons.

- *Many-to-many*: Librarians can have more than one subject area, and, a subject area may have more than one librarian. Jean and Denise are the liaisons to history, and Denise is also liaison to philosophy.

Each of these relationships leads to completely different database structures. In the first example, the database structure could be as simple as one table, with one column (or field) for the librarian's name, and one column for the librarian's subject. You can add additional one-to-one relationships just by adding new columns: for example, Jean's birthday or her phone number (figure 11.6).

If your library starts running short of staff and needs to assign Jean to multiple subject areas, however, the efficient database designer will create an entirely new table that lists subject areas (figure 11.7).

Furthermore, if the university departments grow too large for one librarian to handle, so multiple librarians might serve multiple departments (Jean and Denise will *both* be liaison to history), then a linking table will definitely be required (figure 11.8). Figure 11.9 shows these various relationships as they would appear in an entity-relationship diagram, which is the standard way to illustrate a database structure. Each time the relationship between liaison and subject changed in this example, your programmers would need to write new database query

**Figure 11.6** A one-to-one relationship

| Librarian | Subject | Birthday |
|-----------|------------|------------|
| Jean | Philosophy | 09/12/1975 |
| Denise | History | 08/31/1948 |

**Figure 11.7** A one-to-many relationship

| Subjects | | | |
|---|---|---|
| **Subj_ID** | **Subject** | **Lib_ID** |
| 1 | History | 1 |
| 2 | Philosophy | 1 |
| 3 | Political Science | 2 |
| 4 | Religion | 3 |

| Librarians | |
|---|---|
| **Lib_ID** | **Name** |
| 1 | Jean |
| 2 | Denise |
| 3 | Richard |

**Figure 11.8** A many-to-many relationship

| Librarians | |
|---|---|
| **Lib_ID** | **Name** |
| 1 | Jean |
| 2 | Denise |
| 3 | Richard |

| Librarian-Subject Linking Table | |
|---|---|
| **Lib_ID** | **Subj_ID** |
| 1 | 1 |
| 2 | 1 |
| 2 | 2 |
| 3 | 3 |
| 3 | 4 |

| Subject | |
|---|---|
| **Subj_ID** | **Subject** |
| 1 | History |
| 2 | Philosophy |
| 3 | Political Science |
| 4 | Religion |

**Figure 11.9** Examples of simple entity-relationship diagrams

One-to-one relationship

One-to-many relationship

One-to-many relationship

Many-to-many relationship

strings and both designers and programmers would need to alter the administrative interfaces used to assign librarians to subjects. In this example, anticipating and specifying the most complicated database structure from the start would save time in the long run.

# Working with programmers

Once your team has finalized the technical requirements and programming specifications, the programming can begin. Ideally, your team has also finalized the database specifications; if not, the programmers will temporarily need to use static content as placeholders for data that will end up being database-driven.

During the programming phase, the project manager needs to be ready to provide immediate feedback to programmers. You want to do what you can to enable them to keep working steadily. Stop by regularly to see if they need anything. They may not think they need your help, or may even seem irritated at the interruption. In updating you about their progress, however, they'll have to explain problems in layperson terms, which is a good exercise for thinking through something that might not be working right. Programmers may be concentrating so hard on fixing a tiny coding problem that they forget to take a break or try to think through the issue another way.

Here are some ways your regular visits can help, even if you don't know one whit of code:

- In explaining a problem to you, the programmer may realize an answer herself.

- You may realize she has been spending hours trying to accomplish something that was an 'optional' feature of the product.

- She explains that she can't figure out how to meet some aspect of the specifications, although she's come close. She couldn't get an expandable panel to work and wishes the specifications had called for a simple drop-down menu. Together, you realize that the specifications could easily be revised in this area to use a drop-down menu instead.

- You realize that someone else on the team can help.

If none of the above happens, you've at least shown that you're available and you're interested, and you're staying up to date about the programmer's progress.

## Programming languages and environments

 Most libraries will already have a server and a web programming environment in place for their regular website. As project manager, you should understand these different environments when communicating with your programmers about their work, as well as when evaluating open source and turnkey applications. Several environments are described below, along with aspects you should consider.

### *Linux/Apache/MySQL/Perl (LAMP)*

This environment may use Linux, Unix, or one of their variants as an operating system. Apache is the name of a popular open source web server (*http://www.apache.org*), which is easy to set up and configure. MySQL is an open source database server (*http://www .mysql.com*); there are several other open source database servers that might be used in its place. Perl is an interpreted programming language, meaning you can read and edit the source code files directly in a text editor, but they must be processed 'on-the-fly' by the Perl interpreter before they run (*http://www.activestate.com/ activeperl/*). Other interpreted languages might be used instead of Perl, such as PHP. You can run Perl and PHP programs on any web server, provided that the Perl and PHP interpreters are installed. Some characteristics of this environment include:

- There's more than one way to do everything, providing unlimited flexibility, but you might not find documentation for what you choose to do.

- All of these tools are financially free. The cost comes in staff time.

- You won't find official support, although the users in this community are quite friendly and user forums abound on the web.

- Although some graphical interfaces exist for managing the server, databases, and programs in this environment, most users rely on text editors and command-line interfaces.

### Windows ASP.NET

This environment typically uses a Windows IIS web server and object-oriented programming languages like C# or Visual Basic. The database server will most likely be SQL server, although many options are possible. Unlike Perl and PHP, no interpretation needs to happen before the code is executed by the server. This theoretically speeds up the execution of the application for end users, but means you need to run the compiler after every edit before uploading a new version. You can only run .NET programs on a web server that has the .NET environment installed.

- While there are some options for how you do things, there are more standards in this environment.

- Although you can theoretically edit C# and Visual Basic programs in text editors, most programmers use some type of graphical editor like Microsoft Visual Studio.

- Windows server and SQL server are not free. The .NET environment and programming languages are free, and there's even a free visual editor (*http://www.microsoft.com/Express/*).

- Since you've bought Microsoft products, you get official technical support when something goes wrong.

- Active Server Pages combine Visual Basic or C# code with HTML and are processed by the server before displaying in the user's browser.

### Java

The term 'Java' refers to a system of products and specifications from Sun Microsystems that can be deployed across multiple types of computing platforms. The Java programming language can run on multiple operating systems, as long as you install the Java Development Kit (*http://java.sun.com/javase/downloads/index.jsp*) to compile your code. The Java community is large and diverse, with an active open source contingent (*http://java-source.net/*). These are some of its features:

- The Java Development Kit and its documentation are free under the GNU General Public License.

- You can use a variety of database servers.
- You can write code in a simple text editor, or use a development tool, such as Visual Editor (*http://www.eclipse.org/vep/*).
- Java Server Pages combine Java code with HTML and are then compiled as Java 'servlets' when first requested by a user.
- Java 'applets' are programs embedded in a web page using the <applet> element.

## Collaboration and communication with the technical team

If you are lucky enough to have more than one programmer, part of your role is making sure they communicate with one another as well as with the rest of the team. The programming specifications will go a long way toward reducing confusion between your programmers by specifying field names and values, filenames, and other technical decisions. Specifications, however, do not take the place of regular communication while the programmers work.

In addition to multiple programmers, you may also have designers who need to be involved in the programming. Object-oriented programming environments like Visual Studio and Flash can intertwine design and programming so your programmers are designing more and your designers are programming more. One person with both skills, for instance, may create graphical elements within Flash and then animate those elements using ActionScript. The two parts of the project— graphics and programming—are created at one time. In any programming environment, your programmers can specify stylesheet attributes, or they can rely on the designers to do so. By including the designers in technical team communication, you help to prevent duplication of effort and confusion.

Before the programming begins, you should sit down with all technical team members to decide how to divvy up the work. Programming skills will often dictate who does what. For example, if you have a Flash programmer, he will surely handle the Flash work. If you have a programmer strong in database design, she will likely handle the code most closely related to the database. You may also designate a lead programmer who will provide daily monitoring and advice instead of the project manager. Other divisions of labor you might consider include:

- *By user*: Many applications have a front-end that end users see versus a back-end which library staff use to edit and administer the application.
- *By centrality*: Most applications have one or more areas that users see most often versus supplemental areas like help and error handling.
- *By internal stakeholder*: Some projects have different internal stakeholders. An example might be the online catalog, where reference staff may care most about the ability to search and circulation staff may care most about status messages.
- *By release*: If your project is large, one person may work on the first phase, then someone else could take over for the next phase. This may sound unusual, but with the hybrid positions common in academic libraries, it may help balance workload.

## Using code comments to collaborate

Writing code is usually a solitary pursuit, requiring concentration and individual effort. Yet your programmers and designers can communicate with each other easily with comments within their code. Web designers should use comments in their stylesheets and HTML, and programmers should include extensive comments in their source code. Plain-language descriptions of what each section of code does will help the original programmer edit code later, and will be invaluable if a second programmer needs to edit the files at any time. Programmers should also note any tricks they used to get something to work, fixes to tricky bugs, and references to any online documentation which illuminated a particular challenge.

Communicate with your technical team members about expected comments and documentation. Find out what is important to them about one another's documentation, and agree to a plan. Then, when they show you how a web page is developing, take a look at the code; if it's a compiled web application, ask the programmer to send you the code file as well. Some programming languages have 'self documenting' code features and may even be able to pull out embedded comments and generate a separate document (Bean Software 2009). Even if you don't understand the programming language, you should see a generous sprinkling of plain-language explanations.

Here are some other ways in which members of your technical team can collaborate even as they work individually:

- Create a shared addendum to the programming specifications with decisions that were not specified in the documentation. This can just be a Word document which all programmers can edit and that the entire team can read.

- Plan to take coffee breaks together. Your programmers cannot code 100% of their time; they need to take breaks. That time is ideal for brainstorming a solution to a thorny problem.

- Touch base with 15-minute stand-up meetings daily. Even if your programmers work in the same physical area, you may find that they neglect to communicate about the project. You can encourage this with your own daily visits.

- Stagger work times so that one programmer works and uploads changes in the morning while the second programmer works and uploads changes in the afternoon.

As project manager, you can keep an eye on potential conflicts and bridge the gap between different work styles.

# Testing the project

Your role as project manager is also to plan which types of tests are required for your project, to be sure the project timeline includes time for testing, and to confirm that the tests are carried out thoroughly. All aspects of your project need testing: usability testing (discussed in chapter 9, 'Getting user input'), accessibility testing (discussed in chapter 10, 'Overall and design specifications'), and proofreading (discussed in chapter 12, 'Web content specifications'). Each of these are also described in more detail by Ashley Friedlein (2001, 204), along with two types of testing related to programming and development: functional testing, and load and security testing.

The purpose of testing associated with programming is to find functional and operational problems. It should not be misused as a place to make changes to the specifications unless you explicitly planned to do so. Friedlein emphasizes the importance of establishing a milestone after which no new content or changes will be accepted, so that you can concentrate on testing (2001, 202). This goal may be challenging to achieve in an academic library, particularly when you are using the inclusive project teams that we recommend. You will recall from chapter 6, 'Library web team dynamics', that your team will likely have many individuals who are thorough and have high standards based on common MBTI® types among librarians and programmers. Most of your users, though, will be thrilled by even small improvements to websites and applications. Once you've entered into the testing stage, save any requests for functional or content changes for a later version or even another project. Don't let all the issues you find and new feature ideas discourage or delay you from launching the project. Iterative improvement is the key.

## Functional testing

Functional testing is, in simplest terms, looking for things that don't work, or bugs. There are two keys to a successful bug-finding mission. First, you need a checklist or troubleshooting script. We have posted a sample script online (see *http://sites.google.com/site/pm4web/Home/book*). This script outlines the steps to take to navigate through every interaction with the system. You start on the entry page and follow every link and perform every function to be sure it is what you expect. If there are multiple options that can be set on a search screen, you'll need to have a line in your testing script for each combination of items.

Creating this script can be more tedious than actually performing the test. However, a testing script greatly improves the quality of the work and makes the process much faster. If you have a script that you are confident in, you can get help from student workers and other colleagues. Having a script also means that when new revisions are ready for launch, you have a clear record of what you tested last time. You will just re-use the script for each new round of testing. You will also use the same testing script for each browser brand and version that you intend to support. In other words, you will create the script once and use it many times.

At a minimum, the test script should include information about:

- which browsers to check
- specific pages to view at the screen resolutions you intend to support
- using a broken link program to test for broken links
- checking load times for each page in the project; some web statistics tracking tools will report load times automatically
- checking the printed results pages for specific pages that a user might wish to print

- checking all navigation links to confirm that they match specifications
- filling out every form field normally and submitting the form
- leaving all fields blank and submitting the form
- putting junk—HTML code, content pasted from a word processor, and a string consisting of every special character on your keyboard ('~!@#$%^&*()__+-=`{}[]:';<>?,./|\)—into each field and submitting the form
- checking to see what happens if you 'refresh' the browser and use the 'back' button
- how to perform every combination of functions possible with an application; for example, if you can search by title or author, then sort by publication date or relevance, you must:
  - do a title search, then sort by publication date
  - do a title search, then sort by relevance
  - do an author search, then sort by publication date
  - do an author search, then sort by relevance.

If different users should see different behavior, be sure to test the project using each different user role. Such a checklist could easily become quite long, but it is much easier—and less embarrassing—to fix bugs now than after you have released the finished project to your users.

The second element to a successful bug-finding mission is getting lots of people involved in the testing effort. Many hands make light work, and many eyes will find more bugs. Having multiple people use the system at once will test its capabilities for handling multiple simultaneous users. Do you know someone in your organization who sends in lots of trouble reports or bugs? Now is the time to invite them to participate in testing the application! Don't give this group the checklist; have them try to use the system as they think it was intended, and encourage them to try anything they like. Encourage them to try to break the system. While the commercial world does not always fully appreciate testing (Friedlein 2001, 203), library staff care about finding bugs in advance since they will likely be regular users of this project. Allow time in your schedule for at least two iterations of multi-user testing. If the first testing session finds either a very significant error or a sufficient number of errors, you may need to stop testing, allow time for your programmer to fix the bug(s) found, and then have a subsequent testing session.

Your web programmers can only help with testing in this area to a certain extent. They are at the same disadvantage as a writer proofreading her own work. Your programmers have been debugging their program constantly as they've been working. Even after working with code they've written for days, they simply cannot be expected to find all the errors. They also have extremely specific ideas of how the program is supposed to work. They may not be able to find certain bugs because they are going to use the program exactly how it was written. They may never try some wacky combination of steps because it would simply never occur to them. Finally, they will have plenty to do fixing the bugs that are found. If you're a one-person web project team, consider dividing your functional testing activities from your programming activities. First make your bug list; then go through it all at once.

## Load and security testing

Although load testing and security testing are different activities, they are grouped together here because the same person, a system administrator, will likely handle both items. If your system administrator is not already on your project team, be sure to discuss the project with her in advance, and collaborate with her to choose tests for load and security issues.

The idea behind load testing is to simulate what it will be like when thousands of users are hitting your finished web project, instead of just the handful of folks on your web project team or participating in your multi-user testing sessions. Automated tools are available to help (see callout 'Tools for load testing'), and your server administrator should know about them.

---

### Tools for load testing

- 'Web Site Test Tools and Site Management Tools' (*http://www.softwareqatest.com/qatweb1.html #LOAD*) offers a list of load and performance testing solutions, including some open source options.

- WebLOAD (*http://www.radview.com/solutions/HTTPLoad-Testing.aspx*), a load testing tool for internet applications, can be evaluated for free.

- NetMechanic (*http://netmechanic.com/products/SCP_FreeSample .shtml*) will perform an eight-hour free trial evaluation of your web server's performance.

---

For security testing, you or your team can perform some basic checks, including:

- filling out web forms with text that includes special characters and code
- verifying that information that is supposed to be encrypted, such as passwords, is in fact encrypted
- verifying that e-mails are being sent to the correct addresses
- viewing the HTML source code through the browser to ensure there are not comments with sensitive information
- confirming that any planned security or privacy statements display to the user.

If the project you are working on makes use of sensitive information, such as student records, you'll want to be sure to enlist the help of your campus IT department before you even begin your project. Although it would be unusual, there are companies whose business it is to try to break through a site's security, and one of them could be hired as a consultant to try to breach your system. Your web project is also susceptible to hackers who target your site randomly.

In addition to finding bugs, and checking for load and security issues, a good testing plan communicates respect to your technical personnel. Expect some irritation when problems are discovered, and be ready to let it roll off your back. If necessary, remind everyone it's better to find issues before launch than afterwards! Also, be ready to offer frequent praise and admiration for successes.

## Using a tracking system

Have a system to track the testing phase. Your team can use one of the many freely available and inexpensive software tools to track bugs and provide status reports and feedback. Wikipedia offers a helpful comparison of different issue tracking systems at *http://en.wikipedia.org/wiki/Comparison_of_issue_tracking_systems*.

This book's authors use an open source tracking application called Issue Tracker (*http://www.asp.net/downloads/archived/starter-kits/issue-tracker/*). Since it is installed on a shared server, anyone on the project team can leave comments, create new issues, assign issues to others, update issues, and specify who should receive e-mail notifications of updates. This particular application also lets you divide your issues into different projects, each with its own set of users and status messages.

Although this book advocates using the tools you have at hand for many tasks, don't rely on e-mail for tracking the bugs you discover while testing. A tracking system provides for effective organization, archiving, and access by your whole group. As a project manager, you will appreciate having such communications separate from the rest of your work. Use a system.

Once you have a tracking system in place, set a plan for how reported bugs will be handled. The software you've chosen will dictate some of your options, but you should at least decide who will report bugs and issues as they are found. Ideally, your entire technical team does so along with you. How much information do they need to submit? Can the person submitting a bug set a priority level for the bug? What priority categories will you use? Who will be responsible for double-checking a fixed bug? Remember, you don't have to do all the testing, all the reporting, all the double-checking, and all the re-testing. Your role as web project manager is not to conduct all the tests. Your role is to plan and coordinate this testing effort, generate enthusiasm among the testing group, buoy your team's spirits as the bug reports roll in, help track the project through its quality assurance stage, and confirm that someone on your team is responsible for double-checking bugs as they are fixed.

# Conclusion

Clearly written technical requirements, programming specifications, and database specifications serve as excellent communication tools between you and your technical personnel. As web project manager, it will be your role to check in regularly as technical work begins in order to identify problems, help troubleshoot, and facilitate communication between people hard at work. You also have the obligation to ensure that the work gets tested thoroughly. You yourself do not have to engage with every technical detail, but you should have enough knowledge to know when your team is doing the job well. Your role is to set up communication pathways, procedures, and documentation to ensure each piece of minutiae is dealt with according to its importance.

# Recommended readings

Hower, Rick (2009) Web site test tools and site management tools, *http://www.softwareqatest.com/qatweb1.html.*

Lauesen, Soren (2002) *Software Requirements: Styles and Techniques.* Harlow, England: Addison-Wesley.

Litwin, Paul (2003) *Fundamentals of Relational Database Design.* September 7, *http://r937.com/relational.html.*

Myers, Glenford J., Corey Sandler, and Tom Badgett (2004) *Art of Software Testing.* Hoboken, NJ: Wiley.

# References

Bean Software (2009) *Automatic Documentation Generation in ASP.NET Applications, http://www.beansoftware.com/asp.net-tutorials/ automatic-documentation-vb.aspx.*

Fowler, Martin (2000) *UML Distilled: A Brief Guide to the Standard Object Modeling Language.* 2nd ed., Reading, MA: Addison-Wesley.

Friedlein, Ashley (2001) *Web Project Management: Delivering Successful Commercial Web Sites.* New York: Morgan Kaufmann.

# Web content specifications

## Introduction

Academic libraries are rich with web content. Library websites provide access to top information sources, search tools, and guides to information. The staff within libraries—librarians and support staff alike—are subject area liaisons, writers and communicators, and service area experts. Every web project has some kind of content. Web projects within an academic library will frequently have *considerable* amounts of content. This chapter reviews the project manager's responsibilities with respect to the content of a web project. Some of the possible content responsibilities for a web project manager in an academic library include:

- knowing the peculiarities of library content
- drafting a site map
- creating a content inventory and content plan
- identifying sources for content
- helping colleagues understand issues related to formats
- understanding content management systems
- reviewing content.

In academic libraries, web project management may not yet be well understood and many different people are capable of creating content. Make sure no one assumes that you as the project manager will provide the web content. This is, in fact, an ideal time to involve others in the organization beyond your project team.

Like the two previous chapters in this book, this chapter about content specifications presents techniques and tools that help you communicate the details of your web project, especially with those most closely associated with this aspect. More so than the design and technical specifications chapters, most aspects of the content specifications apply to your project even if you are implementing a third-party application or creating a static website. Just about every project has some type of content. As with the other two areas, choose the tools in this chapter that best fit your project's needs.

# Academic library web content is different

When thinking about content for an academic library web project, consider that libraries have access to an enormous amount of licensed content with both opportunities and restrictions. Electronic databases and journal platforms usually offer ways to integrate content into the library website, but these may not be immediately obvious to non-technical librarians. Examples of ways that licensed content could be integrated with a library website include:

- RSS feeds of new titles or search results displayed on library web pages
- input boxes which launch searches into specific databases
- links into database or journal platforms made with custom URLs so that the user sees a specific section of the database or predefined search parameters.

If your library has an electronic resources librarian, you may wish to enlist his assistance for advice and implementation. If not, you may need to investigate your options with the vendors of licensed resources.

Another peculiarity of library content is that library website information is often kept in separate databases. A good portion of the content on library websites comes from the library catalog, institutional repositories, journal lists, and other database-driven systems. Many web projects will need to draw information from these systems, but each system comes with its own technical requirements and limitations. Web project managers may need to assume a coordinating role between library systems, technical services, and the web project team in order to effectively use this data. Your content specifications, then, will indicate any external content to be integrated into the project, while the technical specifications will detail exactly how it happens behind the scenes.

Copyright and licensing restrictions are another area of importance related to content. As members of educational institutions, library staff have considerable leeway in using others' content under fair use provisions of copyright law and licensing agreements. Publishing that same content on the web, however, is a new and quite different use. For example, suppose an instruction librarian wants to post class handouts online. She has some examples of scholarly and non-scholarly full text articles that she usually passes out in class. Is it okay to post these on the website? Suppose a library wants to use book cover images from Amazon.com on its website—is that okay? As web project manager, while you may not be an authority on copyright, you may be the one who becomes aware of potential issues and coordinates the process of finding the answer. You may need to involve your library administration or university's legal department to answer the questions that you uncover. As you identify legal issues related to the content that you access, be sure to document those issues in either your content specifications or within site-wide guidelines for future reference.

Librarians already know to be cautious when providing medical, legal, and business information. As web project manager, you can help to be sure this caution also applies to the use of content within your project. Your organization may want to consider a standard disclaimer for use on the website. The callout 'Examples of library website disclaimers' gives a list of libraries that have chosen this option and example clauses from their disclaimers.

## Examples of library website disclaimers

 **Association of Academic Health Sciences Libraries,** *http://www.aahsl.org/mc/page.do?sitePageId=81755*

'The information posted here should not be considered medical advice and is not intended to replace consultation with a qualified medical professional.'

**North Carolina State University,** *http://www.lib.ncsu.edu/disclaimer/*

- 'The information provided... within the www.lib.ncsu.edu domain... does not represent the official statements or views of NCSU Libraries...'
- 'Information is... provided "as is" with no warranties of any kind.'
- 'NCSU Libraries shall not be liable for any damages of any kind.'

> **Princeton University,** *http://www.princeton.lib.nj.us/legal/disclaimer.html*
>
> 'In choosing sources to link to its Web site, the Library follows its materials selection guidelines. Beyond this, the Library does not monitor or control information accessible through the Internet. The Library is not responsible for the content or changes in content of the sources to which the Library pages link, or for the content or changes in content of sources accessed through secondary links.'
>
> **The University of Edinburgh,** *http://www.lib.ed.ac.uk/disclaimer.shtml*
>
> 'The information contained in these pages is, as at the date of its inclusion in these pages, believed to be accurate and free from error, but the author(s) provide no warranty to this effect, nor will the author(s) be liable to any party for the consequence(s) of any reliance placed thereon by such party, other than to the extent that the same shall result in a legal liability, unavoidable at law. The inclusion of any commercial logo, banner or link does not imply endorsement. Freedom of Information: see University of Edinburgh Freedom of Information Publication Scheme (*http://www.pubs.recordsmanagement.ed.ac.uk/*).'

# Documenting your content needs

The content specifications document attempts to identify the content needs for your project, where your team will get that content, and plans for future additions and maintenance. More so perhaps than the other two types of specifications, the content specifications may list existing content—even if it will be removed from a website as part of your project—as well as content not yet created. These content considerations are similar to those for websites outside of libraries, too, although libraries frequently have large amounts of content.

## Site maps

A site map, also called a content map, illustrates the major content areas and the hierarchy of web pages on a site. It can be arranged to represent the actual file structure on the server or the navigation and chunks of content seen by the user. As with most diagrams, the site map can be created using software or hand-drawn like the one in figure 12.1. When

**Figure 12.1**  Example of a simple, hand-drawn site map

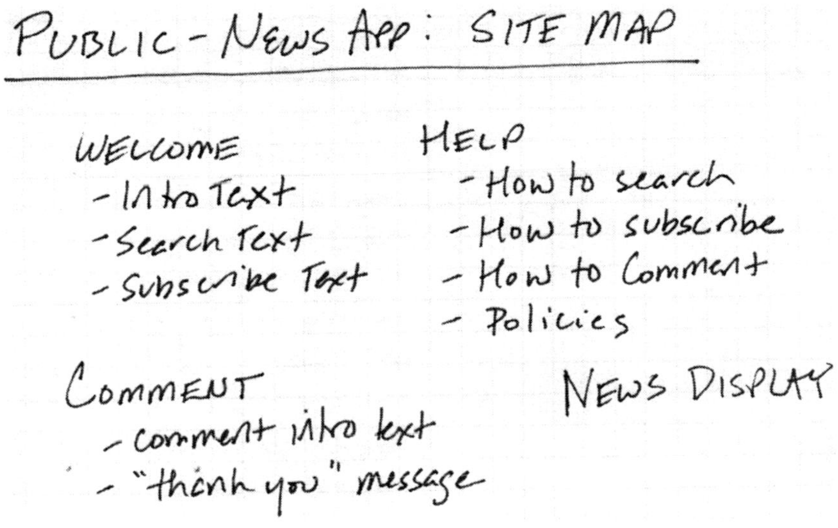

PUBLIC - NEWS APP: SITE MAP

WELCOME
- Intro Text
- Search Text
- Subscribe Text

HELP
- How to search
- How to subscribe
- How to Comment
- Policies

COMMENT
- comment intro text
- "thank you" message

NEWS DISPLAY

illustrating a current site in anticipation of a redesign, this diagram can highlight illogical navigation and weak areas of a website in need of more content. You can also use a site map for brand-new projects as a reminder of the different areas that need attention. In figure 12.1, for instance, the grouping of text associated with 'help' is an excellent reminder to ask someone on your project team to write the help text for that area.

## Content inventories

A content inventory is simply a descriptive list of a particular project's content (figure 12.2). For a full redesign of a large website, a content inventory reflecting the current site can be lengthy, particularly if your website is a collection of individual files as opposed to database-driven. Creating one for an existing website can help your project team identify groupings of content for a site map. Creating your content inventory in a spreadsheet, with a row for each page or type of content, gives you options like sorting rows and hiding columns. You can identify each item of content by systematically clicking through your website, using lists of files from statistics tracking software, or using lists of files from

**Figure 12.2** Portion of a content inventory

| ID | File Type | Path/File | Title | Last mod date | Author | Type of content | Audience | Note |
|----|-----------|-----------|-------|---------------|--------|-----------------|----------|------|
| 1.1 | asp | /smith/ auth/auth.asp | None | 01 Apr 2005 | Wilson | | | Orphan |
| 2.3 | asp | /circulation/ index.asp | Circulation Services | 01 Mar 2009 | Nichols | Service | All | |
| 1.2 | aspx | /about.aspx | About the library | 16 Mar 2009 | Brown | Promo | Faculty | Revise |
| 3.1 | asp | /smad/ masscomm .aspx | Research Guides: Media Arts & Design: Film | 16 Mar 2007 | Keach | Instruction | Students, faculty | Update |

automated software that crawls your site to find broken links or create site maps. Capture as much information from automated systems as is possible. If you decide that you don't need that information after all, you can always hide that column.

Depending on the information you choose to include for each piece of content, a content inventory can serve many planning and maintenance purposes. It can help you document (and then delete) files that are on your server but no longer used, as well as redundant and outdated content. A content inventory can also help you identify groups of similar files that could be managed better by a database or content management system. As your project proceeds, your content inventory can also provide the framework for a content plan, as described later in this chapter.

Carefully consider your available time when embarking on a content inventory and when deciding how much detail to include. Inventories have their place for certain types of projects, but creating complete ones for large websites is time-consuming.

## Content plans

A content plan is similar to a content inventory but looks forward to the content that you need. Creating it ensures that you and your team have thought through the content-related requirements of the project early in the process. The following list, expanded from Friedlein (2001, 119), includes the major features of a content plan:

- an inventory of the content to be included
- who will be providing the content
- the expected format of the content
- to whom the content should be provided
- how often content will be updated
- deadlines for content providers.

Friedlein strongly urges project managers to be clear about content requirements. Assumptions about content, he says, should be reflected in the budget, timeline, and project specifications. If initial samples of content differ greatly from what you were expecting, you may need to adjust the timeline (2001, 90–3). Creating content and editing old content, just like designing and programming, are not trivial tasks.

Your content editor will need to brief your contributors on how their work fits into the plan. Since librarians and library staff are not full-time web writers, the content editor will need to be sure they have plenty of time to complete writing assignments. Set clear deadlines and send regular reminders of when content is due. Make sure that contributors from outside your project team know where they can go if they need technical help or a better understanding of the entire project.

For large projects, or if the project will be ongoing, Friedlein (2001, 155) also suggests a tracking system for web content. This system might include the following:

- e-mail procedures such as acknowledging receipt of content by e-mail, and guidelines about which e-mails to save
- a systematic process for saving, organizing, and archiving submitted content, including e-mail attachments
- procedures for saving and archiving content contained in the text of an e-mail
- a good back-up plan for both original and production files.

You may use one or all of these techniques, depending on the project. What's important is that you've planned for the content.

## Content style guides

You read about documenting design decisions and technical decisions in style guides in the two previous chapters. You should also document content style decisions for this project within your content specifications and refer your content creators to any content style guide for your entire site (see figure 12.3).

**Figure 12.3** Excerpt from a content style guide on writing

| Writing advice | Why |
|---|---|
| Both of these sentences are correct in their use of off-campus/off campus: <br><br> 'Students have off-campus access to online resources.' <br><br> 'Students have access to online resources from off campus.' | When used as an adjective, as in the first sentence, use a hyphen. <br><br> When used otherwise, no hyphen. |
| *'LEO Library Catalog'* or *'LEO'* is the preferred way to refer to the catalog. <br><br> Some non-preferred ways are: 'Leo,' 'Leonardo,' 'LEO Libraries Catalog,' 'LEO Card Catalog,' 'LEO Online Catalog,' 'LEO Catalog.' | Although LEO is not an acronym for anything, it has historically been in all-caps. It is referred to as LEO Library Catalog on its own front page as well as in most places throughout the website. |
| If in doubt about a general word or grammar question, refer to the library's most recent editions of: <br><br> *The Associated Press Stylebook and Briefing on Media Law* (Carrier Ref. PN4783.A83 2002) <br><br> *Webster's New World College Dictionary* (Carrier Ref. PE1628.W5629 1997) | These are the style guides adopted by our university for all publications. |
| Break up large chunks of text for readability. | Usability testing suggests that sentences of less than twenty words and paragraphs of less than six sentences are most readable. |

Types of content decisions that might be included in an entire site style guide include:

- proper names that refer to parts of your website like your catalog, journal list, and database list

- spelling and capitalization rules associated with the name of your library and university

- the preferred use of capitalization and compound words commonly used on the site

- an authoritative source to answer additional questions of usage and spelling.

## Determining guidelines and responsibilities for updating content

To prevent a completed web project from becoming dated, identify early in the process who will be responsible for updating the content after the project is completed. Although someone else may be responsible for ongoing maintenance of the completed project, as project manager you will have the clearest understanding of what content updates will be needed in the future.

Some of the questions you'll want to answer with your project sponsor include:

- Will content authors update the content directly?

- Will content authors instead send some or all new content to a technical staff person?

- Does the new content go through an approval process? If so, by whom? Ensure that you train technical staff in the system and in the guidelines for posting content.

If content authors will update the content directly, be sure to specify details about the administrative interfaces and user permissions in the design and technical documents. Also, plan for training sessions and documents to prepare them for their task. Even if they will be using a fairly intuitive web editor like Dreamweaver, or web forms in a content management system, they will need training. Training is also a good time to review best practices such as following accessibility standards and your website's style guide.

# Identifying sources for content

In chapter 5, 'The academic library web team,' you read about the importance of having someone responsible for web content on your team. That person may be the creator of the content, solicit content on behalf of the project, and coordinate editing and proofreading. The following sections present just some of the available sources.

## Existing graphical content

Although your project will likely include original textual content, you may choose to seek out existing graphics that fit your needs. Seek out free websites with high-quality images or shop at the websites of the many online stock photo vendors. Seek out local photographs from your colleagues in the library as well as your campus public relations or marketing office. As you gather your images, note your sources and any restrictions related to their use in your content specifications. Remember to get appropriate permissions when using existing photographs, as discussed in chapter 9. For archival purposes, consider burning a CD with all the original graphics when a project concludes.

## Team contributions

One person or more on your team may work on the project's content. Let's say you're planning some new entry web pages for specific user groups such as 'For Students,' 'For Faculty,' and 'For Distance Learners.' You could ask a subset of your project team to work on these pages in order to facilitate brainstorming and decision-making. Group work can also be a good way to balance people's strengths. For example, if Amy tends to be very wordy, and Donald always wants to add poor graphics to his web pages, putting them on a team together may reduce the need for *you* to discourage Donald from his graphics or to ask Amy to tighten up her prose.

## Public relations

If your library has someone who serves as a public relations officer, your content editor should contact that person. This marketing person can play a key role with respect to written web content and may also have a collection of logos, photographs, and other images you can re-use. They may coordinate press releases, official announcements, and have easy access to your library's facts and figures. They may have some ready-made content designed for print publications which you can adapt for the web. They may also be interested in reviewing new content to verify its accuracy and consider whether it should also be issued as a press release. They can help you be sure that new content avoids political pitfalls.

## Soliciting contributors

For large web projects, your content editor may solicit additional writers and artists. In academic libraries, you have a wealth of colleagues who are experts in specific areas and are interested in writing about those topics. You likely also have some colleagues with graphic skills. Colleagues who do not usually work on web projects may especially enjoy being asked to contribute in these areas.

One approach to consider is personally inviting people to contribute content. If you aren't sure the invitation will be welcomed from you personally, consider having the project sponsor issue the invitations. Either way, be sure to explain clearly how the new content will enhance library services. Don't be shy about highlighting the person's strengths as reasons why you thought they would make a good contributor.

Another approach is a mass invitation where you send out a list of things that need to be done, and invite volunteers to take on tasks. In a large library, there may be people who would make excellent contributors but whom you don't know well. Also, depending on your library, there could be a tendency to think first of librarians as contributors. Don't make the mistake of overlooking talented colleagues who don't happen to be librarians!

## User-contributed content

Increasingly, websites are opening up ways for users to contribute directly to the content found online. Tagging, comments, ratings, and reviews are just a few of the ways users enhance sites like Amazon.com, Netflix, and the Internet Movie Database. Sites like Wikipedia are almost entirely composed by users. While some of today's academic libraries are hesitant to offer user-contributed content, others are creating custom applications specifically to support this feature.

The following list includes policy, feature-related, and technical issues for your project team to think about when considering content contributions from users:

- What will happen to a student's contributed content after she graduates?

- Can a user delete his own content?
- Can a user decide to keep her contributions private or share them only with a certain group?
- Will the library review user-contributed content?
- How will the library prevent spamming?
- Will the library 'seed' and maintain the site with librarian contributions to encourage user contributions? If so, who will do this?

User-contributed content may be of interest to many parts of the library, and policies related to this type of content may need to be defined at the organizational level, not just for your current project. If you're not sure who should be involved with issues related to user-contributed content, check with your project sponsor or library administration.

---

## Libraries offering user-contributed content

 PennTags at the University of Pennsylvania, *http://tags .library.upenn.edu/*
'PennTags is a social bookmarking tool for locating, organizing, and sharing your favorite online resources. Members of the Penn Community can collect and maintain URLs, links to journal articles, and records in Franklin, our online catalog and VCat, our online video catalog.'

MTagger at the University of Michigan, *http://www.lib.umich.edu/ mtagger/*
'MTagger is the U-M Library's tagging tool—it allows you to save and label things you find on library web pages, the library catalog (Mirlyn), digital images, or any other web page.'

Library Suggestion Blog at Virginia Commonwealth University, *http://blog.vcu.edu/libsuggest/*
A variation of the traditional suggestion box.

MyDiscoveries at the University of Chicago, *http://lens.lib.uchicago .edu/*
Within the library catalog, 'can make lists of, rate (1 to 5 stars) and add reviews for books and other library materials. Lists can be made for your private use or to share with others. You can also tag library materials to make finding them easier. All public lists, all tags, reviews and ratings are visible to all users.'

---

# Working with different web content formats

The format of web content can greatly affect the design and execution of a web project. Neither your team members nor your content authors may be familiar with format issues such as:

- Will the content for the web project be database-driven or static?

- What formats will the content include? Text, images, video, audio?

- Do new versions of content need to be created? For example, is the client hoping to have a set of documents in PDF format that are currently in Microsoft Word?

Be sure to get examples of the content that will go into the web project. If you're creating a database, get some test data to populate it. If it's a static website, get examples of the text, images, videos, or other types of formats. Not only will this help you develop prototypes, you'll also get an idea for how speedily the content will be delivered and you'll be able to check assumptions about the content. For example, a set of navigation button images may be submitted in a low-quality JPG format, and they may need to be re-created as transparent GIFs. Or, you may receive a spreadsheet of data to include in the new database only to find that it contains inconsistent, non-standardized data. You can overcome these problems, but it's easier to address them earlier in the project than later.

Checking the content early is important even when it already exists and is being re-purposed. For example, suppose you are redesigning an area of the library's website and expect to move the old content to new templates. The 'old' web pages may be full of nonstandard HTML or outdated tags. If you plan to move old content to new templates, ask one of your technical team members to convert a few pages and look for any major problems. You can also consider whether student workers would be able to assist with a big content move-over, or whether too many decisions will be involved with each page. Be sure to allow time in your schedule for content transfer!

The following sections briefly outline specific considerations for various formats of web content.

## *Text*

Naturally, you would assume that content contributors would send textual content for a website in electronic form, flawlessly edited, in a highly compatible document format. Be sure to check this assumption. If text must be converted into a database, and the amount of material is large, consider creating Microsoft Access forms with validation enabled. You can also use this program's spell check feature.

If the project entails the creation or use of PDF documents, experiment early with the creation or conversion process to make a good estimate of the time required. See Adobe's support website (*http://www.adobe.com/support/*) for details about PDF creation and display. Be aware that you can change many parameters to regulate the appearance of PDFs within a site (Parameters for Opening PDF Files, *http://www.adobe.com/devnet/acrobat/pdfs/pdf_open_parameters.pdf*).

## Writing for the web

Writing for the web is different than writing for print and your content editor may need to help authors adjust their style. First, there are physical considerations. In most cases, web pages display in 'landscape' orientation as opposed to the portrait orientation of most print publications. Second, text on screens looks continuous, but is actually grainy. In most displays, light shines out from the screen into readers' eyes. For these reasons, reading online is tiring and reading speed decreases by about 30% (Sammons 2004, 18). When using the web, people tend to operate in scanning mode, which your authors can facilitate with brevity, conciseness, and chunking of information. Your users may also prefer a more casual, direct, and personal style on websites than they do in print, conflicting with the desire of academics to maintain certain language standards. For example, using the second person pronoun 'you' and active language directs statements to users and adds a personal tone. Consider the difference between 'You can renew books online' and 'The library catalog facilitates renewals.'

Like other websites, academic libraries will have a variety of reader levels in their audience. Faculty may expect a high level of professionalism and appropriate terminology, while new students may not yet be familiar with the language of their major's discipline, let alone library jargon. Refer to 'Library Terms that Users Understand' (*http://www.jkup.net/terms.html*), a clearinghouse of recommended library terminology drawn from usability tests, which suggests easy-to-understand words to replace common library jargon. To accommodate both expert and novice reader levels, consider combining technical terms and jargon with linked definitions (Sammons 2004, 3–4) or defining jargon on the same page with explanatory text.

Your content editor should also encourage a simple writing style. Jakob Nielsen and Hoa Loranger recommend writing home pages and other entry pages to a sixth-grade reading level (2006). Pages at a deeper level can be written at an eighth-grade reading level. Keep in mind that while 'most users *prefer* clear, simple language, site visitors with poor reading skills *need* it' (2006, 265). Beyond the considerations of library jargon offered earlier in this chapter, consider how your readers will comprehend technical explanations such as configuring a web browser to access library databases. Some of Nielsen's other tips for web writing are (2006, 258–283):

- Use simple language.
- Tone down marketing hype.
- Summarize key points and pare down.
- Format text for readability:
  - Highlight keywords
  - Use concise and descriptive titles and headings
  - Use bulleted lists and numbered steps
  - Use short paragraphs
  - Be sure the most important point on a web page is stated within the first two lines.
- Keep paragraphs short.

These tips help all your readers better understand what you are trying to share.

## Chunking and organizing information

Your content editor and your information architect should both assist with organizing content on the page. 'Chunking' content into smaller parts is one way to meet user expectations for easy-to-scan text on websites. Figure 12.4 shows a model of chunking information about information ethics, while figure 12.5 shows a real-life example of how chunked information improves readability. Note how the example in figure 12.5 uses bullets to emphasize important text.

As you are chunking, consider also the ordering of sections on the page. Will you use an alphabetical arrangement? A numeric arrangement with steps numbered 1, 2, 3? Does the topic lend itself to organization from simple to complex? Or, will you need to use a combination of all these methods? The important thing to do is review these concepts with your contributors and make conscious decisions based on user needs.

**Figure 12.4** A model for chunking information

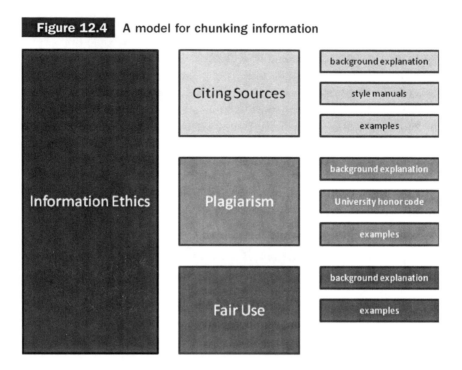

**Figure 12.5** Example of a chunked text

**Citing sources**

When you quote or paraphrase the idea of another person in your research paper, speech or PowerPoint presentation, you must provide a proper citation for the source in a bibliography or list of references to:

- give credit to the author or creator and
- enable a reader to locate the source you cited.

Providing references for sources you used also lends credibility to your work, especially if you use authoritative sources. Be sure to provide full citations to all types of sources you use, including:

| | |
|---|---|
| ✓ books | ✓ government documents |
| ✓ articles | ✓ nonprint media (dvds, videotapes) |
| ✓ Internet sites | ✓ images |
| ✓ interviews | ✓ data sources |

*Source*: Go for the Gold, *http://www.lib.jmu.edu/gold*; used with permission

According to Sammons (2004, 8–20), other techniques to assist readers include:

- *Use introductions and summaries to condense the main gist of a page into a quick description*: Academic libraries are familiar with article abstracts; consider using them to assist users on lengthy library web pages as well! Summaries are not just limited to page introductions. They can be used in sidebars, tables of contents, lists of related topics, and more.

- *Use an 'inverted pyramid' writing scheme*: Present the main point first, then give a brief overview of topics, then a brief statement of the context, then finally background information and links to details and examples.

- *Use topic sentences*: If you've got a page with several paragraphs, consider bolding the first sentence of each or inserting headings to help users decide whether they need to read each section.

# Images

You can read many full-length books about using images on the web (see 'Recommended readings' at the end of this chapter). This section highlights just a few basics.

## Resolution

Try to get the highest resolution possible for source images. If necessary accept a print graphic from someone and scan it to a high resolution rather than use a low resolution file. Although you'll be saving the final image at a lower resolution (usually 72 dpi), by having the higher resolution available, you'll be able to edit and resize the image much more professionally.

## Capturing images

While plenty of commercial screen-capture software exists, in a pinch you can use the keyboard combination Alt-PrintScreen on a PC or Command-Control-Shift-3 on a Mac to capture an image of your desktop. Windows Vista and PCs with Office 2007 can use the Windows key plus 'S' to capture a rectangular area drawn with your mouse. All these actions place the image in a clipboard from which you can paste into a graphics editor. Free image editors such as GIMP (*http://www .gimp.org/*) offer affordable alternatives to the full-featured and expensive Adobe Photoshop.

## GIFs and JPGs: what's the difference?

 The following chart, paraphrased from Ashley Friedlein (2001, 149) lists the major practical distinctions between GIF and JPG formats:

**GIF**

- best for graphics with large areas of flat color such as logos

- supports transparency

- can only support 256 colors

- cannot specify the level of compression.

**JPG**

- best for photographs or other images with lots of colors

- cannot support transparency

- supports up to 16 million colors

- can specify level of compression to trade off quality for smaller file sizes.

## *Audio and video*

With the advent of YouTube (*http://www.youtube.com*), video has become increasingly popular on academic library websites. Tools like Viddler (*http://www.viddler.com*) even allow users to post text and video comments at specific points within the video. For projects using audio or video, be sure the content plan specifies whether any audiovisual recording or editing is necessary, and where the content will be stored. Collect samples of the expected audio and video content early so your team can anticipate file formats, clip lengths, and quality. For projects with audio or video, consider designating a video/audio content editor on your team as suggested in chapter 5. If someone will be creating the content specifically for your project, ensure that your video/audio content editor updates the content plan with the details of what, who, when, where, and how this will be done.

Several free tools exist to help with audio and video. Audacity (*http://audacity.sourceforge.net/*) is a good open source tool that can be used to create and edit audio. Windows Movie Maker and Video Edit Master are free tools for Windows users, and can be found at *http://www.download.com*, while iMovie (*http://www.apple.com/ilife/imovie/*) is the standard for Macs. Quick Media Converter is a free download to convert video formats on Windows machines (*http://www.cocoonsoftware.com/*).

When choosing the type of format and player, consider your end users. Do you mind if they have to install a plug-in to access the content? What connection speed do they have? Will the material be streaming or downloadable? Some licensed content may only allow for streaming, but downloading is a nice option for users with slow connections or mobile devices. Consider providing transcripts or alternative texts for both video and audio. Not only will you be making your content accessible to more users, you will also increase the searchability of the content. Chapter 10 discussed the importance of accessibility in more detail.

## Third-party content and widgets

Libraries increasingly make use of third-party content, widgets, and tools such as Google Maps, Amazon.com book covers, and vendor search interfaces. For widgets that are clearly meant for re-use, be sure you read any details about the original party's right to track and record user interactions. For third-party content that's not obviously meant for re-use, such as Amazon's book covers, seek out any use restrictions. Save the information you find and date it for future reference. If you can't find this information, write the company and ask.

# Content management systems

While a discussion of content management system selection and implementation is beyond the scope of this book, this section will briefly discuss some of the things you should know in your role as a web project manager. A content management systems (CMS) stores content in databases that feed content into templates, creating dynamic pages on the fly. You may choose to implement a small-scale CMS for a specific use or a complex, feature-rich one to support an entire website. Here are just a few examples of how content management systems are sometimes used in academic libraries:

- for publishing news and announcements
- for presenting a library's electronic resources in subject categories
- for allowing librarians to create and maintain subject web pages
- for hosting an institutional repository.

When you completed a content inventory of your current site or mapped out your content needs for your current project, you may have noticed that large amounts of content were near-identical in format. For example, suppose your web project involves creating or redesigning subject guides maintained by your librarians. At a small library with few authors and infrequent updates, it might make sense to leave these guides as static web pages. At a large library with many authors, daily updates, and shared content between the guides, it may make sense to implement a CMS. Using a CMS or other database-driven pages can allow for:

- adherence to controlled vocabularies so that everyone uses consistent terminology
- common elements which appear on each similar page
- simplified steps for pulling in content from a library database or integrated library system
- searching by specific fields within the database of content.

Your team will evaluate the potential use of a CMS just as it would evaluate any technical solution:

- Determine whether a given project might call for some type of CMS.
- Evaluate the interoperability of the CMS with other library systems or the website.
- Recommend in-house development or a third-party CMS.
- Write specifications for implementing a CMS.
- Plan for the support, training, and maintenance for the CMS.

There are several issues to consider when deciding whether or not to use a third-party CMS. First, the cost: even open source content management systems will require staff time. Second, customizability: many CMS-driven sites look similar even though they may offer some customization capabilities. Third, performance and reliability: by adding another layer to your website, you're adding another piece that can go wrong. You'll want to contact current customers about this issue. Staffing is a fourth consideration. Implementing a CMS will require not only staff to implement and launch the system on day one, but also staff to provide ongoing technical support and training. Perhaps the most important issue is the ease of migration. Ensure that you can get content in and out of a CMS for future changes. See the 'Recommended readings' section at the end of this chapter to learn more. In particular, Wayne Powel and Chris Gill (2003) offer an excellent introduction to content management systems in higher education.

# Reviewing content

Proofreading the content on a new website is separate from functional testing. This step requires someone who is 'in the know' about the content area and can find factual errors as well as typographical problems and quality issues. You should charge your content editor and audio/video content editor with reviewing newly submitted web content. If needed, the testing should include fact checking. For instance, if re-used text states that circulation is responsible for the campus delivery service, your editors should confirm that this statement is still true. They should also review all video and audio content for both accuracy and quality.

In addition to checking for errors and quality issues, your editors should review the content with the overall project and content specifications in hand. Confirm that the content satisfies all stated expectations including:

- content style regarding standard language and writing style
- design style guides, stylesheets, and standard templates
- licensing, copyright, and permissions
- accessibility standards.

This content review step can be just as time intensive as the testing associated with the programming, particularly if your project includes a large amount of content.

# Conclusion

Each web project presents unique content challenges for the web project manager. Identify experts who can help you with specific issues related to your web project, and enlist them into your team or as consultants. These experts may come from outside the library, perhaps from a different campus department or even another library entirely. Publicly available websites can provide current best practices for working with specific types of web content such as images, video, and audio. Refer to them to test your understanding about content needs. Above all else, make sure no one assumes that you are the web content provider for your library just because you're the project manager. This is an area where your non-technical team members and others in your library can share the load.

# Recommended readings

Austin, Andy, and Christopher Harris (2008) Drupal in libraries. *Library Technology Reports* 44.

Bourne, Jennie, and Dave Burstein (2008) *Web Video: Making It Great, Getting It Noticed*. Berkeley, CA: Peachpit Press.

Eden, Bradford Lee, ed. (2008) *Content Management Systems in Libraries: Case Studies*. Lanham, MD: Scarecrow.

Luini, Jon, and Allen Whitman (2002) *Producing Audio for the Web*. Thousand Oaks, CA: New Riders Publishing.

Slaybaugh, Matt (2001) *Professional Web Graphics*. Boston: Course Technology.

# References

Friedlein, Ashley (2001) *Web Project Management: Delivering Successful Commercial Web Sites*. New York: Morgan Kaufmann.

Kupersmith, John (2008) *Library Terms That Users Understand*, *http://www.jkup.net/terms.html*.

Nielsen, Jakob, and Hoa Loranger (2006) *Prioritizing Web Usability*. Berkeley, CA: New Riders.

Powel, Wayne, and Chris Gill (2003) Web content management systems in higher education. *Educause Quarterly* 26 (2): 43–50, *http://net .educause.edu/ir/library/pdf/eqm0325.pdf*.

Sammons, Martha C. (2004) *The Internet Writer's Handbook*. 2nd ed. New York: Pearson Longman.

# 13

# Planning the work

## Introduction

When you work on a project by yourself, you may sketch out a few notes, keep specific details in your head, and mentally revise as you proceed through the work. When you are leading a team through a project, however, you should more carefully plan and document the steps to success. Doing so keeps team members and colleagues informed, helps to prevent misunderstandings, and keeps everyone on track.

Most books about project management will encourage you to produce considerable documentation. This can be intimidating and lead you to throw the whole PM idea out the window. This book acknowledges that you are not a full-time project manager. You may also be answering questions at the reference desk, teaching classes, and attending committee meetings. You may also be serving in some of the roles that we described for your web project team in chapter 5. In this book, we've listed only the most likely documents which you will pursue. These, in our opinion, are the documents that pack the most punch. If you are a full-time project manager, be sure to check out the references at the end of the chapter to learn more about additional project management documentation and deliverables.

Despite their value, the tools we describe are not used by all web project managers in libraries. The most commonly reported techniques in response to a survey by the authors included identifying milestones and creating work breakdown structures (see table 13.1) (Keach and Fagan 2008). Both of these techniques are part of formal project management, and they can also be done more informally. Fewer respondents budgeted for staff time or external costs, or created Gantt charts or PERT charts. Many respondents mentioned there was not always enough time or staff to engage in formal project management techniques. Some of them came from a background where they used these techniques, but were no longer doing so in their current libraries.

**Table 13.1** How often project management techniques are used in academic libraries

| Technique | Frequently (%) | Sometimes (%) | Rarely (%) | Never (%) |
|---|---|---|---|---|
| Identify milestones (n=79) | 49 | 34 | 13 | 4 |
| Create work breakdown structures (n=79) | 38 | 29 | 22 | 10 |
| Budget for in-house staff time (n=78) | 26 | 23 | 26 | 24 |
| Budget for outsourcing, hardware, and software costs (n=80) | 15 | 26 | 29 | 26 |
| Create a Gantt chart or schedule (n=79) | 14 | 27 | 14 | 43 |
| Create a PERT chart (n=78) | 1 | 13 | 17 | 62 |

And, some felt that these techniques were just not needed for the projects they tackle.

This selective use of project management techniques holds true outside of libraries, too. A 2002 survey of 236 project managers working with all types of projects and in all types of industries found that Gantt charts were used by 64% of the respondents, but work breakdown structures by only 32% (White and Fortune 2002, 8). As you read this chapter, you should find yourself wondering how these project managers were able to create Gantt charts without work breakdown structures. Some of this discrepancy may simply be a matter of definition. A selective list of the most popular techniques and tools according to the survey by White and Fortune is offered in table 13.2.

**Table 13.2** How often project management tools are used across all industries

| Technique/Tool | (%) |
|---|---|
| Gantt bar charts | 64 |
| Work breakdown structure | 32 |
| Critical path method | 30 |
| Program evaluation and review technique | 10 |

Source: White and Fortune 2002, 8

The most important trend to notice here is that not all project managers use all the techniques. In White and Fortune's survey, the top four factors most commonly cited as critical to the project's outcome were clear goals and objectives, support from senior management, adequate funds/ resources, and a realistic schedule (White and Fortune 2002, 7). In Chapter 4 you read about encouraging clear goals and objectives with a project overview. This chapter gives you tools to set realistic schedules and to support requests for adequate funds and resources.

Finally, software specifically designed for project management is optional. Some of the techniques we describe in this chapter are easier to document within Microsoft Project than without (if you understand how to use the software), but few of the techniques require specialized tools. In fact, you will experience a steep learning curve for most software and you may even find that the software gets in the way of your thinking. If you plan to manage many projects, that learning curve may make sense. You will find that Microsoft Project is the most popular tool, but not the only one. Explore some of your options at the website 'Project Management Software Review' from TopTenReviews (*http://project-management-software-review .toptenreviews.com/*). Most importantly, remember that using project management software does not make you a good project manager just as using word processing software does not automatically make you a better writer. Use the software when it makes sense, but stay open to low-tech solutions.

# Work breakdown structure

The work breakdown structure (WBS) is simply a breakdown of your project by activities in the form of tasks and outcomes. Documenting the tasks is part of what allows everyone on your team to move forward independently rather than wait on you to tell them what to do each step of the way. You can format a WBS as a concept map diagram or as an outline. See figures 13.1 and 13.2 for examples of each style using sample tasks within a larger project.

For the WBS, you don't have to list the tasks or 'work packages' in order. At this point, you don't even need to know who will do what or how long each task will take to complete. The WBS is an attempt at a complete listing, though, and you will eventually transfer each task to a schedule that you will monitor as you progress through your project. In its comprehensiveness, the WBS attempts to define the tasks that are in-scope for your project. Creating a WBS gives you and your team a clear

**Figure 13.1**  Concept map WBS (created in Microsoft Word)

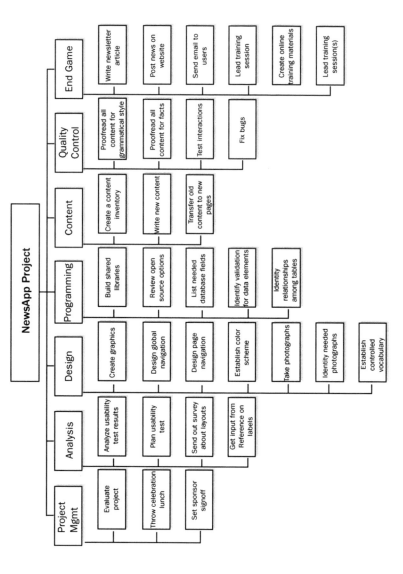

**Figure 13.2** Outline WBS (created in Microsoft Word)

NewsApp Project
- Project Mgmt
  - Evaluate project
  - Throw celebration lunch
  - Get sponsor signoff
- Analysis
  - Analyze usability test results
  - Plan usability test
  - Send out survey about layouts
  - Get input from Reference on labels
- Design
  - Create graphics
  - Design global navigation
  - Design page navigation
  - Establish color scheme
  - Take photographs
  - Identify needed photographs
  - Establish controlled vocabulary
- Programming
  - Build shared libraries
  - Review open source options
  - List needed database fields
  - Identify validation for data elements

understanding of your project, helps you create cost and time estimates, and clarifies responsibilities of your team (Verzuh 2003, 105–7).

Your project specifications will dictate the categories of work for your project, but for most web projects, you will often find that your work falls into the following general areas:

- *Project management*: Throughout the entire project, you will have tasks such as communicating about the project, managing change requests, reviewing progress with the project sponsor, coordinating meetings, and maintaining the project page. Many of these tasks will fall to you as the project manager, but you should still list them. Refer back to chapter 8, 'Planning for organizational communication,' for a reminder of the work associated with a communication plan.

- *Analysis*: Although you have completed the bulk of your analysis in order to create the project specifications, you will be seeking and analyzing new information as the work proceeds. Examples include testing your project in-process with users, getting input from colleagues, and watching the market for new solutions. Refer back to chapter 9, 'Getting user input,' for details about research that happens both before you've written your project specifications and while you are creating the finished product.

- *Design*: As part of the overall project specifications, your designers specified layout and graphical elements. Now, they will have to complete the final layout, color schemes, stylesheets, and graphics. They will also finalize navigation, the organization of links, and other information architecture decisions.

- *Programming or implementation*: If your project includes custom programming or databases, then you will need a list of tasks associated with creating the code. If you are implementing a turnkey system, then your team will need to learn how to use the system and customize it for your environment.

- *Content*: During the analysis phase, your team did a content inventory to understand the project. Now you will specify tasks such as moving content into the new system, writing and editing, and creating graphics. You might also have tasks associated with controlled vocabulary and the text of error messages in this category or in the design category.

- *Quality control*: As programmers finish coding and as content coordinators finish inserting text and graphics, your tasks will include testing for bugs and proofreading for errors.

- *End game*: As the project begins to gain shape, promotional tasks such as training and marketing still remain.

The next hierarchical level and any additional sublevels of the WBS list the individual activities that need to be accomplished. Usually, the work packages at the very bottom of the WBS offer a task and a deliverable: create graphics, test interface, lead training, write newsletter article, or post minutes. Each of these is actively written and clear about expectations in order to improve the chances the person assigned to the task will remember what he is being asked to complete. These tasks and deliverables are based on everything you learned during the gathering data and analysis phase, as documented in the project specifications.

The skills and work styles on your team influence how granular your work packages should be. For instance, if you have more than one person who is likely to handle content, you might list fairly small tasks so you can distribute and coordinate the work among many:

- Compose text about circulation policies.
- Compose text about interlibrary loan policies.

- Revise existing text about reserves policies.
- Get approval from director about changes in policy text.

By listing out each chunk of content, you ensure that none of it is overlooked. Also, if one part of the content depends on another and will be completed by different people, listing the tasks out in detail helps to ensure that the stepping stones are all accounted for.

On the other hand, if you know that the individuals who are likely to write the different pieces of text work closely together, or that a single person will handle it all, you might instead list a single, larger task:

- Finalize policy text.

Similarly, if you have only one experienced programmer on the project, you may also choose to create relatively large work packages because the same person will be doing all the work and the person is an expert in that work:

- Program search functionality.
- Create database for policies.

These large work packages are composed of many smaller steps and deliverables. The work, in fact, can't be done without the smaller steps that lead up to the deliverables listed above. Because your programmer is both experienced and working alone, though, you may decide that listing the smaller steps is unnecessary.

Another factor that will influence the size of your work packages is how much control you expect to have over the schedule. Jolyon Hallows, in *Information Systems Project Management*, writes: 'Obviously, activities can be broken into levels of detail so fine that each hour of each team member's day for the duration of the project is planned. Just as obviously, such a plan will be obsolete by the end of the first day' (2005, 125). You are unlikely to track progress down to the hour. According to Hallows, some experts recommend defining tasks so they can be completed within two weeks. In academic libraries, especially due to most people's multiple responsibilities, you may have tasks that last for a month or longer with no need of breaking them down into subtasks, such as the programming examples above. The goal is to list tasks using enough detail so that you, as the project manager, are satisfied that the work is manageable (2005, 126). Your own instincts rather than steadfast rules should decide how granular your work packages should be.

Creating the WBS is a valuable activity to do as a team for a number of reasons. You need to tap the knowledge of those who will be doing the work. The process also helps to demystify what needs to happen and is a way for the team to get involved in nitty-gritty planning. A complete WBS can also be quite reassuring to your team members. Some of them may have never worked on a web project before and may still be uncertain of the different steps that are ahead of them. As they identify activities as a team, they will start to understand more fully how they will be contributing to the project. It can be reassuring to those who have worked on web project teams before, too. They may know full well all the work that needs to be done and may be wondering if everyone else knows what needs to happen. By listing out all the tasks, your experienced team members will be reassured that everyone is on the same page.

## Creating a work breakdown structure with sticky notes

 Even project managers who use specialized software will use low-tech sticky notes to brainstorm with a project team and plan out the work. In the series of callouts in this chapter, you'll learn how you can do so, too.

1. Bring your team together to write tasks on sticky notes until no one can think of new ones. This will take awhile.

2. Group the tasks into the following categories as you work: project management, analysis, design, programming, content, quality control, and end game.

3. Your tasks should be in the form of task + deliverable.

4. Ask everyone to review others' tasks as they work to reduce duplication and inspire more tasks.

5. Document all your tasks in a spreadsheet or transfer the sticky notes to the insides of manila folders for safekeeping.

You will read about one way to create a WBS in the callout, 'Creating a work breakdown structure with sticky notes.' You may choose instead to brainstorm and create a WBS in an outline format. Again, this process doesn't need any special tools; you can just create an outline in your word processing software. Doing so is not quite as fun as the sticky-note method, but it gives you two options. You can create an outline WBS outside of meeting time and use it to start a more detailed in-meeting discussion, or create one together within a meeting and then ask individuals to break work areas down into a list of work packages outside the meeting.

You may eventually use software to document your WBS, but we recommend that you brainstorm your WBS in a low-tech way. You will more easily enlist all your team members and you won't get caught up in the aesthetics of your WBS before you've really thought through the content. Even books that help you use Microsoft Project may recommend using Microsoft Word first to outline your WBS (Biafore 2007, Section 4.4). You can copy and paste Word and Excel text into Project or other software if you decide to use the more specialized tools.

# Assigning tasks

With a long list of tasks before you, the next natural step is to parcel the work out to members of your team. As discussed in chapter 5, you can create your web team using the following list of key roles:

- project manager
- project sponsor
- end users
- webmaster
- library application manager
- graphic designer
- interaction designer
- information architect
- programmer
- database programmer
- specialty programmers
- content editor
- video/audio content editor
- testing organizer
- marketing coordinator
- training coordinator.

Now that you have a more accurate list of *what* needs to be done, you will find out how well you predicted *who* you would need!

As a member of your team, you will have most of the project management tasks assigned to you. This is a great way for other team members to understand your role in the project. If they aren't 100% sure how substantial your tasks are, hopefully they will know by the end of the project. You can, of course, also take on additional tasks, but don't be in a rush to do so. Based on your knowledge of your team members,

### Assigning tasks using sticky notes

 The next step after creating a work breakdown structure with sticky notes is to assign tasks.

1. Prepare a folder for each team member including you. Add another folder called 'outsource.'

2. Ask everyone on your team to distribute the sticky note tasks in your WBS to the different folders. If no one is sure who does a particular task, it goes in the outsource folder.

3. As a team, review each person's folder. Encourage moving some tasks from the more populated to the less populated folders. The most populated folder is not necessarily the folder with the most work. A folder with nothing in it, though, is a team member with nothing to do.

4. As project manager, you should help to populate the folders of team members who are still unsure of their contribution.

5. For tasks that are in the outsource folder, add the word 'Outsource' to the note and then assign to someone on the team to take the lead on finding someone from outside the team to do the task.

6. Each team member takes their sticky notes away with them after this meeting. They should initial their tasks, and if you have decided to ask them to do so, indicate a time estimate for each task.

try to be objective about whether or not you are the best team member for the job. In fact, consider delegating some of your project management tasks to others on your team if it makes sense.

# Estimating time and money

You will recall that when you created the project overview document (chapter 4), you provided a ballpark estimate on timeline and costs. These estimates were created not based on the work needed to be done— you didn't actually know yet what needed to be done—but on the available time and money. Now that you have a complete listing of activities, you can create a new estimate for both time and money based on the actual tasks (Verzuh 2003, 115). This new estimate will be the more accurate of the two and the detail will allow you to track your progress, making adjustments as needed.

Estimating financial costs is straightforward. If the required activity is to outsource work or to purchase hardware, the team member assigned to the task does the required research to identify likely or actual costs. It may be time-consuming to track down the details, but most cost outlays can be estimated with relative accuracy.

Estimating time, on the other hand, is a significant challenge. According to Scott Berkun, one reason for this is that 'few people enjoy estimating complex things that they will be held accountable for' (2008, 34). In fact, if your team has never estimated schedules before, they may be very reluctant, even displaying anger or indifference. You should be clear with yourself as well as with the team that an estimate is just that— an estimate. It is not a promise. It is not a guarantee. It is not binding. It is, instead, an educated guess with which you will be planning the work. After explaining this, then, be sure to keep to that philosophy. Review and revise time estimates as the work proceeds with an understanding that individual activities can't always be completed according to rigid schedules.

We all have issues with time management, deadlines, and schedules, but don't assume that everyone on your team has the same issues as you. The four Keirsey temperaments discussed in chapter 6, for instance, provide insight into how varied these issues can be. The SJs can tend to be strict about schedules, meaning they'll usually be on time, but they may be hesitant when you ask them to estimate a schedule. The other types— NTs, SPs, and NFs—may not be as tied to a schedule. NTs may spend ample time estimating a schedule, but then find it difficult to follow through. SPs can tend to be adaptable with their schedules, leading to estimates that they expect to change frequently. The NFs may accept any schedule handed to them, regardless of how realistic it is, because they don't want to say no (Kroeger, Thuesen, and Rutledge 2002, 182). While you're likely to have all types on your team, remember the more common temperaments for librarians and programmers are NT and SJ. You'll need to be on the lookout for how these two different work styles mesh. SJs may get frustrated with NTs who don't end up following through, and NTs may not understand SJs' lack of flexibility.

Each person on your team may estimate time needed for tasks in a different way. Some will hope to protect their reputation and pad all realistic estimates by 15% (Shelford and Remillard 2003, 107). Others will try to fit the work into the allotted time, creating overly optimistic estimates that will likely fail. Others will just make wild guesses based on little but your request for an estimate. In the first case, the estimated schedule unnecessarily produces a completion date well beyond the realistic estimate. In the second, your project may only be halfway done by the time the planned completion date arrives. In the last method, you have no idea when your project might be done. Even though these methods could be more accurately described as guesses than as estimates, you may still choose to use them. If you do, however, you should be clear with your team and with your project sponsor about the certain lack of accuracy.

## More accurate estimates

The field of project management uses relatively simple techniques to estimate a schedule and increase the odds that you will meet deadlines and make accurate promises to others. Both of the techniques described here start with estimating the amount of time needed for each activity under three scenarios: optimistic, realistic, and pessimistic. Each is exactly how it sounds. The optimistic estimate is based on the best-case scenario. If everything goes well, this is how long the activity should take. The realistic estimate is the most likely. The pessimistic estimate assumes a worst-case scenario. Individual activities may have a range of days or even weeks (table 13.3).

The first of two techniques described here is to select just one of these three estimates based on how risky you perceive the activity to be. If the work appears to be run of the mill, you might use the optimistic estimate. If the activity is original—you've never done it before—then you would use the pessimistic estimate. You record all three estimates on your end schedule, but you plan your timeline based on just one of the estimates.

**Table 13.3**  Example of optimistic, realistic, and pessimistic estimates

|  | Optimistic estimate | Realistic estimate | Pessimistic estimate |
|---|---|---|---|
| Proofread all text for grammatical errors | 3 days | 7 days | 21 days |

A second method, which starts with the same three estimates, is a major component of the Program Evaluation and Review Technique (PERT) (Thomsett 2002, 205). In this technique, instead of choosing just one of the three estimates, you compute a new expected estimate. The equation used is:

$$\text{Expected} = (\text{Optimistic} + 4 * \text{Realistic} + \text{Pessimistic}) / 6$$

In this technique, you are weighting your realistic estimate the heaviest, but also giving yourself some wiggle room with the other two estimates. The final number depends on how far away the optimistic and pessimistic estimates are from the realistic estimate (table 13.4).

Before your team members run off to estimate the amount of time needed for each task, you need to first discuss how to measure that time. You want to be sure that everyone is estimating in a similar way. One option is to estimate *periods* (also called duration). This is the length of time allowed for the task, regardless of how many people are assigned to the task (Hallows 2005, 137). The other option is to estimate *effort*. A time estimate for effort is the number of hours that someone—anyone—needs to work on the project. If you can assign more people to the task, then you can shorten the effort time estimate. These two styles of considering time can produce dramatically different estimates.

Traditional project management will tell you to estimate both period and effort. However, unlike design and software firms where clients are billed by hours worked on a project, employees in academic libraries do not typically track the number of hours to complete a specific task. Also, if you have created a lean team without much duplication of skills, you will usually have just one person per task. That means that you are unlikely to add someone to a task to speed up the completion of that task. If you are looking for a shortcut when working with your academic library web team, consider asking your team members to estimate period, not effort.

Your estimators may also try to account for distractions while they are estimating, but you should dissuade them from doing so. In a typical day,

**Table 13.4**  Example of calculating estimates

| | Optimistic estimate | Realistic estimate | Pessimistic estimate | Calculated (expected) estimate |
|---|---|---|---|---|
| Proofread all text for grammatical errors | 3 days | 7 days | 21 days | 9 days |

after all, most of your team members will not be working 100% on this project. Suppose that only 50% of a work day is spent on new tasks. The other half is spent handling interruptions and routine tasks. Ask them to estimate their time as if they were focused entirely on the task at hand rather than within the context of all their other work, and without distractions and interruptions. Doing so helps to ensure that the estimate is accurate even if the project moves to a different time of year when workloads are different, or even if the task moves to a different person. You will factor in the amount of time that the person assigned to the task actually has for a task later on when you combine all the estimates into one schedule.

The internal dialog for estimating the period required for a work package labeled 'finalize policy text' might go something like this:

> It will take me one to two hours to write a first draft of that policy. My boss should review it within two days. She might ask me to make a few edits or to follow up with others, so that might take me an additional hour to request and accept that input. I'd call that an optimistic two days, a realistic three days, and a pessimistic four days when measured by period.

The size of the work package will dictate if the estimates are in hours, days, or weeks. Encourage your estimators to use what makes sense to them for the given task.

Finally, you may or may not ask your team members to estimate time needed for all tasks. Formal project managers will likely suggest that you estimate time for *all* the tasks, and that does create the most accurate end schedule. If you can accept a less accurate but still better-than-nothing schedule, you could instead ask your team members to estimate time only for the tasks they predict will be lengthy. You could also just ask your core team members, as well as yourself, to estimate time needed for all assigned tasks. That core team will likely be the busiest during your project and stands the greatest risk of being overloaded.

## Task dependencies

After estimating time needed for each task, the next logical step is to identify which work packages need to be completed before other work packages, and which ones can happen at the same time. As you created the WBS you may have found your team putting the tasks in some type of order within each work category. As you review the WBS as a project team, the successors and predecessors should be relatively clear. Look for dependencies between work areas as well as within work areas. For example:

- You can't train your users on how to search until after the search function is completed.
- You can't complete the search until it has been tested.
- You can't test the search until after a first version is created.

You may find yourself erring on the side of caution, thinking that everything needs to be done in a sequential order. In fact, many of the tasks can be done in parallel, and some are relatively independent of everything else—they just need to be done by the end of the project. You can illustrate the dependencies with boxes (or sticky notes) and arrows showing the connections. This diagram is often called a network diagram.

---

## Creating a network diagram with sticky notes

 The next step after assigning tasks with sticky notes is to create a network diagram.

1. Confirm that your team members put their initials on their assigned tasks before you begin to work.

2. Arrange your sticky note tasks on flip-chart paper or on a white board in sequence. Tasks that need to be done early in the project go to the far left. Tasks to be done at the end of the project go to the far right.

3. Some of your tasks will have no predecessors—you could start on these things right away if the team had nothing else to do. Those go all the way to the left.

4. As you identify tasks that can only be accomplished after a previous task is done, put those sticky notes near each other and in order, left to right. You'll gradually start to see a sequence of tasks taking shape.

5. You may have neglected to write down some tasks earlier. If so, create a new sticky note and slot it in.

6. Some tasks will need to happen, or can happen, at the same time as another task. Put those sticky notes in parallel paths.

7. Draw directional arrows between tasks to indicate tasks that need to happen in a particular order.

8. If you plan to continue working in a second meeting, leave the sticky notes in place for your next meeting if you can. If not, photograph your work and carefully transfer your sticky notes to folders.

As you create your network diagram, you'll gradually start to see a sequence of events taking shape. If you find that you have one big line of tasks snaking across the work surface, look for places where that single line of tasks can be split up. Do you really need to wait until all programming is done before you start marketing the project to the users? Do you really need a place to put the content before you start writing new content? Question each task on the board and place the sticky note at the earliest possible spot in your sequence.

While working on your network diagram you may discover you have not broken some of your work packages down to small enough sizes. For instance, you may have originally listed 'hold training sessions' as one of your work packages. You clearly can't complete that until the main design and functionality of your project is done, but you can invite users and schedule the room well before the design and programming is completed, and you can create training handouts while the programming is still underway. You could break the original work package down into the following steps:

- Coordinate training sessions (invite users, schedule the room).
- Create training handouts.
- Train users.

Similarly, you may break the programming down into smaller work packages:

- Program main functionality.
- Develop search options (secondary navigation).

This will help you identify at what point other work can proceed.

# The schedule

## *Preliminary project schedule*

More complicated versions of your network diagram could be produced using standards associated with Project Evaluation Review Technique (PERT), the Critical Path Method (CPM), and the Precedence Diagram Method (PDM). A simplified version serves the purpose of predicting your schedule, though. You now have a big-picture view of what needs to happen in sequence and you can identify the sequence of events which represent the longest path through your project from start to end. This is the aptly named 'critical path.' Add up the time estimates along the critical path and you discover the earliest date you can complete your project. Everything else has a certain amount of 'float.' The float work packages can happen slightly earlier or slightly later, and the project will still finish on time. If one task along the critical path takes longer than expected, and if you can't shorten something else along the critical path, then your completion date will be delayed as well.

Traditional project managers will usually switch over to software at this time to perform calculations and create a detailed project schedule. Plugging all this information into software like Microsoft Project will allow you to propose exact start and end dates for each task, and discover the target finish date in the process. Software also gives you the opportunity to add details about available work time for each team member so you can identify trouble spots where one or more people are overtaxed. This step is called 'leveling resources.' Some software will also help you create attractive network diagrams. Most will create Gantt charts for you, where each task is represented on a timeline (see figure 13.3). Most project management programs, however, are complex and require a significant amount of time and patience to learn. Without knowing

**Figure 13.3** Example Gantt chart (created in Microsoft Project)

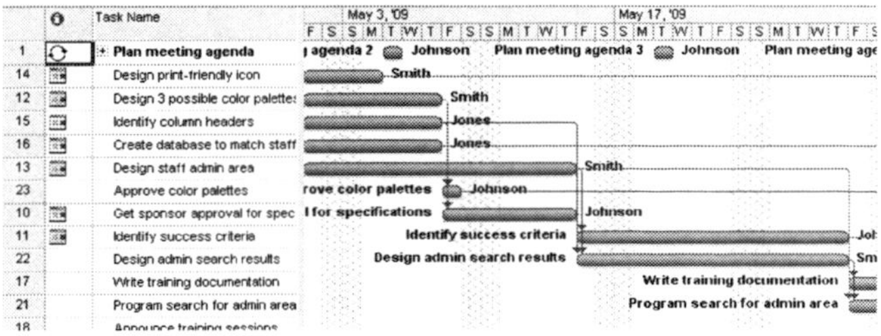

## Planning a project schedule with sticky notes

 After creating a sticky note network diagram, you can then create a sticky note project schedule.

1. Make sure that the team members who are most likely to be overtaxed are included in this meeting. Invite your project sponsor to this meeting.

2. Identify your critical path: the sequence of tasks that must happen one after another that snake across your diagram. Each of these tasks has a preceding and subsequent task from the project beginning to project end. If two parallel tasks are in that path, the one that takes the longest is the one in the critical path.

3. Mark the tasks along the critical path for your project with a marker.

4. If you have not already done time estimates for those tasks, do so now and write those estimates on the sticky notes.

5. Consider how frequently you plan to check in with your team. Use that time period for the next step. For instance, if you are meeting every other week, you will mark two-week periods of time.

6. Starting at the far left, follow the time estimates on the critical path forward by your chosen time period and write that date on the flip-chart paper or white board. Repeat until you reach the end of your project. This is your estimate of your earliest completion date.

7. If your estimated completion date is past your original estimate, review your critical path for any activities that can actually happen in parallel.

8. If your estimated completion date is still beyond your original estimate after reviewing the critical path, you will want to review your schedule, scope, and resources with your project sponsor. Find more on this topic later in this chapter.

9. As a team, review the tasks within each marked time period, considering the amount of work required for each team member. If a team member requests it, total up their time estimates for the period.

10. Adjust the workload of your team members ('level resources') one or more of the following ways:

    a.    Shift non-critical-path tasks to a less busy time period for the same person. If you do this, be sure to shift all predecessor tasks, too.

    b.    Reassign tasks to someone who doesn't have as many tasks.

    c.    Identify tasks that can be outsourced to a colleague outside the team and reassign.

    d.    As a last resort, delay a task along the critical path, shifting the rest of the schedule forward.

what you are doing, the software could make calculations that are incorrect and you would then be worse off than when you started.

As a part-time project manager, you might instead choose to continue to work with sticky notes to plot out your project by month or week, and make educated guesses about workload. Alternately, you could use the software to identify overload issues for only the core members of your project team—the ones who are spending most of their time on this project. You can establish an effective project schedule with just your sticky notes and a white board, as explained in the callout, 'Planning a project schedule with sticky notes.'

This process should help your team come up with a complete, if still estimated, project schedule. You'll have a clear idea of the critical path that sets the minimum time necessary for the project, and you'll have more confidence that your team members can accomplish their assigned tasks within the project timeline.

## Balancing scope, schedule, and resources

The preliminary project schedule can be a sobering view of your project. Unless you padded your initial timeline considerably, your completion date is probably well beyond your target date. Resist the urge to claim that you can accomplish the project on schedule anyway by shortening your time estimates. All evidence suggests that you cannot. This estimate should instead encourage you to adjust your expectations.

All projects have a triangle of three factors that you can potentially adjust: scope, schedule, and resources. Your job as a project manager is to collaborate with the project sponsor to identify which of these three factors can be adjusted. Pull out your project overview and project specifications documents. All three of these factors are listed there, hopefully with notes you previously made about the importance of each one.

- *Scope* is the listing of features and objectives for the project. You identified the primary objectives on the project overview document when you first started. You developed the feature list more fully in the project specifications. Review both documents with your project sponsor to identify any secondary features that may only be optional, particularly ones that require a large amount of time to complete. Also look for required features which could come at a later date (and be treated as another project).

- *Schedule* is the target date that you gave your project sponsor or that she provided to you when she first asked for this project. It is also documented in the project overview document. How was that target date identified? Can it be changed to match your preliminary schedule target date?

- *Resources* involve both money and people. Are there any parts of the project that can be outsourced to a commercial company or purchased off the shelf? Is there any advantage to adding another colleague to the project team?

Whether your project sponsor knows it or not, she has already mentally weighted the importance of these three factors in her head. To identify her priority, ask which factor she would like to explore first. As you consider options for cutting scope, extending the schedule, or adding more resources, adjust the preliminary schedule to determine if the change brings the project in line. You may find that you identify some features to cut, outsource some piece of the project, and also agree to a slightly longer timeline than you first expected. Once you've come up

---

## Iterative approaches to project management

 In this book, we've based our approach on what is sometimes called the 'waterfall model' (Thomsett 2002, 17). This method spends a significant amount of time planning out the work and getting approval from a project sponsor before proceeding. This is the way that much of the literature and practitioners suggest that you should manage projects. It is not foolproof and it is not the only way.

Rapid Application Development (RAD) and Extreme Programming (XP) are two alternatives. Both advocate for iterative and rapid changes with short project time frames and less planning up front. Berkun (2008, 29–30) and Shelford and Remillard (2003, 91–2) offer concise descriptions of these alternatives and how they contrast with traditional project management. For more complete methodologies, consult the recommended readings at the end of this chapter.

with the compromise, document it on a revised project overview document and ensure that your project sponsor agrees.

## Documenting the schedule

Throughout this chapter, we've described working with sticky notes to establish your schedule. Once you are ready to finalize your plan, you'll need to transfer your information to a more portable and editable format. If you choose to invest in the time and money for project management software, you will be able to create an attractive and dynamic schedule as a Gantt chart or task list. For many of the software options available, you will be able to adjust time actually spent on tasks and your entire schedule will adjust to reflect the change. You can also create a Gantt chart in Microsoft Excel, although it will typically be more of a static display than a dynamic tool. The website 'Vertex42: A guide to Excel in everything' (*http://www.vertex42.com/ExcelTemplates/excel-gantt-chart .html*) offers an attractive template for creating a Gantt chart in Microsoft Excel along with links to other Gantt chart tools. You can also find tips for creating a Gantt chart within Microsoft Excel 2007's help files. Just go to the help area and search for Gantt. If your team is using a shared calendar or task list, you can also transfer all your tasks and deadlines to that application.

As we have often suggested in this book, however, you can accomplish the same goal—sometimes more efficiently—with immediately familiar tools. Consider documenting your schedule in a simple spreadsheet with columns for ID numbers, the tasks and dependencies, start and end dates, assigned team members, and status, as in figure 13.4. The ID numbers will help you document the dependencies in whatever format you choose to transfer your schedule to. Although you can devise a logical schema for your ID numbers based on category of work or phase

**Figure 13.4** Documenting a schedule using a spreadsheet

| ID | Task | Predecessors | Successors | Start date | Due date | Assigned | Status |
|----|------|--------------|------------|------------|----------|----------|--------|
| 1 | Plan meeting agenda (each month) | | | May-09 | May-09 | Johnson | Done |
| 2 | Get sponsor approval for specifications | | 3 | May-09 | May-09 | Johnson | Done |
| 3 | Identify success criteria | 2 | 154 | May-09 | May-09 | Johnson | In process |
| 4 | Design 3 possible color palettes | | 54 | May-09 | May-09 | Smith | |
| 5 | Design staff admin area | | 13, 14 | May-09 | May-09 | Smith | |
| 6 | Design print-friendly icon | | 54 | May-09 | May-09 | Smith | |
| 7 | Identify column headers | | 14 | May-09 | May-09 | Smith | |
| 8 | Create database to match staff authors to approved categories | | 12 | May-09 | May-09 | Jones | |

of the project, you can also simply begin with the number one. You can also designate the work packages along your critical path with a different color or font.

Using such a simple schedule and saving it to a shared work area allows anyone on your team to consult it quickly for their own next task. Each team member can sort the schedule by the 'Assigned' column to see their tasks at a glance, or by due date to see what needs to happen before they start a specific task. Your goal should be to create not a work of art for framing, but a document that everyone on your team can access quickly and efficiently.

# Tracking the work

Part of your job as project manager is to complete the tasks assigned to you on your schedule, just like the rest of the team. You also have the ongoing jobs of monitoring progress, coaching your team through tough spots, and making decisions on the fly. These tasks are difficult to articulate in the schedule, but don't neglect to make the time to do them. The team meetings, one-on-one meetings, and team workspaces that you read about in chapter 7 will also help your team stay in touch with each other and with you. Rather than simply demanding status reports with each interaction with your team members (a sure way to have them start hiding from you), your regular check-ins with your team members can also serve to motivate and facilitate the work. In *Making Things Happen* Scott Berkun offers an inspiring and straightforward list of ways to 'get people's best work' (2008, 187). His list is a superb guide to what you should be looking for when you are communicating with your team. He suggests that you: follow advice, challenge/make demands, inspire, clear roadblocks, remind them of your respective roles, remind them of the project goals, teach, and ask. Rather than paraphrase his clear and thoughtful descriptions, we recommend that you get a copy of *Making Things Happen* and read it for yourself.

## Adjusting the plan

As your work proceeds, trust that you will need to adjust your plan. The most precise schedules are still only estimates of what you expect to happen. An important regular step in anticipating changes is to monitor your progress against your schedule. By regularly reviewing your schedule with your entire team, you will be able to work together to recognize variance and brainstorm on solutions. When you meet to review, look at what was scheduled to be completed since the last check-in as well as the work scheduled to come before the next meeting. Looking both backwards and forwards helps remind your team members to mention new information that might affect the project. It also serves as a reminder of the commitments each team member made. Remember that unexpected delays can come from inside the project—for example, a difficult-to-resolve programming bug—or outside the project—such as a team member's illness. Either type of delay creates the same end result: a need to examine the tasks that relied on the one that was delayed.

A delay in a specific task does not always need to lead to a major schedule adjustment. If the delayed task is one that has few dependencies, then completing it by the next review meeting might be sufficient. The person assigned to that task should consider if they have room in their workload to move the task forward or if doing so will then delay other tasks. If a delayed task is along the critical path, however, pay special attention. Remember that the critical path is frequently composed of tasks that are of long duration and highly connected to other tasks. When one of these tasks is delayed, look for opportunities to shorten the time spent on other tasks to get that line of tasks back on schedule.

Delays in already-identified work packages, of course, are not the only reason that your plan changes. As you complete each work package, you also gain information that potentially changes your design, technical, and content specifications. A usability test may reveal that your planned page layout is ineffective. After you've purchased a turnkey system, you may discover that some features aren't working as you initially understood. As you receive content back from subject experts, you may find that you have much more, or much less, content than you anticipated. Each of these situations may lead to adjustments to your schedule or to the project specifications.

As you adjust the plan midstream, consider what to communicate to your project sponsor. Remember earlier in this chapter when you learned about balancing scope, schedule, and resources? Your sponsor's priorities again come into play as your project progresses. If you have a clear understanding of your project sponsor's priorities, you will be able to make educated guesses as you consider the options with your team. If the deadline is the most important aspect of this project to your sponsor, for example, then suggest cutting features or request more resources. After you've brainstormed with your team about your options for adjusting your project, you can then propose changes to your project sponsor with confidence that you are suggesting changes aligned with her priorities.

## When your project sponsor is the one changing the plans

In the authors' 2008 survey of web project managers in academic libraries, inadequate staffing tied for first place with unclear or changing priorities by upper administration (Keach and Fagan 2008). Project overviews and project specifications both help to clarify priorities for individual projects, and getting sign-off on those (in theory) helps to prevent constantly shifting priorities. However, not all project sponsors will honor that commitment, and project goals can change over the time span of a project. Constantly shifting priorities can be a sticky situation due to reporting lines, power structures, and politics; you'll want to be careful as you address these issues.

As discussed in chapter 2, your role as web project manager is likely to be just a part of what you do. Usually when you think about your relationship with your supervisor or library administration, you're thinking about your complete role and position in the organization. It can be hard to separate issues relating to other aspects of your job from your role as a web project manager if one of these powerful positions is also serving as your project sponsor. Yet separating those aspects of your job is important if you are going to have a focused discussion. When you meet with your project sponsor to discuss proposed changes, focus solely on the direction for the project at hand, large or small. As web project manager, you are looking out for the needs of the *project*, not your personal needs or even the needs of your team members—except as they affect the project.

If your project is not receiving the expected resources (in money, staff, or support), then you can again use the strategies related to scope, schedule, and resources. Receiving less support than you expected will require a change in the project plan. So you'll need to make sure your understanding of the importance of the project is in agreement with upper management. And, you'll need to be clear with them how the varying levels of support will affect the project. A scenario is given in the callout, 'A conversation with your project sponsor about shifting priorities.'

---

### A conversation with your project sponsor about shifting priorities

 *You*: 'When you and I last talked, we agreed that the project team should only pursue open source software options because of available financial resources and because you had already researched the subscription options and none of them matched our needs. You've now recommended several subscription products for us to review. I'm wondering if you've had a change of heart.'

*Project sponsor*: 'Well, I thought they looked interesting.'

*You*: 'They do look interesting. Are you offering them as examples of features that might also be available in open source options, or were you thinking we should consider these subscription resources as options?'

*Project sponsor*: 'Well, I just think we should consider both options—keep our minds open.'

---

*You*: 'Okay, I'm 100% behind open minds. So far in the project, we've made some assumptions based on going with one of the three open source products. If we step back to evaluate the subscription products as well, it could add an additional two months to our timeframe since we'll have so many more options to consider. How would you feel about that?'

*Project sponsor*: 'Would it really take that long? You know I wanted this in place by next semester.'

*You*: 'The subscription products have even more features than the open source products, so if we're going to look at them all fairly, it really would take that much time. If we *choose* one of those options, then we'd rework our plan to fit the new solution. That said, after evaluating, we might still go with the open source options. In that case, we'd pick up where we left off on the current plan.'

*Project sponsor*: 'Maybe I shouldn't have so firmly steered you away from a subscription option to begin with! We don't actually have the funds for a new recurring cost, so please consider the subscription options as examples of features, but continue with your plan to implement an open source solution. I'd like us to stick to the schedule.'

If your project sponsor is also one of your team members, you are ahead of the game for decision-making and communicating. Even if everyone on your team and your project sponsor are at the meeting where you agree to changes, though, be sure to create revised versions of your schedule and your project specifications so that the working documents reflect the current plan. If the change substantially alters the information documented on the project overview, consider creating a revised project overview so you continue to have a current document communicating your project to those outside the team.

# Conclusion

If the level of planning described in this chapter is new to you, you may now feel overwhelmed. Experiment with the planning tools in this planning chapter little by little. For instance, if you create a work breakdown structure, assign the tasks to your team members, and then roughly order the work packages by month, you have made a significant step toward distributing work amongst your team members and creating an efficient tool to monitor your progress. If you embrace the relationship between scope, schedule, and resources, you move much closer toward leading a successful project than if you had never considered how the three are related. If you tap the expertise of your team members in planning the work as well as monitoring it, rather than developing elaborate plans in isolation, then you have accomplished plenty.

# Recommended readings

Beck, Kent (2004) *Extreme Programming Explained: Embrace Change.* 2nd ed. Reading, MA: Addison-Wesley.

Highsmith, James A. (2002) *Agile Software Development Ecosystems.* The Agile Software Development Series. Boston: Addison-Wesley.

Larman, Craig (2004) *Agile and Iterative Development: A Manager's Guide.* Agile Software Development Series. Boston: Addison-Wesley.

Poppendieck, Mary, and Thomas David Poppendieck (2006) *Implementing Lean Software Development: From Concept to Cash.* Addison-Wesley Signature Series. Upper Saddle River, NJ: Addison-Wesley.

Shore, James, and Shane Warden (2008) *The Art of Agile Development.* Sebastopol, CA: O'Reilly Media, Inc.

# References

Berkun, Scott (2008) *Making Things Happen: Mastering Project Management.* 2nd ed. Sebastopol, CA: O'Reilly.

Biafore, Bonnie (2007) *Microsoft Project 2007: The Missing Manual.* Farnham: O'Reilly, *http://proquestcombo.safaribooksonline.com/.*

Hallows, Jolyon (2005) *Information Systems Project Management: How to Deliver Function and Value in Information Technology Projects.* 2nd ed. New York: Amacom.

Keach, Jennifer, and Jody Condit Fagan (2008) *Survey of Web Project Managers in Academic Libraries.* Web survey conducted June 9 – July 1, 2008.

Kroeger, Otto, Janet M. Thuesen, and Hile Rutledge (2002) *Type Talk At Work: How 16 Personality Types Determine Your Success on the Job*. Revised and updated ed. New York: Dell Publications.

Shelford, Thomas J., and Gregory A. Remillard (2003) *Real Web Project Management: Case Studies and Best Practices from the Trenches*. Boston: Addison-Wesley.

Thomsett, Rob (2002) *Radical Project Management*. Just Enough Series. Upper Saddle River, NJ: Prentice Hall PTR.

Verzuh, Eric (2003) Building the action plan: Scheduling, estimating, and resource allocation. In *The Portable MBA in Project Management*, ed. Eric Verzuh, 98–141. Hoboken, NJ: Wiley.

White, Diana, and Joyce Fortune (2002) Current practice in project management—an empirical study. *International Journal of Project Management* 20: 1–11.

# 14

# Concluding your web project

## Introduction

While you would think projects would simply end when they are done, completing a web project right takes both time and attention. You must first recognize that your project is approaching completion. You must begin to transition the finished project to the final managers. You must continue to focus on communication about the upcoming changes with your colleagues and end users. You must survive the often-stressful launch of the project. You should spend some time thanking your team for their time and work. And, it's an ideal time to conduct a review of how your project management techniques worked. These final steps may be the last things on your mind, but you've worked hard to manage your project from the beginning. Don't mar it by letting the last details fizzle out.

If you are nearing the end of a large web project, consider planning now for a day or two of vacation. You deserve to celebrate; you will need some downtime; and you may need to make a psychological adjustment to returning to the rest of your work after a significant project. You may not be able to schedule a precise day until the launch is over, but clear the idea with your supervisor now.

## How do you know when you are done?

You are done when you deliver the product that you and your project sponsor agreed upon. Review the exit criteria listed in your overall project specifications to decide when you have reached the completion milestone. Remember that when you gained new information about development time and costs, you may have modified those exit criteria. As long as each of those revisions got your project sponsor's approval through a change request process, you should still have clear exit criteria.

You documented this information originally to guide the development and communicate to your team and colleagues. Now you use it to tell you when to stop. These exit criteria should not be a surprise to anyone. By establishing exit criteria early, you have been communicating these criteria to both your team and your colleagues throughout your process.

Even with the best project specifications, your team, colleagues, users, and even your project sponsor will ask you to add new features right up until (and beyond) the official launch day. Even at the end, evaluate each of these requests against your exit criteria and against your schedule and budget. If they won't conflict with required features and won't run the project over time or budget, consider adding the new features. Be cautious in doing so, though, because many small changes eventually add up to significant distractions from the approved goals. To manage the bulk of the last-minute requests, including those that come immediately after the launch date, begin a list of new features to consider as part of an update or as a small but separate project.

This is as good a time as any to encourage your colleagues and team to think of each web project as just one step in improving your library's overall web presence. Although you complete individual projects, each project is just one of many you will likely undertake. Friedlein refers to this continuous improvement cycle as the 'virtuous spiral:'

> Virtuous as used here connotes the opposite of vicious; in a vicious cycle, things spiral downward, each factor contributing to the detriment of the next until the project fizzles out or self-destructs. A virtuous development spiral is one whereby each project builds on the last and contributes to the betterment of the next (Friedlein 2001, 46).

Just as this project will inform and potentially feed into your next, your library will never be truly 'done' with its web presence. The web is a constantly changing and evolving medium with new standards, new needs, and new trends encouraging you to revisit each of your past projects regularly. Embrace this idea as you are tying up your project and you will be better able to defer new requests, knowing that this is not the last time someone will be 'touching' this section of the library web.

# Letting go of your project

As your work on the project begins to draw to a close, you should begin to let go of your ownership of the end product. You will need to spend the time preparing the final caretaker for ongoing maintenance. You'll need to make sure they are also ready to take over related communications, including handling feedback related to the completed project's ongoing existence.

An example may illustrate this best. Suppose you created an internal blog for your reference desk staff by request of the head of the department. You identified the needs with the department head as your project sponsor and selected a free, hosted blogging application. You handled the technology needs such as enabling privacy settings, establishing accounts, and setting up the reference desk computer to log in to the blog automatically. You established information architecture with a starting taxonomy of tags and related links for the blog page. You led a team to create training documents for staff and one member ran training sessions. Unless you agreed with the department head that you would provide day-to-day care and feeding, you should now be handing the blog over to the department head or a colleague chosen by the department head to manage the blog.

It is not enough for *you alone* to know where the line between active project and finished project lies: you, your project sponsor, and the final managers need to all agree. If you haven't already done so during the final review process, you should provide an in-depth tour of the project features. Consider both the user interface perspective and the administrative interface perspective (if applicable). You may find an efficient way to accomplish part of this is to offer a hands-on training session. In addition, Shelford and Remillard (2003, 206) offer a checklist for the types of documentation you should share with the final owner before the final launch. They recommend a meeting where you share a site map, wireframe mockups, style guide, project documentation, application manuals, and a maintenance plan.

To apply this to the example of the reference blog, you would provide:

- A site map listing of each page within the blog and their relationships. You should have created a site map for the project specifications that you can re-use.

- A wireframe mockup of each different page explaining the types of content that went into each area. You may have also created this for your project specifications.

- A style guide including the taxonomy of the tags, page colors, location of the template or stylesheets, location of any images, and any established font conventions. These decisions should be found in your project specifications, although you may want to reformat them for the final managers.

- Project documentation so the final owner understands the choices made during the project and can make new choices with confidence. Examples include changing the tagging conventions, moving links, and choosing different privacy settings with confidence. If you created a project website and stored notes from activities along with all your official documents there, you already have this in place. Provide a tour to the new owner and insure that he can find it again.

- Training documents, FAQs, and other help documentation designed for both making changes to the blog as well as using it. In this example, you would probably simply link to the documentation provided by the hosted blog, with additional site-specific details such as usernames and passwords. You may also document some of the decisions made about settings in these documents.

- An inventory of maintenance that you anticipate will be needed. For the blog project, maintenance might be an annual review and consolidation of tags, training for new staff, and regularly checking any auxiliary links.

Engage the project sponsor or their appointed representative to identify the types of tasks included in ongoing maintenance and who tasks will be assigned to. Otherwise, the finished website may languish, with everyone wondering why you aren't doing something about it. With a clear handoff, others will know who carries which responsibilities.

If you are your library's webmaster, you will likely have some ongoing responsibilities related to the website, including each of the projects you managed. This situation makes the separation between project and production more challenging. In the reference blog example, the reference department would likely still serve as the owner and provide day-to-day maintenance. As part of your webmaster role, you might be tapped for minor adjustments to layout and settings. If a significant change was called for—moving to a new application or an overhaul of navigation— you then would revisit the blog as a potential new project.

# Communications related to project launch

As the project is nearing completion, you will be at your busiest responding to unexpected issues and tying up loose ends. You will also be announcing the launch of the project. Chapter 8 talked about preparing for launch as part of your communication plan. Now is the time to implement that plan.

## What to say and to whom

In the weeks leading up to your launch date, your team should be composing messages related to the launch so they are ready to go. Since you identified stakeholder groups (see chapter 4) and maybe even personas (see chapter 9), you'll already have a list of possible target audiences. You may craft a different message and delivery method for each of those audiences. For example, you might plan for and prepare listserv announcements for your library, blast e-mails to students and faculty, and a training session for public services library staff. As you read in chapter 8, as you are creating your message related to the launch you may be able to re-use parts of your planning documentation—flow diagrams, the project overview, exit criteria, and more. You will find you have a lot to say about the project, but probably no one cares as much as you do about all of the details together! Your challenge is to say everything you need to say, but not write such a long message that no one will read it.

Luckily, you have numerous means for sharing your message:

- *E-mails to your internal user groups, pre- and post-launch*: These can reference a project website as needed. Have at least two announcements ready to go on launch day: a pre-launch announcement to let everyone know the project is going live, and a post-launch announcement to alert everyone that it's accomplished.

- *The project website*: This is a great place to put final documents, including launch messages too long and wordy for an e-mail, or messages only a select few will want to reference. This is also a great place to have a 'Frequently Asked Questions' page, information about whether this project will continue to be developed or is 'closed,' future features for consideration, and training documents. The project website is also a good place for before-and-after screenshots.

- *Pre- or post-launch e-mails and website announcements targeting external user groups*: Depending on your organization, you may need to send these through your library administration, your outreach librarian, or other colleagues.

- *Announcements to specific individuals or groups*: You will likely want to send an e-mail to your whole project team lauding details of their accomplishments that would be too lengthy for the entire organizational listserv. You may want to stop by your project sponsor's office to thank her for her support. You'll probably want to just say 'thank you' to a number of people who really pitched in.

For any and all of these announcements, consider including the following information:

- *A concise description of the project and how it benefits its users*: You'll need to write this differently for internal and external users.

- *The URL of the web project itself*: Like attaching files to e-mails, this is surprisingly easy to forget.

- *Thanks and praise*: This is the time to highlight the contributions of your project team, other contributors, and your library administration. You're going to come up with some names immediately, but take some time to think through the list of names that don't come to mind right away. Was there a reference librarian who covered a lot of your team members' desk shifts so they could come to meetings? Did your library's administration run interference, provide resources, or even just give you a lot of authority on this project? Think of who to thank publicly in which announcement. For example, you definitely want to highlight your web programmer in your internal e-mail announcement, but it might be your dean or director that gets star treatment in the e-mail that is sent to the larger institution.

- *Who to contact with questions about the project*: You'll probably want to include a technical contact and a content-expert contact. For example, if the project is a new reference services website, the technical contact might be your webmaster, and the content-expert contact might be the head of reference.

- *The URL of the project website for more information*: This might go to internal users as well as selected colleagues on campus and beyond.

## When to communicate

Another issue to consider is *when* you make your communications about the launch. For example, you might set these timeframes for a public website project:

- Two months before launch:
  - Update internal stakeholders about the date of launch. You've been working with them throughout the project, but ensure they've heard from you lately.
  - Schedule training sessions and announce the dates to the entire library. Include details of the project since this may be the first time some staff members have heard about the project.
- One month before launch:
  - Confirm date of launch with team.
  - Remind or update entire library about date of launch and training sessions.
- One week before launch:
  - Confirm date of launch with team.
  - Remind entire library about date of launch.
  - Send blast e-mail to faculty and students.
  - Hold training session for public services staff.
- Day before launch:
  - Remind entire library of launch.
- Day of launch or day after launch:
  - Send blast e-mail to faculty and students after a successful soft launch. If anything went differently than you expected, e-mail library or specific library staff with updates.

All this planning may seem like overkill, but after you've sent multiple e-mails and done multiple presentations, you may begin to forget to whom you have told what. You ensure that you've included all your stakeholders by creating a plan to guide you on the front end rather than winging it on the back end.

## Who will send launch announcements?

As project manager, you have probably been responsible for sending updates to your colleagues throughout the project, including at the launch. You should discuss with your project sponsor if you should also be the one responsible for preparing and sending communications to external audiences. You may collaborate with or hand this task over to a marketing committee, the library's public relations staff, the project sponsor, internal stakeholders, or library administration. Be sure to clarify responsibility for both launch-related communications and ongoing marketing and promotion of a web project. A long-term marketing plan is typically led by the owner of the finished project and would fall outside of your project management responsibilities.

For practical reasons, the project sponsor or library director might want to announce the web project to the library or campus community. She might want to frame the project launch within a larger context. She may want to incorporate the news of your project's launch with some other announcements or even showcase your project as an example of how the library is supporting the larger organizational mission or strategic plan. Your project sponsor or library director may not initially think she wants to send such an announcement, but as time passes she may think of ways to weave it into the larger organization's affairs. As the launch date approaches, even if you created a communication plan ahead of time (as discussed in chapter 8), you should confirm the plan again before sending out any announcement yourself.

In addition to deciding who sends launch announcements, anticipate responses to those announcements. Whoever sends the launch announcements will receive most of the feedback. Agree in advance who will be responsible for responding to feedback. Tell the sender if you are interested in receiving copies of any comments received. Imagine your director sending the announcement to your campus community and receiving 20 'great job!' e-mails. She may tell you about them—but wouldn't it be nice if you could share them directly with your team? She may be willing to forward on all such notes if you ask, but might not think to do so otherwise.

---

## 'But we weren't notified about this project...'

 Because you are intimately familiar with the status of your project, it can be tough to remember that others in your organization may not understand the extent of the changes that you are introducing to the library website. Even with a carefully crafted communication plan, there will likely be someone on the day of launch who complains that the impending change was a surprise to them. Your colleagues may not have considered the implications of the expected change or may not have even understood what you attempted to explain. Depending on their workload, they may have only skimmed their e-mails and may not have attended any sessions demonstrating the changes.

If you've planned for and carefully implemented both ongoing and launch-related communications, complaints about not enough communication can be especially deflating and you may be tempted to discredit the complaint. Although the input may come at an inopportune time, do not create bad relations by responding poorly or taking the feedback personally. The intense time of the launch is not the best time for you to evaluate your communication plan. If you can identify a way to quickly address the perceived lack of communication, do so. Otherwise, courteously give thanks for the feedback and return your focus to the launch. Soon after the launch, review your communication plan with the complainants and ask for input on how it could be better.

# Day of launch

After you have worked so hard to plan for the launch day, do not be surprised if it is more stressful than the rest of the project so far. Regardless of how well you have planned the project, you will have a list of last-minute tasks—ones that came as a surprise and ones that you put off—that need to be completed. During the last week of the project, your timeline suddenly becomes compressed. Throughout the project, your team may have been committing a few hours a week to the project and checking in bi-weekly. In the last week, members of your core team will suddenly be spending all their time on the remaining tasks and checking in daily or even hourly. Keep organized with the tools you already put into place. If you are using bug tracking software, consider listing the remaining tasks in that system so that everyone on the team can see the status of each item. Doing so will also allow a team member with extra time to step in to help.

If you can choose the launch date, the worst day of the week for Monday to Friday work weeks is obviously Friday. If things don't go well, no one wants to stay late on Friday; no one will be around on Saturday to fix anything that's broken the next day; and your organization will be less aware of changes that happen late on a Friday afternoon since they are wrapping up their week and heading out for the weekend. The best day of the week is Tuesday: you have three days to live with the launched project before the weekend. The disadvantage of

Monday is that your organization is less likely to deal well with change: 'I showed up Monday and the site was totally different!' They will also still be sorting through their e-mail and planning their week. On Monday, you can send out a reminder that the web project will be launching and you can check in with all your team members. If you are planning the launch for the early morning hours, it's also just a little easier to get in early on a Tuesday than immediately after a weekend!

If your project has been residing on a development server, start with a soft launch before unveiling the site to your users. Move all files to the final destination for a final test and final approval from the project sponsor but do not create public links to your project yet. Revisit the testing scripts you used earlier and test everything again. Ask all members of your project team to spend time interacting with your finished product in its final home with all links live. Look for unexpected missing graphics, broken links, missing navigation, and broken functionality. Problems associated with differences in the server environments and absolute links can arise for the first time and files can always be accidentally left behind on the development server. This soft launch also reduces the stress associated with the public launch. When all systems are go, you will just be renaming a few files to make the project live.

Once your soft launch is successful, it is time for the public launch of the finished project. If this is a large project, the feeling can be both terrifying and exhilarating. The public launch is a real-life test of both your user-centered design and your technical testing. Send your announcement to the library that it is now live, and invite any reports of problems. Be sure to indicate who should be contacted about problems, perhaps even after regular business hours. Also send or post any planned announcements for end users outside the library.

It should go without saying (but we are going to say it anyway) that you and your core team need to be available on the day of the launch for any problems that arise, and probably for a few days afterwards. Despite all your testing, once the full population of users begins using the final product, they may find problems. This is true whether you have implemented a turnkey solution, built an application, or redesigned a website. You will have last-minute fixes that are top priority. As project manager, you need to be available to announce any delays, make decisions about priority levels of fixes, and coordinate the unexpected. You will be the one who knows when the intensity of launch day is over. Depending on the size of the project and the size of the audience, 'launch day' can last for just an hour, the whole day, or through the week and beyond.

# Adjourning your team

When the rush of a successful project is behind you, it's time to adjourn your team. You may recall from chapter 6, 'Library web team dynamics,' that this is a final and important stage of any team. Remember that your team members added your project onto their already-busy schedules. Take the time to adjourn the team by celebrating and thanking them. Among the things you might consider doing:

- Treat everyone to lunch, along with the project sponsor.
- Provide a small memento related to the project (figure 14.1).
- Nominate the team for appropriate university and library awards.
- List all team members' names in an authorship page within the project.
- List all team members' names in e-mails announcing the final product.

Regardless of fun additional activities, you should write a letter of thanks to each team member with a copy to the person's direct supervisor and to the project sponsor. This letter should offer at least one example of what the person contributed to the project. Copying the direct supervisor and the project sponsor increases the chances that this person's contribution is mentioned both informally and during an annual review.

**Figure 14.1**    Thank-you postcard (created with Wordle, *http://www.wordle.net/*)

# Evaluating your process

After you have weathered the launch day, handed the project off to the final manager, and thanked your team, you are still not done. For the good of your project, your reputation, your professional development, and your library, you should evaluate both the product as well as the entire project management process. If you are a tenure-track librarian, this could be the start of a presentation or publication.

## *Early project evaluation*

You can't truly evaluate the success of most projects until a semester or more has passed. If you are comparing site visits to an earlier benchmark, surveying users, or asking for anecdotal evidence from your colleagues, your users need to have had time to become accustomed to the changes and you need enough data to make accurate comparisons.

Soon after the project launch, however, you can quickly 'take the temperature' to ensure everything is running smoothly. This evaluation step can be as simple as asking for problem alerts from your colleagues most likely to observe user problems. Send an e-mail, call a meeting, or ask in an already scheduled meeting. This does not need to be formal. Depending on your project, you may also check to see if anyone is using it:

- If it's a room scheduling system, are any rooms scheduled?
- If it's a blog, are any messages posted?
- If it is a search, do your search logs show activity?

If you are using log analysis software which tracks visits to pages and paths through your site, look there for unexpected statistics:

- Are your users visiting all of the new pages? If not, maybe you forgot to include a link to new content.
- Are your users reaching error pages from the new pages? If so, can you reproduce that error?
- Are your users exiting the site unexpectedly from one of the new pages? If so, maybe your users are encountering problems just before they exit.

You want to make sure that you discover problems that need to be fixed quickly, even if your colleagues or users neglect to mention them. Your colleagues may think you already know, you are too busy to do anything about issues, or you can't do anything about issues.

## Personal review of the project management process

You'll recall that you recorded success criteria in your project overview and project specifications. In the weeks after your project is completed and the major bugs are fixed, it is time to pull those documents out and evaluate your success—at least for all aspects you can evaluate this early. Check off what you believe you accomplished and make notes about what you know you did not accomplish. For criteria that require more data, commit to making that evaluation by scheduling it on your calendar.

You may have incorporated some project management aspects into your success criteria such as keeping to the schedule or staying within budget. Evaluate those items and also consider what went right and what went wrong with your project management. Review the different activities you documented on your project website:

- Did any of your work seem to be a waste of time?
- Were you surprised to find the project took longer than you expected?
- Did you spend adequate energy on user input?
- What might you do differently next time?

Give yourself an honest assessment from your own perspective, but remember to give yourself credit for trying a new technique, even if it was only partially successful. Be especially sure to hold yourself accountable on what you said you would do, not on the parts of the project that appeared midstream. Anything else you accomplished is pure bonus.

## Review of the project management process with others

After you have looked inward, look outside yourself by asking your project team, your colleagues, and finally your project sponsor about the process. Although your perception might be that the project went off without a hitch because no one complained, you may have been unavailable to receive complaints during the final phases. The opposite is also possible. You may be beating yourself up for mistakes along the way, but you may have just led the best project your organization has ever seen. You can't temper your own internal evaluation without some external input.

**Figure 14.2** Example evaluation questions (created with Google Documents)

I felt well-informed about this project.

| | 1 | 2 | 3 | 4 | 5 | |
|---|---|---|---|---|---|---|
| Strongly disagree | ○ | ○ | ○ | ○ | ○ | Strongly agree |

I believe that this project was important to undertake.

| | 1 | 2 | 3 | 4 | 5 | |
|---|---|---|---|---|---|---|
| Strongly disagree | ○ | ○ | ○ | ○ | ○ | Strongly agree |

I felt that I was asked for my input at appropriate stages.

| | 1 | 2 | 3 | 4 | 5 | |
|---|---|---|---|---|---|---|
| Strongly disagree | ○ | ○ | ○ | ○ | ○ | Strongly agree |

I felt that input I offered was given appropriate consideration.

| | 1 | 2 | 3 | 4 | 5 | |
|---|---|---|---|---|---|---|
| Strongly disagree | ○ | ○ | ○ | ○ | ○ | Strongly agree |

I am looking forward to using the new site/application.

| | 1 | 2 | 3 | 4 | 5 | |
|---|---|---|---|---|---|---|
| Strongly disagree | ○ | ○ | ○ | ○ | ○ | Strongly agree |

How often did you visit the project team page?

| | 1 | 2 | 3 | 4 | 5 | |
|---|---|---|---|---|---|---|
| Never | ○ | ○ | ○ | ○ | ○ | Weekly |

With both your project team and the rest of your colleagues, be sure to provide a comfortable method for providing constructive criticism and feedback. You might consider an anonymous survey (figure 14.2), a team meeting, or one-on-one meetings with those who have already offered criticism. You might also enlist an impartial colleague to facilitate this process (Berkun 2008, 325). Regardless of what you discover, be open to their input and reflect on the input you receive.

Spend some additional time evaluating the completed project handoff with the final caretaker. If you have not provided adequate training or documentation, the weeks immediately after the launch are the time to discover and correct the situation. A meeting with the caretaker is a great opportunity to both evaluate the project and to confirm the final handoff of the completed project.

Finally, meet with your project sponsor for a debriefing. Share a short summary of what you think went right and what went wrong, the input received from your team and colleagues, and future plans for evaluation. Use your project sponsor as your final check. Did you meet your project sponsor's expectations? If not, how might you improve the process next time?

# Conclusion

As you wind down your project, spend time now to close out your project documentation. If you have a project webpage, post any final announcements about the launch and the results of your process evaluation. Indicate what and when the next steps of evaluating the project will be, and plan to post the results of those later evaluations on the same project page. Gather and post any missing documents. It will be increasingly difficult to fill in any documentation holes as time passes, so do these final tasks now— or risk never doing them. Finally, move the project from the in-progress column to the completed column and take a few minutes to pat yourself on the back. Schedule some extra time for yourself when your work is done, whether in celebration or relaxation. Plan to go out to lunch with good friends. Take two hours in the middle of a day to work out, take a walk, or attend an event on campus. Congratulate yourself as well as your team for the completed project.

Becoming a good project manager is an ongoing process, filled with trial and error of what works for you and for your organization. Build on each success by continuing to experiment and repeat what works. If you successfully implemented just one piece of advice you found in this book during your project, then you have succeeded in developing as a project manager. Congratulations!

# References

Berkun, Scott (2008) *Making Things Happen: Mastering Project Management.* 2nd ed. Sebastopol, CA: O'Reilly.

Friedlein, Ashley (2001) *Web Project Management: Delivering Successful Commercial Web Sites.* New York: Morgan Kaufmann.

Shelford, Thomas J., and Gregory A. Remillard (2003) *Real Web Project Management: Case Studies and Best Practices from the Trenches.* Boston: Addison-Wesley.

# References and recommended readings

Adair, John (2003) *Concise Time Management and Personal Development*. London: Thorogood.

Agada, John (1998) Profiling librarians with the Myers-Briggs Type Indicator: Studies in self selection and type stability. *Education for Information* 16 (1): 57–69.

Alessandra, Anthony J., and Michael J. O'Connor (1996) *The Platinum Rule: Discover the Four Basic Business Personalities—And How They Can Lead You to Success*. New York: Warner Books.

Alexander, Ian (2002) *Writing Better Requirements*. Boston: Addison-Wesley.

Allen, David (2001) *Getting Things Done: The Art of Stress-free Productivity*. New York: Penguin.

Austin, Andy, and Christopher Harris (2008) Drupal in libraries. *Library Technology Reports* 44.

Bailey, Robert (2006) Applying usability metrics. Conference paper presented at Usability Metrics: How to Measure Performance and Progress, Washington, DC.

Bean Software (2009) *Automatic Documentation Generation in ASP.NET Applications*, http://www.beansoftware.com/asp.net-tutorials/automatic-documentation-vb.aspx.

Beck, Kent (2004) *Extreme Programming Explained: Embrace Change*. 2nd ed. Reading, MA: Addison-Wesley.

Berens, Linda V. (2000) *Understanding Yourself and Others: An Introduction to Temperament*. 2nd ed. Huntington Beach, CA: Telos Publications.

Berkun, Scott (2008) *Making Things Happen: Mastering Project Management*. 2nd ed. Sebastopol, CA: O'Reilly.

Biafore, Bonnie (2007) *Microsoft Project 2007: The Missing Manual*. Farnham: O'Reilly, http://proquestcombo.safaribooksonline.com/.

Bordac, Sarah, and Jean Rainwater (2008) User-centered design in practice: The Brown University experience. *Journal of Web Librarianship* 2 (2): 109–138.

Bourne, Jennie, and Dave Burstein (2008) *Web Video: Making It Great, Getting It Noticed.* Berkeley, CA: Peachpit Press.

Bouwman, Harry, Bart van den Hooff, Lidwien van de Wijngaert, and Jan A. G. M. van Dijk, (2005) *Information and Communication Technology in Organizations: Adoption, Implementation, Use and Effects.* Thousand Oaks, CA: Sage.

Bowers, Michael (2007) *Pro CSS and HTML Design Patterns.* Berkeley, CA: Apress.

Bradbary, Dan, and David Garrett (2005) *Herding Chickens: Innovative Techniques for Project Management.* San Francisco: Harbor Light Press.

Brandon, Dan (2006) *Project Management for Modern Information Systems.* Hershey, PA: IRM Press.

Bunch, Nancy J., Anne Marie Casey, Frances A. Devlin, and Lana Ivanitskaya (2006) Project management and institutional collaboration in libraries. *Technical Services Quarterly* 24 (1): 17–36.

Centers for Disease Control and Prevention (2008) *US Public Health Service Syphilis Study at Tuskegee, http://www.cdc.gov/tuskegee.*

Cooper, Alan (1999) *The Inmates Are Running the Asylum.* Indianapolis, IN: Sams.

Covey, Stephen R. (2004) *The Seven Habits of Highly Effective People: Restoring the Character Ethic.* New York: Free Press.

Croneis, Karen S., and Pat Henderson (2002) Electronic and digital librarian positions: A content analysis of announcements from 1990 through 2000. *Journal of Academic Librarianship* 28 (4): 232–236.

DeRosa, Cathy, Joanne Cantrell, Janet Hawk, and Alane Wilson (2005) *College Students' Perceptions of Libraries and Information Resources.* Dublin, OH: OCLC, *http://www.oclc.org/reports/pdfs/studentperceptions .pdf.*

Eden, Bradford Lee, ed. (2008) *Content Management Systems in Libraries: Case Studies.* Lanham, MD: Scarecrow.

Falks, Angi, and Nancy Hyland (2000) Gaining user insight: A case study illustrating the card sort technique. *College & Research Libraries* 61 (4): 349–357.

Flynn, Nancy, and Tom Flynn (2003) *Writing Effective E-mail.* Fifty Minute Series. Rev. ed. Menlo Park, CA: Crisp Learning.

Foster, Nancy Fried, and Susan Gibbons, eds. (2007) *Studying Students: The Undergraduate Research Project at the University of Rochester*. Chicago: Association of College and Research Libraries, *http://www.ala.org/ala/mgrps/divs/acrl/publications/digital/Foster-Gibbons_cmpd.pdf*.

Fowler, Floyd J. (2002) *Survey Research Methods*. Applied Social Research Methods Series. 3rd ed. Thousand Oaks, CA: Sage Publications.

Fowler, Floyd J. (1995) *Improving Survey Questions: Design and Evaluation*. Applied Social Research Methods Series. Thousand Oaks, CA: Sage Publications.

Fowler, Martin, and Kendall Scott (2000) *UML Distilled: A Brief Guide to the Standard Object Modeling Language*. 2nd ed. Reading, MA: Addison-Wesley.

Frame, J. Davidson (2003) *Managing Projects in Organizations*. San Francisco, CA: Jossey-Bass.

Friedlein, Ashley (2001) *Web Project Management: Delivering Successful Commercial Web Sites*. New York: Morgan Kaufmann.

Gamma, Erich, Richard Helm, Ralph Johnson, and John Vlissides (1995) *Design Patterns: Elements of Reusable Object-oriented Software*. Reading, MA: Addison-Wesley.

Garrett, Jesse James (2002) *The Elements of User Experience*. Indianapolis, IN: Pearson Education.

Garton, Colleen, and Kevin Wegryn (2006) *Managing Without Walls*. Lewisville, TX: MC Press.

Greenbaum, Thomas L. (2000) *Moderating Focus Groups: A Practical Guide for Group Facilitation*. Thousand Oaks, CA: Sage Publications.

Hallows, Jolyon (2005) *Information Systems Project Management: How to Deliver Function and Value in Information Technology Projects*. 2nd ed. New York: Amacom.

Harris, Richard M. (2006) *The Listening Leader: Powerful New Strategies for Becoming an Influential Communicator*. Westport, CT: Praeger.

Highsmith, James A. (2002) *Agile Software Development Ecosystems*. The Agile Software Development Series. Boston: Addison-Wesley.

Holzner, Steven (2006) *Design Patterns for Dummies*. Hoboken, NJ: J. Wiley & Sons.

Hoppe, Michael H. (2006) *Active Listening*. Greensboro, NC: Center for Creative Leadership.

Houghton, Sarah (2005) I've been framed! Designing a library web site within a government frame. *Computers in Libraries* 25 (6): 6–8.

Houghton-Jan, Sarah (2008) Twenty steps to marketing your library online. *Journal of Web Librarianship* 1 (4): 81.

Hower, Rick (2009) Web site test tools and site management tools, *http://www.softwareqatest.com/qatweb1.html*.

Kaluzniacky, Eugene (2004) *Managing Psychological Factors in Information Systems Work: An Orientation to Emotional Intelligence*. Hershey, PA: Information Science Publications.

Karn, John. S., Sharifah Syed-Abdullah, Anthony J. Cowling, and Mike Holcombe (2007) A study into the effects of personality type and methodology on cohesion in software engineering teams. *Behaviour & Information Technology* 26 (2): 99–111.

Katzenbach, Jon R., and Douglas K. Smith (2004) The discipline of teams. In *Harvard Business Review on Teams that Succeed*, 1–25. Boston, MA: Harvard Business School Publishing.

Keach, Jennifer, and Jody Condit Fagan (2008) *Survey of Web Project Managers in Academic Libraries*. Web survey conducted June 9 – July 1, 2008.

Keirsey, David, and Marilyn Bates (1978) *Please Understand Me: An Essay on Temperament Styles*. Del Mar, CA: Promethean Nemesis Books.

Keyton, Joann (2004) *Communication and Organizational Culture: A Key to Understanding Work Experiences*. Thousand Oaks, CA: Sage.

Kinkus, Jane (2007) Project management skills: A literature review and content analysis of librarian position announcements. *College & Research Libraries* 68 (4): 352–363.

Kliem, Ralph L. (2007) *Effective Communications for Project Management*. Boca Raton: Auerbach.

Kneip, Jason (2007) Library webmasters in medium-sized academic libraries. *Journal of Web Librarianship* 1 (3): 3–23.

Koch, Peter-Paul (2003) The ideal web team (part 1). *Digital Web Magazine*, April 10, *http://www.digital-web.com/articles/the_ideal_web_team_part1/*.

Kroeger, Otto, Janet M. Thuesen, and Hile Rutledge (2002) *Type Talk at Work: How 16 Personality Types Determine Your Success on the Job*. Revised and updated ed. New York: Dell Publications.

Krug, Steve (2006) *Don't Make Me Think! A Common Sense Approach to Web Usability*. 2nd ed. Berkeley, CA: New Riders.

Kupersmith, John (2008) *Library Terms That Users Understand*, *http://www.jkup.net/terms.html*.

Larman, Craig (2004) *Agile and Iterative Development: A Manager's Guide*. Agile Software Development Series. Boston: Addison-Wesley.

Lauesen, Soren (2002) *Software Requirements: Styles and Techniques*. Harlow, England: Addison-Wesley.

Lencioni, Patrick (2002) *The Five Dysfunctions of a Team: A Leadership Fable*. San Francisco: Jossey-Bass.

Levine, Stuart (2006) *Cut to the Chase—And 99 Other Rules to Liberate Yourself and Gain Back the Gift of Time*. New York: Currency Doubleday.

Litwin, Paul (2003) *Fundamentals of Relational Database Design*. September 7, *http://r937.com/relational.html*.

Lombard, Emmett, and Lesley A. Hite (2007) Academic library web sites: Balancing university guidelines with user needs. *Journal of Web Librarianship* 1 (2): 57–69.

Luini, Jon, and Allen Whitman (2002) *Producing Audio for the Web*. Thousand Oaks, CA: New Riders Publishing.

Lyons, Michael L. (1985) The DP psyche. *Datamation* 31, August 15: 103–105.

Meyer, Eric A. (2007) *CSS: The Definitive Guide*. Sebastopol, CA: O'Reilly.

Meyer, Eric A. (2004) *More Eric Meyer on CSS*. Indianapolis: New Riders.

Meyer, Eric A. (2003) *Eric Meyer on CSS: Mastering the Language of Web Design*. Indianapolis: New Riders.

Miller, Brian Cole (2007) *More Quick Team-building Activities for Busy Managers*. New York: AMACOM/American Management Association.

Morgan, David L. (1997) *Focus Groups as Qualitative Research*. Qualitative Research Methods Series. 2nd ed. Thousand Oaks, CA: Sage Publications.

Morville, Peter, and Louis Rosenfeld (2006) *Information Architecture for the World Wide Web*. 3rd ed. Sebastopol, CA: O'Reilly.

Myers, Glenford J., Corey Sandler, and Tom Badgett (2004) *Art of Software Testing*. Hoboken, NJ: Wiley.

Myers, Isabel Briggs (2000) *Introduction to Type: A Guide to Understanding Your Results on the Myers-Briggs Type Indicator*. 6th ed. Oxford: Oxford Psychologists Press.

Myers, Isabel Briggs (1998) *MBTI Manual: A Guide to the Development and Use of the Myers-Briggs Type Indicator*. 3rd ed. Palo Alto, CA: Consulting Psychologists Press.

Nauman, Ann K. (1991) *Making Every Minute Count: Time Management for Librarians*. Berkeley Heights, JC: Library Learning Resources.

Nielsen, Jakob (2006) *Quantitative Studies: How Many Users to Test?*, *http://www.useit.com/alertbox/quantitative_testing.html*.

Nielsen, Jakob (2000) *Why You Only Need to Test with 5 Users, http://www.useit.com/alertbox/20000319.html.*

Nielsen, Jakob (1994) *Usability Inspection Methods.* New York: John Wiley & Sons, Inc.

Nielsen, Jakob, and Hoa Loranger (2006) *Prioritizing Web Usability.* Berkeley, CA: New Riders.

Parker, Glenn M. (1994) *Cross-functional Teams: Working with Allies, Enemies, and Other Strangers.* Jossey-Bass Management Series. San Francisco, CA: Jossey-Bass.

Parker, Glenn M., and Robert Hoffman (2006) *Meeting Excellence: 33 Tools to Lead Meetings That Get Results.* San Francisco, CA: Jossey-Bass.

Pickering, Peg (2001) *How to Make the Most of Your Workday.* Franklin Lakes, NJ: Career Press.

PMI Standards Committee (1996) *A Guide to the Project Management Body of Knowledge.* Newtown Square, PA: Project Management Institute.

Pollar, Odette (1999) *Organizing Your Work Space.* Los Altos, CA: Crisp Publications.

Poppendieck, Mary, and Thomas David Poppendieck (2006) *Implementing Lean Software Development: From Concept to Cash.* Addison-Wesley Signature Series. Upper Saddle River, NJ: Addison-Wesley.

Posner, Barry Z. (1987) What it takes to be a good project manager. *Project Management Journal* 18 (1): 51–54.

Powel, Wayne, and Chris Gill (2003) Web content management systems in higher education. *Educause Quarterly* 26 (2): 43–50, *http://net.educause .edu/ir/library/pdf/eqm0325.pdf.*

*Project Management for IT Professionals* (2005) Mission, KS: CompuMaster.

Ragsdale, Kate W. (2001) *Staffing the Library Web Site.* Washington, DC: Association of Research Libraries.

Ricigliano, Lori, and Renee Houston (2003) Men's work, women's work: The social shaping of technology in academic libraries. Paper presented at ACRL Eleventh National Conference, Charlotte, NC.

Rushton, Erin E., Martha Daisy Kelehan, and Marcy A. Strong (2008) Searching for a new way to reach patrons: A search engine optimization pilot project at Binghamton University Libraries. *Journal of Web Librarianship* 2 (4): 525–547.

Sammons, Martha C. (2004) *The Internet Writer's Handbook.* 2nd ed. New York: Pearson Longman.

Scherdin, Mary Jane (2002) How well do we fit? Librarians and faculty in the academic setting. *Portal: Libraries & the Academy* 2 (2): 237–253.

Scherdin, Mary Jane (1994) Vive la différence: Exploring librarian personality types using the MBTI. In *Discovering Librarians: Profiles of a Profession*, 125–156. Chicago, IL: Association of College and Research Libraries, American Library Association.

Seidman, Irving (2006) *Interviewing as Qualitative Research: A Guide for Researchers in Education and the Social Sciences*. 3rd ed. New York: Teachers College Press.

Shelford, Thomas J., and Gregory A. Remillard (2003) *Real Web Project Management: Case Studies and Best Practices from the Trenches*. Boston: Addison-Wesley.

Shore, James, and Shane Warden (2008) *The Art of Agile Development*. Sebastopol, CA: O'Reilly Media, Inc.

Slaybaugh, Matt (2001) *Professional Web Graphics*. Boston: Course Technology.

Sostre, Pedro, and Jennifer LeClaire (2007) *Web Analytics for Dummies*. Hoboken, NJ: Wiley.

Spool, Jared M. (1999) *Web Site Usability: A Designer's Guide*. San Francisco: Morgan Kaufmann Publishers.

Stewart, David W., Prem N. Shamdasani, and Dennis W. Rook (2007) *Focus Groups: Theory and Practice*. Applied Social Research Methods Series. 2nd ed. Thousand Oaks: Sage Publications.

Taylor, James (2004) *Managing Information Technology Projects: Applying Project Management Strategies to Software, Hardware, and Integration Initiatives*. New York: American Management Association.

Taylor, Mary K. (2000) Library webmasters: Satisfactions, dissatisfactions, and expectations. *Information Technology & Libraries* 19 (3): 116.

Thomsett, Rob (2002) *Radical Project Management*. Just Enough Series. Upper Saddle River, NJ: Prentice Hall PTR.

Tidwell, Jenifer (2005) *Designing Interfaces: Patterns for Effective Interaction Design*. Sebastopol, CA: O'Reilly Media.

Tidwell, Jenifer (1999) Common ground: A pattern language for human-computer interface design, *http://www.mit.edu/~jtidwell/interaction_patterns.html*.

Trochim, William M. K. (2006) *Introduction to Validity*, *http://www.socialresearchmethods.net/kb/introval.php*.

Tuckman, Bruce W. (1965) Developmental sequence in small groups. *Psychological Bulletin* 63 (6): 384–399.

Tuckman, Bruce W., and Mary Ann Conover Jensen (1977) Stages of small group development revisited. *Group and Organizational Studies* 2: 419–427.

Tullis, Tom, and Bill Albert (2008) *Measuring the User Experience: Collecting, Analyzing, and Presenting Usability Metrics.* Burlington, MA: Elsevier, Inc.

Turley, Richard T., and James M. Bieman (1995) Competencies of exceptional and nonexceptional software engineers. *Journal of Systems and Software* 28: 19–38.

Tyson, John C. (1988) A study of the personality type of academic library directors in the Commonwealth of Virginia using the Myers-Briggs Type Indicator. Doctor of Arts, Simmons College, Graduate School of Library and Information Science.

US Department of Health and Human Services (2006) *Research-based Web Design and Usability Guidelines, http://www.usability.gov/pdfs/guidelines .html.*

Verzuh, Eric (2003) Building the action plan: Scheduling, estimating, and resource allocation. In *The Portable MBA in Project Management*, ed. Eric Verzuh, 98–141. Hoboken, NJ: Wiley.

Whang, Michael (2007) Measuring the success of the academic library website using banner advertisements and web conversion rates: A case study. *Journal of Web Librarianship* 1 (1): 93–108.

White, Diana, and Joyce Fortune (2002) Current practice in project management—an empirical study. *International Journal of Project Management* 20: 1–11.

Whitehead, Richard (2001) *Leading a Software Development Team: A Developer's Guide to Successfully Leading People and Projects.* New York: Addison-Wesley.

Winston, Mark D., and Tara Hoffman (2005) Project management and libraries. *Journal of Library Administration* 42 (1): 51–61.

Wodtke, Christina (2003) *Information Architecture: Blueprints for the Web.* Boston: New Riders.

# Index